Mass Misunderstandings

Other Titles of Interest from St. Augustine's Press and Dumb Ox Books

Kenneth D. Whitehead, ed., *After Forty Years: Vatican Council II's Diverse Legacy*

Kenneth D. Whitehead, ed., *John Paul II – Witness to Truth*

Kenneth D. Whitehead, ed., *The Church, Marriage, and the Family*

Kenneth D. Whitehead, ed., *Marriage and the Common Good*

Kenneth D. Whitehead, ed., *The Catholic Imagination*

Kenneth D. Whitehead, ed., *Voices of the New Springtime*

Kenneth D. Whitehead, ed., *The Catholic Citizen: Debating the Issues of Justice*

George Marlin, *The American Catholic Voter: 200 Years of Political Impact*

Charles Cardinal Journet, *The Mass: The Presence of the Sacrifice of the Cross*

Richard Peddicord, O.P., *The Sacred Monster of Thomism: An Introduction to the Life and Legacy of Reginald Garrigou-Lagrange, O.P.*

John Paul II, *The John Paul II LifeGuide*™

Dietrich von Hildebrand, *The Dietrich von Hildebrand LifeGuide*™

St. Augustine, *The St. Augustine LifeGuide*™

St. Augustine, *On Order – De Ordine*

Thomas Aquinas, *Treatise on Law: The Complete Text*

Thomas Aquinas, *Commentary on the Epistle to the Hebrews*

Thomas Aquinas, *Commentaries on St. Paul's Epistles to Timothy, Titus, and Philemon*

Thomas Aquinas, *Disputed Questions on Virtue*

John of St. Thomas, *Introduction to the Summa Theologiae of Thomas Aquinas*

Josef Pieper and Heinz Raskop, *What Catholics Believe*

Josef Pieper, *Scholasticism: Personalities and Problems*

Josef Pieper, *The Silence of St. Thomas*

Josef Pieper, *The Concept of Sin*

Josef Pieper, *Death and Immortality*

Josef Pieper, *The Silence of Goethe*

C.S. Lewis, *The Latin Letters of C.S. Lewis*

Jacques Maritain, *Natural Law*

Dietrich von Hildebrand, *The Heart: An Analysis of Human and Divine Affectivity*

Dietrich von Hildebrand, *The Nature of Love*

Florent Gaboriau, *The Conversion of Edith Stein*

Ralph McInerny, *The Defamation of Pius XII*

James V. Schall, S.J., *The Sum Total of Human Happiness*

James V. Schall, S.J., *The Regensburg Lecture*

Peter Kreeft, *The Philosophy of Jesus*

Peter Kreeft, *Jesus-Shock*

Servais Pinckaers, O.P., *Morality: The Catholic View*

Teresa Wagner, ed., *Back to the Drawing Board: The Future of the Pro-Life Movement*

MASS MISUNDERSTANDINGS

THE MIXED LEGACY OF THE VATICAN II LITURGICAL REFORMS

Kenneth D. Whitehead

ST. AUGUSTINE'S PRESS
South Bend, Indiana
2009

Manufactured in the United States of America.

1 2 3 4 5 6   15 14 13 12 11 10 09

Library of Congress Cataloging in Publication Data
Whitehead, K. D.
Mass misunderstandings:
the mixed legacy of the Vatican II
liturgical reforms / by Kenneth D. Whitehead.
p. cm.
Includes bibliographical references and index.
ISBN-13: 978-1-58731-496-4 (pbk.: alk. paper)
ISBN-10: 1-58731-496-7 (pbk.: alk. paper)
1. Catholic Church – Liturgy – History – 20th century. 2. Vatican Council
(2nd: 1962–1965) Constitutio de sacra liturgia. I. Title.
BX1975.W45 2008
264'.02009045 – dc22   2008030711

Some of the material in this book appeared previously in somewhat different form in articles in the *Adoremus Bulletin* and in the *Fellowship of Catholic Scholars Quarterly*.

∞ *The paper used in this publication meets the minimum requirements of the American National Standard for Information Sciences - Permanence of Paper for Printed Materials, ANSI Z39.48-1984.*

St. Augustine's Press
www.staugustine.net

Once Again

To

Margaret

TABLE OF CONTENTS

Part One: Pope Benedict XVI Decides to Revive the Traditional Roman Mass

Part Two: Vatican Council II and the Reform of the Sacred Liturgy

Part Three: The Reform Stands
in Spite of the Unintended Consequences

PART ONE

POPE BENEDICT XVI DECIDES TO REVIVE THE TRADITIONAL ROMAN MASS

Chapter One
The Pope Issues a Motu Proprio, Summorum Pontificum

On 7/7/07 Pope Benedict XVI issued a much anticipated and long-expected apostolic letter in the form of a *motu proprio* ("by his own word"). As many people are well aware, the two-word Latin title usually assigned to such papal documents is normally taken from the first sentence of the document itself. The first sentence of this particular document reads (in English): "Up to our own times it has been the constant concern of the supreme pontiffs to ensure that the Church of Christ offers a worthy ritual to the Divine Majesty . . . " Hence the title of this particular *motu proprio*, taken from this first sentence, became *Summorum Pontificum* ("of the supreme pontiffs").

Since the subject of this new document concerned the offering of what the document's first sentence styled "a worthy ritual to the Divine Majesty," it should perhaps have been no surprise to anyone that, in the Catholic context, this *motu proprio* turned out to pertain to the holy sacrifice of the Mass. Specifically, among other things, *Summorum Pontificum* allows any Catholic priest in good standing to celebrate the Mass, not only in accordance with the current liturgical rules laid down in the revised and reformed Roman Missal issued by Pope Paul VI in 1970 (further revised and updated by Pope John Paul II in 2002), but also in accordance with the old Roman Missal used prior to the liturgical reforms called for by Vatican Council II. This older Missal was thought to have been long superseded.

Concretely, what this new allowance meant was that, under the conditions set forth in the pope's document itself, a Catholic priest no longer needed the specific permission of his bishop to celebrate this older form of the Mass (although the celebration of this or any Mass, as is the case with all the other sacraments of the Church, still remains under the ultimate authority of the bishop).

The old Roman Missal, in accordance with which by Pope Benedict's new ruling the former Mass could now again be more freely celebrated,

dated substantially from the year 1570, when Pope St. Pius V, following the
Council of Trent, codified and regularized the traditional Roman liturgy
that had been transmitted down through the centuries up to that time. This
traditional "Tridentine" Roman Missal underwent only a few minor
changes and adjustments over the next nearly 500 years. The latest revision
of it – which it was thought at the time would be the last, since in the mean-
time the Second Vatican Council, which met in Rome each fall over four
years between 1962 and 1965, was expected to call for a substantial reform
of it, and did in fact call for such a reform of it – was issued by Blessed
Pope John XXIII in 1962.

What Pope Benedict XVI's new apostolic letter *Summorum Pontificum*
now provided for, however, was that:

> The Roman Missal promulgated by Paul VI is the *ordinary* expres-
> sion of the *lex orandi* (law of prayer) of the Catholic Church of the
> Latin Rite. Nonetheless, the Roman Missal promulgated by St.
> Pius V and reissued by Blessed John XXIII is to be considered as
> an *extraordinary* expression of that same *lex orandi* . . . (Art. 1;
> emphasis added).

It is important to take careful note of the meaning and import of the
pope's language here. The current Roman Missal, which was thoroughly
revised in accordance with Vatican Council II's Constitution on the Sacred
Liturgy, *Sacrosanctum Concilium* (issued on December 4, 1963), was to
continue to be the *ordinary* form of Catholic eucharistic worship. Thus, in
no way was Benedict XVI annulling or going back on the liturgical reform
decreed by the Council. Rather, among other things, he was specifically
reaffirming the product of that reform as the ordinary form of the Mass.
Meanwhile, though, he was also now allowing another, older form of
eucharistic worship to be carried on as well, under the conditions which he
then specified in the text of the *motu proprio* itself.

The reform of the sacred liturgy was, in fact, the first subject taken up
by the Second Vatican Council, and *Sacrosanctum Concilium* was the first
conciliar document enacted by the Council. The document specifically
said that the Church's liturgy was to be "revised carefully in the light of
sound tradition" (SC 4). More specifically, *Sacrosanctum Concilium*
directed that:

> The rite of the Mass is to be revised in such a way that the intrin-
> sic nature and purpose of its several parts, as well as the connection

between them, may be more clearly manifested, and that devout and active participation by the faithful may be more easily achieved (SC 50).

The Council Fathers saw the Mass of the day, which they themselves were accustomed to celebrate, as solemn and reverent; but many of them also saw it, as did much of the informed opinion in the Church developed through the liturgical movement of the previous decades, as seeming to be almost entirely the affair of the priest-celebrant on his own, and as leaving too passive a role to the faithful; the priest said virtually all of the prayers in Latin throughout the entire Mass, with responses coming only from the acolytes (Mass-servers) "representing" the people. The people themselves, meanwhile, as often as not, knelt in their pews in silence and perhaps said their rosaries, if indeed they prayed at all while the Mass was going on.

Through the successful catechesis of that day, the people generally did understand that the Mass was a *sacrifice*, a re-enactment of the sacrifice of Jesus Christ on the cross, and they responded accordingly with appropriate reverence and devotion; but otherwise they often had little idea of what was going on at the altar while it was going on. That was why many of them *could* just say their rosaries while the mighty drama of the holy sacrifice of the Mass was unfolding before them!

The Council Fathers desired a liturgical reform which would accord a greater and more active role to the faithful in the congregation in the liturgy which they described as "the summit toward which the activity of the Church is directed; it is also the fount from which all her power flows" (SC 10). *Sacrosanctum Concilium* was the result of their deliberations on this subject. This first of the Council's sixteen documents laid out in careful detail the respects in which the Fathers believed the liturgy needed to be reformed. Reading through it today, one gets the impression of a sound and sensible and at times even beautifully written text. Implementation of it began almost immediately by means of a *motu propio* of Pope Paul VI's entitled *Sacram Liturgiam,* issued on January 24, 1964, a year and a half before the close of the Council itself. In *Sacram Liturgiam,* the pope "ordered and decreed" a number of far-reaching measures which set in motion the reform of the liturgy throughout the whole Church.

By means of this earlier *motu proprio,* among other things, Pope Paul VI established a special commission composed mostly of clerics who were liturgical specialists and experts. They were charged with the task of producing a reformed liturgy designed to encourage on the part of the faithful "the full, conscious, and active participation in liturgical celebrations," which *Sacrosanctum Concilium* declared was the primary aim of the liturgical reform (SC 14). This special commission of Paul VI's later acquired the name of "the Consilium for the Implementation of the Constitution on the Sacred Liturgy." Because of how some of the liturgical reforms in question turned out, however, this "Consilium" and its work later became the object of much criticism.

Nevertheless, the liturgical revisions and texts developed by the "Consilium," after approval by the Sacred Congregation of Rites (later the Sacred Congregation for Divine Worship) – and by the pope – became what Benedict XVI in *Summorum Pontificum* later designated to be the continuing ordinary form of Catholic eucharistic worship in the Roman rite. What Benedict subsequently did with his *motu proprio*, however, to the surprise and even the dismay of some, though to the sincere applause of others, was to allow the celebration of the Mass according to the unrevised 1962 Roman Missal that was in use prior to and at the Council. This older form of the Mass then became designated by Benedict to be the extraordinary form of eucharistic worship.

As Benedict pointed out both in his *motu proprio*, and in an accompanying letter to it that he sent out to the Catholic bishops, the old Missal was never formally and juridically abrogated; it was simply replaced by the new Missal promulgated by Pope Paul VI. At the time, however, it was assumed that the old Missal would no longer be used precisely because it had been replaced by the revised Missal. Few even imagined at the time that this enactment – carried out by legitimate Church authority in response to the mandate of an ecumenical council – might seriously be *opposed* by anybody. It was taken for granted that the changes being decreed were necessary and legitimate. Provision was made at the time for the old Mass to continue to be celebrated by aged or infirm priests celebrating without a congregation. Otherwise, it was simply assumed that the new Paul VI Missal would henceforth simply *be* the Roman rite.

Paul VI himself, for example, seems to have taken this for granted. In two General Audience addresses delivered on November 19 and November 26, 1969, in which he explained the coming liturgical "changes," he also spoke plainly of the "obligation" to celebrate the Mass in the new form, using language making clear that priests "must use" and "must follow" the new rite. It probably never entered his mind that, just because the old Missal was not actually "abrogated," as Pope Benedict XVI would point out some forty years later, the new Missal was somehow therefore not obligatory at the time. Later, in 1974, the Sacred Congregation for Divine Worship would issue an instruction on the "obligation" to employ the new Missal.

Some traditionalists today, however, appear to be interpreting Benedict's words about the lack of any earlier formal abrogation of the old Missal to mean that the liturgical prescriptions that were instituted after the Council by the proper authority of the Church were supposedly *not* actually obligatory on those normally subject to them. But it is hard to credit that this could have been Pope Benedict XVI's meaning. More likely, Benedict's mention of the lack of any earlier juridical abrogation was made in order to make clear that he was not going against any established Church law in again allowing a freer celebration of this older form of the Mass.

Another development that loomed very large at the time all these changes were taking place was that, in addition to going over to the revised new liturgy crafted by Paul VI's "Consilium," and embodied in the new Roman Missal, the Catholic bishops virtually everywhere in the world voted shortly after the Council to celebrate the new Mass in the vernacular rather than in Latin. *Sacrosanctum Concilium* had very plainly said that Latin was to be retained in the Mass (SC 36.1), and this is a passage from this conciliar document that has been very often quoted since, usually reproachfully, since, as things turned out, Latin was *not* retained.

At the same time, however, the Council had also explicitly allowed the celebration of the Mass in the vernacular if the bishops so desired, and if the Holy See approved (SC 36.2). In any event, it turned out that the bishops overwhelmingly did so desire, and the Holy See very soon after the Council acceded to their wishes and granted permission for vernacular Masses virtually worldwide. This was entirely legal, of course, and it is the situation that obtains today.

However, to reintroduce the celebration of the Mass again according to the old Missal thus necessarily also means to re-introduce its celebration in this form exclusively in Latin. While the reformed Mass can be and sometimes is celebrated in Latin, it is typically celebrated in the vernacular. The old Mass, however, can *only* be celebrated in Latin. In the popular mind, in fact, Latin often remains the most salient distinction between the two forms; and hence the whole issue is sometimes and even often framed as a question of whether the Mass is being celebrated in Latin or in the vernacular. But this is not really an exact distinction since the texts of the two Masses differ.

In any case, however, whether it is a question of Latin or the vernacular, of the new Mass or the old Mass, the fact remains that, by re-instituting the regular celebration of a form of the Mass thought to have been left behind by the introduction of a revised form crafted in response to the very definite wish and mandate of an ecumenical council of the Church, Pope Benedict XVI necessarily also changed somewhat the terms by which many of these questions have been normally understood by Catholics. Among other things, the pope's action constituted a belated recognition on the part of the Church's highest authority that the Second Vatican Council, despite its high hopes and ambitions surrounding it, so incessantly and so optimistically trumpeted for so long, had evidently still not really "taken hold" among at least a segment of the Catholic people. The Council was apparently *not* accepted by them as an integral and necessary part of the life and tradition of "the Church." This fact has implications that, as we shall see, extend beyond the question of the Mass as such.

Moreover, how the use of both an "ordinary" and an "extraordinary" expression of the Church's *lex orandi*, or law of prayer, will play out in the future still remains to be seen. The pope's action in setting things up this way surely has to be considered an unusual step creating an unusual situation by almost any standard. It is important to ask why the pope decided to proceed in this manner – to ask what this revival of the traditional Roman Mass is really all about. To answer this question, we shall need to look into the question of why the pope issued *Summorum Pontificum* in the first place.

Chapter Two
Why Did the Pope Issue Summorum Pontificum*?*

How did it come about, then, that Pope Benedict XVI should have decided, more than forty years after the Council, that an earlier form of the Mass should again be more freely allowed and celebrated in Latin as an "extraordinary" form? The pope himself offered an explanation of this in the letter which he sent to the Catholic bishops of the world along with his *motu proprio*. The pope noted in this letter that, following the liturgical reform, "it soon became apparent that a good number of people remained strongly attached to this usage of the Roman Rite, which had been familiar to them since childhood. This was especially the case in countries where the liturgical movement had provided many people with a notable liturgical formation and a deep, personal familiarity with the earlier form of the liturgical celebration."

In other words, Pope Benedict decided to allow a freer celebration of the old Mass because the reformed liturgy had not gained universal approval. What the pope considered to be a significant number of Catholics continued to show that they *wanted* to have the availability of this earlier form of the Mass. In their view, the reform of the liturgy called for by Vatican II had not been a success.

Perhaps more importantly than people simply preferring the old form, though, the pope made the further point that "fidelity to the old Missal became an external mark of identity" for Catholic traditionalists, particularly for those who adhered to a movement founded after the Council by a French Archbishop, Marcel Lefebvre. This Lefebvrist movement, as a result of the illicit ordination by this French archbishop of four other bishops, became, in 1988, the first and so far the only, major formal schismatic movement arising in the wake of Vatican Council II.

Thus, one of Pope Benedict's principal motives in allowing a return to the older form of the Mass, as he explained in his *motu proprio*, as well as in his accompanying letter to the Catholic bishops, was to try to reconcile

all or at least some of the estimated 600,000 Catholics who were currently following the Lefebvrist Society of Saint Pius X (SSPX), and who were
consequently no longer in communion with the Catholic Church. In addition to the SSPX, there were a number of other similar, usually smaller traditionalist groups out there that were also no longer in communion with the
Catholic Church. And there were also not a few traditionally-minded
Catholics who had not actually left the Church, but who remained acutely
dissatisfied with the forms of worship brought about as a result of the
Vatican-II liturgical reforms. The pope's hope and intention was to try to
reconcile all these traditionalists to the Church.

One of the recurring "demands" of the SSPX leadership over the years
has been their claim that every Catholic priest ought to have the "right" to
celebrate the traditional Mass freely, regardless of the Vatican II reforms.
Pope Benedict XVI thus, among other things, by means of his *Summorum
Pontificum,* essentially acceded to this SSPX claim, and granted this
"right" to celebrate the old Mass to all Catholic priests. Whether this concession will in fact serve or help to reconcile the SSPX and other traditionalists separated from the Church remains to be seen; it was certainly welcomed at the outset by not a few traditionally-minded Catholics.

Benedict himself, of course, did not for a moment imagine that the
Mass was the only outstanding issue which had brought about the separation of most of the separated traditionalists from communion with the
Church. He was quite well aware that "the reasons for the break . . . were
at a deeper level" than simply the form of worship preferred. At the same
time, however, he seemed to have decided that the form of worship preferred must not continue to motivate or justify any separation from the
communion of the Church – or to be an obstacle in the way of a possible
return to the Church's communion by those who had already been so motivated.

And as much or perhaps even more than his wish to reconcile
Lefebvrist-type traditionalists to the Church, however, there was the fact
that Benedict himself, before his election to the chair of Peter, quite often
exhibited in his own writings his own great sympathy for the traditional
liturgy and for those Catholics who, even while they remained loyal to and
in communion with the Church, nevertheless preferred this traditional
liturgy. They keenly regretted its replacement by the revised post-Vatican-
II liturgy. In his letter to the bishops, the pope characterized such Catholics
as desiring "to recover the form of the sacred liturgy that was dear to them.
This occurred above all," he added, "because in many places celebrations

were not faithful to the prescriptions of the new Missal, but the latter was actually understood as authorizing or even requiring creativity, which frequently led to deformations of the liturgy which were frequently hard to bear."

Here the pope, with characteristic Ratzingerian delicacy, touched upon what most knowledgeable Catholics had long since understood to have been among the serious missteps and wrong turns which, too often and too widely, were made in the course of carrying out the liturgical reform desired by the Second Vatican Council. In the document he called them "deformations." He could well have used a stronger word, "abuses."

It cannot be denied, in fact, that the Church's liturgical reform, though legitimate, and decreed by legitimate authority, was nevertheless in too many ways far from an unalloyed success. This is something that the Church leadership had not usually been prepared to frankly admit, but it is nevertheless something that most Catholics over the past generation have personally experienced and have been well aware of for some years, even if most of them never reacted as strongly, nor did they take the kind of drastic steps, that some of the Catholic traditionalists decided to take.

For what the pope in his letter so delicately styled "creativity" was sometimes and perhaps even often a good deal more than just "creativity." Sometimes it involved actual liturgical abuses, even gross ones, that could occasionally even border on the sacrilegious, and could cause one to wonder whether the perpetrators of what the pope was so mildly calling "deformations" really any longer themselves even believed that they were truly offering worship to the Divine Majesty.

These kinds of deformations, or abuses, had long since raised questions in the minds of not a few Catholics about whether Vatican II and its reforms could even be considered legitimate. Although in recent years there has generally been great improvement in how the Mass is celebrated since the turmoil of the early post-conciliar years, these questions nevertheless continued and continue to represent an unpalatable fact about Vatican II and its reforms which the Church has had to try to come to terms with virtually since the end of the Council itself.

For the mistakes and abuses which accompanied the Church's revision of the liturgy have long constituted a sore point for many Catholics, and some of the resentments created thereby have persisted up to the present day. Votaries of the new liturgy, including probably most bishops and clergy, have nevertheless too often been reluctant to acknowledge that there really was ever any serious problem. The official line generally held that everything had been just fine and the liturgical reform had uniformly been a great success. Many continue to take that same line today, and hence the typical case has also been that anyone who complained has customarily been taken to be "pre-conciliar" in orientation, and could thus be safely ignored or disregarded.

Occasionally a Roman document might concede that there had been a problem here or there, and might call for a correction. Episcopal documents issued by the bishops, as distinguished from documents issued by the Holy See, have rarely, almost never conceded any such thing. The experience of most of the faithful in the post-conciliar era has therefore been, as often as not, that their bishops would apparently too often side with, or at least tolerate, the perpetrators of abuses, as if these were legitimate features of the reformed liturgy.

Thus, to the dissatisfaction of many Catholics with regard to the reformed liturgy itself, there was sometimes also added an acute consciousness of *scandal* with regard to what even the pope would eventually frankly style "deformations." Too often, unfortunately, some of these deformations seem to have been, in effect, *allowed* in the post-conciliar Church.

No one has consistently been more aware of all this than Pope Benedict himself. All along, first as a theologian, then an archbishop, and then finally as a cardinal, he was one of the few prominent Church leaders willing to speak out frankly about what was so often really going on. He did so, for example, in his well-known 1985 book, *The Ratzinger Report*, in which liturgical "deformations," among other things, were quite frankly and openly recognized and denounced. The same thing proved to be true in other writings of his, especially those on the subject of the liturgy. In his letter to the bishops accompanying the *motu proprio*, to take a case in point, he reminded us that: "I am speaking from experience since I too lived through that [post-conciliar] period with its hopes and confusions. I have seen how arbitrary deformations of the liturgy caused deep pain to individuals totally rooted in the faith of the Church."

For Benedict XVI, then, the consequences stemming from the fact that, not always and in every respect did the Church's liturgical reforms prove to be a complete success, and not always and in every respect did they find complete acceptance in various Catholic quarters, were accordingly very serious consequences – consequences which could not just be ignored. His opening up of a liturgical alternative by means of *Summorum Pontificum* was thus neither a casual nor a superficial thing for him. At the same time, however, we should take careful note of the fact that he did *not* ascribe the problems he recognized to any defects in the revised liturgy itself, as called for by the Council and enacted by the authority of the Church. Rather, he described the deformations he deplored to a failure to be "faithful to the prescriptions of the new Missal." The problem resided not in the new form of the Mass, in his view, but in the failure to celebrate it according to the established rules.

In other words, he did not reinstitute the freedom to celebrate the old form more freely because he thought there was any grave deficiency in the new form. It is true that in his rather copious writings on the subject, Joseph Ratzinger was quite often critical of what he characteristically called "fabricated" or "man-made" liturgies; he was similarly critical of such things as the new practice of the priest facing the people rather than the altar or "the East." Liturgy should develop "organically," he consistently held; it was not something just to be put together by a "committee" or in accordance with somebody's theories. The former cardinal and future pope was nevertheless always fully aware that the Second Vatican Council did call for a reform of the liturgy, and he did not reject the liturgy that was produced as a result of this conciliar call. Rather, he fully accepted and even treasured the reformed liturgy for its positive benefits, and he plainly said so on more than one occasion. For example, in his 1981 book, *Feast of Faith* (published in English in 1986), Joseph Ratzinger wrote:

> Lest there be any misunderstanding, let me add that as far as its content is concerned (apart from a few criticisms), I am very grateful for the new Missal, for the way it has enriched the treasury of prayers and prefaces, for the new eucharistic prayers and the increased number of texts for use on weekdays, etc., quite apart from the availability of the vernacular. But I do regard it as unfortunate that we have been presented with the idea of a new book rather than with that of continuity within a single liturgical history. In my view, a new edition will need to make it quite clear that the so-called Missal of Paul VI is nothing other than a renewed form of the same Missal to which Pius X, Urban VIII, Pius V and their predecessors have contributed right from the Church's earliest history. It is of the very essence of the Church that she should be aware of her unbroken continuity throughout the history of faith, expressed in an ever present unity of prayer.

Thus, the new Missal of Paul VI is "a renewed form" of the *same* Missal as that of Pius X, Urban VIII, Pius V, etc. This hardly suggests that the reforms mandated by Vatican II could perhaps somehow be considered illegitimate! In the context of our present discussion, it is worthwhile adding what the then archbishop of Munich immediately went on to say in his book *Feast of Faith*, namely, that "this awareness of continuity is destroyed just as much by those who 'opt' for a book supposed to have been produced four hundred years ago as by those who would like to be forever drawing up new liturgies. At bottom these two attitudes are identical . . . " And, again, in *Feast of Faith*, with regard to possible remedies for perceived deformations, he wrote that it would not "be right, after the upheavals of past years, to press for further external changes. Therefore, it seems all the more important to promote the kind of liturgical education which will enable people to participate in a proper inward manner . . . "

Thus Joseph Ratzinger on the liturgy. Having been elected to the chair of Peter, it seems that the author of *Feast of Faith* in his *Summorum Pontificum* was rather plainly proceeding to implement some of the same ideas about which he had formerly written in his books. And in his letter to the Catholic bishops, he also wrote, pertinently, that:

> There is no contradiction between the two editions of the Roman Missal. In the history of the liturgy there is growth and progress but no rupture. What earlier generations held as sacred, remains sacred and great for us too, and it cannot be all of a sudden entirely forbidden or even considered harmful. It behooves all of us to preserve the riches that have developed in the Church's faith and prayer, and to give them their proper place.

But the pope then went on to make another very significant point, one which must be clearly understood if the purpose and scope of *Summorum Pontificum* is to be properly understood and evaluated:

> Needless to say, in order to experience full communion, *the priests of the communities adhering to the former usage cannot as a matter of principle exclude celebrating according to the new books.* The total exclusion of the new rite would not in fact be consistent with the recognition of its value and holiness (emphasis added).

We need to take special note of the pope's requirement here that those availing themselves of the new freedom to celebrate the old Mass must accept the licitness and validity of the new Mass. The *motu proprio* further specifies that "priests who use the Missal of Blessed John XXIII must be qualified to do so and not juridically impeded" (Art. 4), in other words, they must be in good standing with their bishops; they cannot be separated or alienated from the duly constituted bishops who by the will of Christ lead the Church. However, these requirements, especially the requirement that the licitness and validity of the reformed liturgy must be accepted, could conceivably remain a serious obstacle in the way of reconciling at least some of the devotees of the old Mass, because there are those among them who do *not* recognize either the validity of the reformed liturgy or that of the Council which called for it.

By specifically including this requirement of acceptance of the new Mass, however, Benedict XVI made abundantly clear in yet one more way – besides designating the two forms as "ordinary" and "extraordinary" – that his primary intention in all this was most definitely not to attempt to go back on the Council and its reforms in any way, nor to try to bring about any kind of "restoration" of the *status quo ante*, as some have imagined and alleged. Rather, the pope seems to have quite genuinely aimed to foster what he considers to be legitimate liturgical pluralism in the Church, a position that he has long advocated. For example, in his *Ratzinger Report*, written more than twenty years earlier, the by-then cardinal-prefect of the Congregation for the Doctrine of the Faith stated that:

> Prior to Trent a multiplicity of rites and liturgies had been allowed within the Church. The Fathers of Trent took the liturgy of the city of Rome and prescribed it for the whole Church; they only retained those Western liturgies which had existed for more than two hundred years. This is what happened, for instance, with the Ambrosian rite of the Diocese of Milan. If it would foster devotion in many believers and encourage respect for the piety of particular Catholic groups, I would personally support a return to the ancient situation, i.e., to a certain liturgical pluralism. Provided, of course, that the legitimate character of the reformed rites was emphatically affirmed, and that there was a clear delineation of the extent and nature of such an exception permitting the celebration of the pre-conciliar liturgy.

This is exactly what Pope Benedict XVI effected more than twenty years later with his *motu proprio.* He has been nothing if not consistent in all of this. He carried his conviction in the matter to the point of insisting, in his letter to Catholic bishops accompanying his apostolic letter, that "it is not appropriate to speak of these two versions of the Roman Missal as if they were 'two rites.' Rather, it is a matter of a twofold use of one and the same rite." The pope seemed especially to want to insist on this point as the answer to the critics who have contended that the *Novus Ordo*, or Mass of Paul VI, itself represented such a deep break with tradition as to be a separate "rite." The pope clearly did not accept or endorse this viewpoint.

Yet he himself, in the rather extensive quotation included above, nevertheless actually referred at one point to the "new rite"! In any case, quite apart from the semantics or terminology being employed at the moment, it could well be that the long-term effect of the pope's action in all this will be the legitimization of what could come to be considered a separate "Tridentine rite" in Latin in the Catholic Church. There are, after all, in the worldwide Catholic Church, a number of separate "rites" besides the Roman rite. In addition to the historical Eastern rites, there is of very recent vintage, for example, the Anglican Use rite, where the Book of Common Prayer has been adapted for those former Anglicans who came into the Catholic Church along with their priests. "Liturgical pluralism" has long been a fact of life in the Catholic Church, in fact, and the Catholic Church is surely big enough to countenance it and even to embrace it.

Only time and practice will show how the consequences of Pope Benedict's action in *Summorum Pontificum* will work themselves out. Liturgical changes of any kind always require time and usage in order to take hold. Failure to understand this was one of the things that helped bring about the dissatisfaction with the revised post-Vatican-II liturgy on the part of many Catholics. What cannot be doubted, however, is the high seriousness and the very careful thought which this pope put into the decision he announced in his *motu proprio*. Contrary to what many press and media reports, and even some supposedly informed commentaries, assumed and alleged about it, *Summorum Pontificum* was no fly-by-night or casual decision. Joseph Ratzinger's own words over many years provide a pretty ample explanation of why as pope he decided to revive the traditional Roman Mass in the way that he did.

Chapter Three
What Does the Motu Proprio *Provide For?*

Pope Benedict XVI's decision in *Summorum Pontificum* to allow a freer celebration of the Holy Mass in the older Roman rite as it was celebrated prior to the reforms mandated by the Second Vatican Council will surely have consequences, some of which cannot perhaps be foreseen. This was to be expected. Nevertheless, we can certainly consider what some of those consequences might be.

First of all, though, we should note that the pope does not seem to have settled upon an exact vocabulary or terminology to describe the new state of affairs that he brought about by his action. In his *motu proprio*, as well as in his letter to the Catholic bishops which accompanied it, he spoke variously of the "ordinary" and "extraordinary" forms of the Roman rite which, by his action, now seem to be firmly established on the basis of, first, the 1970 Missal of Pope Paul VI (further revised by Pope John Paul II in 2002); and, secondly, of the 1962 Missal of Blessed Pope John XXIII as well. Both Missals now appear to be firmly established in place as the authorized liturgical books for use in the Roman rite. It is not quite true, however, that they are both *equally* established, as we shall see.

However, what the pope did not do was to refer to the old and new forms of the Roman rite using the terms that, at least in English, have in fact come into general use in the post-conciliar period. These terms are "Tridentine Mass" for the old form, and "New Order," or *"Novus Ordo,"* for the new form. Ironically, perhaps, the new form, normally celebrated in English, is nevertheless most often today referred to as the *Novus Ordo* by the people who talk and write on the subject. These same people normally use the term "Tridentine Mass" to refer to the old form.

Pope Benedict himself, however, denies that there is even any such thing as a "Tridentine Mass." In his book *Feast of Faith,* from which we have already quoted, Joseph Ratzinger wrote that "there is no such thing as a 'Tridentine' liturgy, and until 1965, the phrase would have meant nothing to anyone. The Council of Trent did not 'make' a liturgy."

However that may be, the term "Tridentine Mass" has nevertheless now come into pretty general usage to describe the pre-conciliar form of the Mass. This form of the Mass was codified and regularized by Pope St. Pius V following the Council of Trent, after all, and the term "Tridentine Mass" therefore does not seem inapt or wrong. In fact, the term seems to have caught on, and everybody knows what is meant by it when it is used. Similarly, when the term *Novus Ordo* or "New Order" is used, everybody knows exactly what is meant by it. So we shall not eschew the use of these terms, even though the pope himself does not employ them.

Furthermore, we should note that, while the celebration of the old form – the Tridentine Mass – is now to be allowed more freely, its use is not entirely unrestricted. For one thing, in the case of private or semi-private Masses, the Missal of Blessed John XXIII may *not* be used for the sacred Triduum – that is, from the Mass of the Lord's Supper on Holy Thursday through the Good Friday services and on through the Masses of Easter Sunday (Art. 2). Yet this sacred Triduum is the single greatest celebration of the Catholic faith.

However, elective Tridentine Masses may otherwise be celebrated with no restrictions and no need for specific permission from the bishop provided the priest is celebrating *without a congregation*. The *motu proprio* specifically says that the "right" of the priest to celebrate the traditional Mass applies only to "Masses celebrated without the people" (Art. 2).

At the same time, though, and perhaps somewhat illogically, any of the faithful who "of their own free will" wish to assist at such Masses celebrated "without the people," may do so (Art. 4). This rather strange provision seems to have been formulated in this way – on the one hand, the priest is supposed to be celebrating without the people, but on the other hand, the people may attend if they wish – in order to prevent the Tridentine Mass from becoming the only Mass offered to the people in some cases or places, the extraordinary form thereby becoming the ordinary form, as it were. This is not envisaged, nor indeed is it allowed. What is allowed is that these prescribed "private" Masses may be, in effect, transformed into "semi-private" Masses, at the wish of those people who desire to attend them of their own volition; but these Masses, for all of that, are quite clearly not to be considered equivalent to "regular" parish Masses. The Tridentine Mass has *not* been made "equal" to the *Novus Ordo*. Nor does it seem to be intended by the pope that it should replace the latter over time.

Article 3 of *Summorum Pontificum* speaks of communities or institutes that might wish to celebrate the old form regularly. This must be decided by the communities in question "according to the norm of law and particular laws and statutes," which have thus in no way been abrogated by Pope Benedict's provisions here.

"In parishes where there is a *stable* group of the faithful who adhere to the earlier liturgical tradition" (Art. 5.1; emphasis added), the pastor is supposed to "willingly accept" their request for a Tridentine Mass, although – another limitation – there may be only one such Mass on Sundays and feast days (Art. 5.2). It is clearly not expected that permission to celebrate the old form will lead to its becoming a parish's principal celebration; on the contrary, it seems to be taken for granted that the numbers opting for a Tridentine Mass will always be small, and will consist mainly of what are perhaps rather curiously styled here as "stable" groups already preferring this form. Benedict XVI seemed principally to have in mind here existing groups already celebrating Tridentine Masses under the special "indult" that Pope John Paul II granted in 1984.

Requests for Tridentine Masses for weddings, funerals, and other special occasions are also supposed to be freely granted (Art. 5.3). I personally know of instances in the post-conciliar period where much unnecessary bad feeling and even hostility towards the Church was generated because a funeral Mass according to the Tridentine form was denied, for example, in cases where the deceased had indeed had a life-long devotion to that form. What could have been the harm in celebrating such a funeral Mass in such cases? Now, where legitimate requests for such a Mass are not granted, the faithful are supposed to be able to appeal to the bishop, who is "strongly requested to satisfy their wishes"; and if he cannot, "the matter should be referred to the Pontifical Commission *Ecclesia Dei*" (Art. 7).

Established by Pope John Paul II in 1988 in Rome to oversee the Tridentine Masses authorized by an indult that he granted, the *Ecclesia Dei* Commission in Rome remains very much in being, and will henceforth presumably oversee the whole phenomenon of expanded Tridentine Masses under Benedict's new dispensation. Bishops are now specifically allowed (and encouraged) to refer questions concerning the expanded permission to celebrate the old Mass to the *Ecclesia Dei* Commission (Art. 8). At the same time, the Commission itself seems to be the entity within the Roman Curia able to deal with whatever problems or situations that may now arise following the issuance of the *motu proprio*.

Another feature of Pope Benedict's new and expanded authorization is that in the case of Tridentine Masses celebrated with congregations, the

Scripture readings may be in the vernacular and may be taken from "editions recognized by the Holy See" (Art. 6). Of course, Scripture readings were already in the vernacular in most places before Vatican II, but some have interpreted this article to mean that they may now also be taken from the Lectionary for the Paul VI *Novus Ordo* Missal as well. This revised Lectionary has a three-year cycle of readings from both the Old and New Testaments in place of the old Tridentine one-year cycle taken from the New Testament only. But it is hard to see how the use of this new Lectionary could be combined with the use of the 1962 John XXIII Missal, where, for example, the old "Sundays after Pentecost" would not correspond to the new "Sundays in Ordinary Time." Perhaps the *Ecclesia Dei* Commission plans to work on ways to integrate the two forms in certain ways, but barring that it would seem that Article 6 simply requires any vernacular Scripture readings to be from vernacular translations approved by the Holy See. Pope John Paul II had even ruled that the two rites could never be "intermingled."

Benedict's *motu proprio* includes yet another provision to the effect that "priests who use the Missal of Blessed John XXIII must be qualified to do so and not juridically impeded" (Art. 5.4). The wording of this provision is somewhat vague, but besides requiring that the priest be "in good standing," it would seem to encompass also the question of whether a priest is *competent* to celebrate a Mass in Latin, that is, whether he knows sufficient Latin to do so, and also whether he is properly trained in the usages and rubrics of the Tridentine Mass. It is here that the bishop's normal authority over the celebration of the Mass would seem to come back into full play, since it would be the bishop's responsibility to see that any priest wishing to celebrate the Tridentine Mass must in fact be qualified to do so.

This certainly cannot be assumed in the case of many and perhaps most priests today, for it has been a good while since thorough training in Latin has been a requirement for ordination. Many of today's younger priests, including many of the young "John Paul II priests" inspired in their vocations by the example of the late pope, would seem to be mostly *not* qualified to celebrate Tridentine Masses in Latin. Some of them, surely, know scarcely a word of Latin!

Pope Benedict XVI appeared to be fully aware of this situation. In his letter to the bishops, he noted, correctly, that "the use of the old Missal presupposes a certain degree of liturgical formation and some knowledge of the Latin language; neither of these is found very often." The pope went on to add, significantly: "Already from these concrete presuppositions, it is clearly seen that the new Missal will certainly remain the ordinary form of the Roman rite, not only on account of the juridical norms, but also because of the actual situation of the communities of the faithful." Benedict quite evidently did *not* envisage a mass movement of the faithful going back to the Tridentine Mass; he seemed to be concerned, rather, with the proper celebration of the Mass in the old form for those who were involved.

The requirement that the priest must be proficient in Latin if he is to celebrate the traditional form properly surely constitutes yet another reason why, as noted above, Article 8 urges the bishop to contact the *Ecclesia Dei* Commission in Rome if and when he is "unable" to satisfy a legitimate request to have a Tridentine Mass. Many and perhaps even most bishops today may not have any priests at all competent to say the Tridentine Mass properly. The same thing could be true of the pastor who is supposed to provide a Tridentine Mass to any "stable group" in his parish requesting it, according to Article 5.1 of the *motu proprio*. What Pope Benedict seemed to envisage here, therefore, was the idea that the *Ecclesia Dei* Commission could assist bishops and pastors being asked to provide a Tridentine Mass by putting them in touch with such groups as the Priestly Fraternity of Saint Peter composed of Tridentine-Mass priests who remain in communion with the Church. (Another avenue to follow here, of course, would for interested diocesan priests to seek training in Latin and in the Tridentine-Mass rubrics, as some seem to have done in the case of the "indult" Tridentine Masses allowed earlier by Pope John Paul II.)

Pope Benedict XVI's *motu proprio* includes a few other provisions, for example, pastors may use the older ritual in administering baptism, penance, marriage, and anointing (Art. 9.1), and bishops may do the same in administering confirmation (Art. 9.2). It is again significant, however, that *ordination* is not mentioned and is evidently not to be conferred according to the old form, since it is not listed along with the sacraments that specifically are mentioned. It is evidently *not* contemplated, in other words, that there should now be created a new class of "Tridentine Mass" priests specifically ordained to take advantage of the new permission that Pope Benedict XVI decided to grant.

The old Roman Breviary may again be used by clerics (Art. 9.3). Bishops may even erect special "Tridentine" parishes in their dioceses if they judge this to be helpful or opportune (Art. 10). But it is certainly not required that this be done.

What emerges from all these provisions would seem to be the clear intention of Pope Benedict XVI to allow the revival of the pre-Vatican–II Mass and sacraments for those members of the Catholic faithful who strongly desired them – some of whom have been alienated from the Church in varying degrees in their absence. However, the pope not only does not appear to have wished or expected a general or even perhaps a very widespread return to the old ritual. He appears, rather, to have taken for granted that the great majority of Catholics will continue to follow the reformed ritual of the Paul VI Mass in the vernacular. His primary motive thus truly does seem to have been the reconciliation of disaffected and alienated Catholics who had not been won over to the reformed rite.

Thus, the pope's action cannot really be classed as an attempt to turn back the clock, repudiate Vatican II, disfavor the *Novus Ordo*, or go back on the extensive revision of the Church's liturgical books. Rather, the pope seems truly and sincerely to hold for what he calls "liturgical pluralism." He certainly meant to encourage at the same time, though, a greater sympathy for traditionalist-type Catholics than has generally been the case up to now in the post-conciliar era.

In his letter to the bishops accompanying *Summorum Pontificum*, speaking of the temporary and contingent provisions for the celebration of the Tridentine Mass that his predecessor, Pope John Paul II, had made two decades earlier, Benedict explained that John Paul had "primarily wanted to assist the Society of St. Pius X to recover full unity with the successor of Peter, and sought to heal a wound experienced even more painfully. Unfortunately," Benedict added, "this reconciliation has not yet come about. Nonetheless, a number of communities have gratefully made use of the possibilities provided by the *motu proprio*."

However, as Pope Benedict also pointed out at the same time, his predecessor's actions had not included "detailed prescriptions" or "juridical norms" for the continued celebration of the older form of the Roman rite; and hence, another one of Benedict's motives for issuing *Summorum Pontificum* was to remedy this lack. This new document thus now does contain the necessary "detailed prescriptions" and "juridical norms" for the regular celebration of the Tridentine Mass. In addition, as we have seen, the *Ecclesia Dei* Commission remains in existence to oversee the implementation of the new provisions, and to help in the solution of any difficulties that might be encountered. Bishops are specifically requested to seek the assistance of the Commission if problems or difficulties arise for them in the carrying out of the new provisions (Arts. 7 & 8). It is to be

hoped that they will do precisely that rather than allow the pope's new prescriptions to go by the board for lack of anyone to carry them out properly.

Finally, as Pope Benedict XVI stressed in his letter to the bishops
accompanying *Summorum Pontificum*, "the new norms do not in any way
lessen your own authority and responsibility, either for the liturgy or for the
pastoral care of your faithful. Each bishop is the moderator of the liturgy
in his own diocese . . . "

The pope also invited the bishops to report to him on how the *motu
proprio* has worked out for them three years after the effective date of the
document itself, which was on the feast of the Exaltation of the Holy
Cross, September 14, 2007. No doubt this date will mark only the beginning of what must be considered a new liturgical era inaugurated by Pope
Benedict in his *motu proprio* entitled *Summorum Pontificum*, according to
which both an "ordinary" and an "extraordinary" form of the Roman rite
is now henceforth authorized in the Roman rite.

Chapter Four
Pope John Paul II and the
Ecclesia Dei *Commission*

The problems that Pope Benedict XVI was endeavoring to deal with in *Summorum Pontificum* have been around for most of the post-conciliar era; but they are problems that the Church's leadership, by and large, has generally been reluctant even to recognize, let alone deal with. It is interesting to compare, for example, the action Benedict XVI has now taken with the actions that his predecessor, Pope John Paul II, thought that he had to take in order to deal with essentially the same problems related to disaffected and alienated Catholics on the traditionalist side.

What Pope John Paul II decided that he had to do when significant numbers of Catholics made clear their profound dissatisfaction with the Vatican II reforms as they were experienced by them in their churches – and also when not insignificant numbers of those same disaffected and alienated Catholics were joining up with schismatic groups that among other things celebrated the Tridentine Mass – was to allow, under quite limited conditions, the licit celebration of the old form of the Mass, the Tridentine Mass. What Pope Benedict XVI would later authorize on a much wider scale, Pope John Paul II had already allowed under narrower circumstances.

Under John Paul II, the conditions for a limited celebration of the Tridentine Mass were first laid out in a document, *Quattor Abhinc Annos*, which the Congregation for Divine Worship and the Discipline of the Sacraments issued on October 3, 1984. This document was the result of an inquiry begun four years earlier by the Holy See inquiring about the reception of the Missal of Paul VI by the faithful, and investigating reports of "opposition to the reform that may need to be overcome." At first it seems to have been concluded by the Holy See that opposition to the new Mass was negligible; but this was a conclusion that was impossible to maintain in the face of increasing adherence by tradition-minded Catholics to Tridentine Mass groups such as the SSPX headed by the dissident French

Archbishop Marcel Lefebvre as well as to other groups headed by other "Tridentinists."

Actually, except for the well-known, indeed almost legendary, traditional Roman slowness, this inquiry about "opposition to the reform" should probably have been instituted *years* sooner than it was. In retrospect, it is hard to see why opposition and even resistance to the liturgical reforms was not immediately obvious to the officials of the Roman Curia (and, indeed, the Catholic bishops generally). However that may be, permission was eventually though still quite reluctantly granted to bishops in *Quattor Abhinc Annos* to grant an indult, or special permission, allowing the celebration of the old Mass according to the Missal of 1962 under certain strict conditions (called norms). These norms were laid out as follows:

> 1. There must be unequivocal, even public evidence that the priest and people have no ties with those who impugn the lawfulness and doctrinal soundness of the Roman Missal promulgated in 1970 by Pope Paul VI.
>
> 2. The celebration of Mass in question must take place exclusively for the benefit of those who petition it; the celebration must be in a church or oratory designated by the diocesan bishop (but not in parish churches, unless, in extraordinary instances the bishop allows this); the celebration may take place on those days and in those circumstances approved the bishop, whether for an individual instance or as a regular occurrence.
>
> 3. The celebration is to follow the Roman Missal of 1962 and must be in Latin.
>
> 4. In the celebration there is to be no intermingling of the rites or texts of the two Missals.
>
> 5. Each bishop is to inform his Congregation of the concessions he grants and, for one year from the date of the present indult, of the outcome of its use.
>
> The pope, who is the father of the entire Church, grants this indult as a sign of his concern for all his children without prejudice to the liturgical reform that is to be observed in each ecclesiastical community (*Quattor Abhinc Annos*).

It is again to be noted that "the liturgical reform" of Vatican II is taken to be the norm in this Roman document. This liturgical reform was *not* something that a band of renegade "liberal," or "Protestant," or Masonry-influenced clerics carried out apart from the regular channels of authority in the Church; it was something instituted *by* the rightful and legitimate authorities in the Church.

For a document that was supposed to be a concession, however, John Paul II's *Quattor Abhinc Annos* certainly seemed to be quite severe in both tone and content. It does not seem that very many indults were granted (or requested) under its stringent norms, in fact – as if Church authority continued to be reluctant to grant any – and, indeed, some of the traditionalist groups celebrating the Tridentine Mass were apparently themselves quite unwilling to accept the conditions laid down in the document or avail themselves of the privileges John Paul II was so reluctantly granting.

Nor does it seem that very many bishops were willing to attempt to deal with groups that might request it, which they generally saw as celebrating illicit "motel Masses" outside the normal jurisdiction of the Church. Indeed, it was the Catholic bishops nearly everywhere who, after the Council, had rather unceremoniously "banned" the old Mass as soon as the liturgical reforms came into effect. As we have seen, Pope Benedict XVI noted that the old Mass never was "abrogated"; what he apparently meant is that the Holy See never formally abrogated or abolished it as such. As a practical matter, however, it was to all intents and purposes "banned" by the bishops nearly everywhere from the time that the reformed liturgy first came in.

Nor was it only by the bishops that the old Mass was "banned," for the Sacred Congregation for Divine Worship, on October 28, 1974, itself issued a Note on the Obligation to Use the New Roman Missal, as we have already briefly noted. The document in question did establish what it called an *obligation* to use the new Missal. It employed language that no Catholic bishop receiving the document from Rome could have imagined was somehow merely optional and not prescriptive. The Latin title of this document was *Conferentiarum Episcopalium*, and it was quite conspicuously included in Father Austin Flannery's widely used collection of the conciliar and post-conciliar documents, so it cannot be said to have been an obscure or unknown document. It stated that once a vernacular version of the Mass was approved by a particular bishops' conference, "Mass may *not* be celebrated, whether in Latin or in the vernacular, save according to the rite of the Roman Missal promulgated by the authority of Paul VI . . . " (emphasis added).

So it was not just the bishops who "banned" the old form. Rome too officially made it obligatory. The bishops, though, seem to have been virtually unanimous in wanting the new Missal used exclusively. They also evidently saw themselves as acting strictly in accordance with explicit instructions from the competent congregation in Rome. Nor will it do to cite the names of individual officials in the Congregation for Divine Worship at the time, as some traditionalists have done, as if identifying such officials as, e.g., freemasons, might somehow invalidate the instructions which the Congregation officially and undeniably issued. How was the average priest, or even the average bishop, to conclude anything else but that "Rome" had indeed "banned" the Tridentine Mass?

At the Council itself, the American bishops had not been in the forefront of those pressing either for liturgical reform or for the vernacular Mass. On the contrary, those American bishops who happened to speak out at the Council on the subject, such as New York's Cardinal Francis J. Spellman, were generally ardent defenders of the then standard Latin Mass. Once the liturgical reforms were put in place, however, most American bishops suddenly became quite adamant in rejecting even the indult that later allowed the celebration of the Tridentine Mass; and many if not most of the American bishops similarly rejected the idea of celebrating even the *Novus Ordo* in Latin. Nor were suitable liturgical books ever issued in Latin by the bishops' conference for the proper celebration of the *Novus Ordo* in Latin. There should never really have been any problem about this – Latin had *not* officially been banned! – but in the minds of most of the American bishops of the day, apparently there was a problem with allowing Latin Masses of any kind.

And so, suddenly, it turned out that Latin itself was, indeed, "banned"; it became *verboten*. It might still be, officially, "the language of the Church," as some conservatives kept tirelessly repeating, but it nevertheless was "banned" for all practical purposes in the Church's official worship in America, as well as in many other places. The Catholic bishops may not have known how to impose discipline on Catholic theologians publicly denying Catholic doctrine; but with regard to anyone who might want a Latin Mass, they knew exactly what they wanted; they were strict disciplinarians; they were veritable tigers! As a result, the response to *Quattor Abhinc Annos*, at least in America, seems to have been really quite minimal. The American bishops of the day apparently did not find it easy to sympathize with anybody who might want a Latin Mass.

Thus, authorized Latin Tridentine Masses under John Paul II's 1984 indult were really quite minimal in the United States. Nor was the problem limited to America. In his *God and the World*, published in 2002, while he was still prefect of the Congregation for the Doctrine of the Faith, Cardinal Joseph Ratzinger observed that:

> Anyone who nowadays advocated the continuing existence of this [Latin] liturgy or takes part in it is treated like a leper; all tolerance ends here. There has never been anything like this in history; in doing this, we are despising and proscribing the Church's whole past. How can one trust her present if things are that way? I must say, quite openly, that I don't understand why so many of my episcopal brethren have to such a great extent submitted to this rule of intolerance, which for no apparent reasons, is opposed to making the necessary inner reconciliation within the Church.

Thus did the future Pope Benedict XVI speak out on the subject of the Latin Mass. For his part, he clearly wished to make "the necessary inner reconciliation within the Church." It should have been clear, long before he was elected to the papacy, in fact, where he stood on such matters. He certainly showed where he stands with the promulgation of his *motu proprio*. His predecessor had only allowed the licit celebration of the pre-Vatican-II Mass on a much more limited basis. Benedict was prepared, however, to expand this authorization quite significantly in *Summorum Pontificum*.

In the case of Pope John Paul II, it was the disobedient and unlawful ordination by Archbishop Marcel Lefebvre of four bishops on June 30, 1988, that finally moved the Polish pope, two days later, on July 2, 1988, to issue his *motu proprio* entitled *Ecclesia Dei*, by which he announced the excommunication of Archbishop Lefebvre and the four new bishops that the latter had illicitly ordained. It was at the same time and by means of the same document, that John Paul established the *Ecclesia Dei* Commission. This Commission was intended to reconcile as many of the followers of the now accomplished Lefebvre schism as possible to the re-establishment of communion with the Catholic Church.

The pope stated in *Ecclesia Dei* that the task of the Commission was "to collaborate with the bishops, with the Departments of the Roman Curia, and with the circles concerned for the purpose of facilitating full ecclesial communion of priests, seminarians, religious communities, or individuals until now linked to the fraternity founded by Mons. Lefebvre who may wish to remain united with the successor of Peter in the Catholic Church . . . "

Significantly, Pope John Paul II also emphasized in *Ecclesia Dei* that "respect must everywhere be shown for the feelings of all those who are attached to the Latin liturgical tradition by a wide and generous application of the directives already issued some time ago by the Apostolic See for the use of the Roman Missal according to the typical edition of 1962" – the pope was referring here, of course, to *Quattor Abhinc Annos*.

Thus, it was only in response to an actual schism that Pope John Paul II finally called for "a wide and generous application" of the indult provisions allowing the celebration of the Tridentine Mass that he had authorized so narrowly some four years earlier. With the encouragement of the new *Ecclesia Dei* Commission, celebration of the Tridentine Mass in accordance with this indult finally did become somewhat broadened. In particular, a number of tradition-minded members of the faithful, including not a few priests, *did* become reconciled to the Church at this point, once it had become clear that the Lefebvrists now actually were in schism with the excommunication of their bishops by the Holy See. So long as Archbishop Lefebvre himself was still engaged in negotiations with the Holy See concerning his status in the Church, many tradition-minded Catholics, and, especially, some of the priests among them, found it possible to reconcile adherence to his movement with their own consciences. Once the archbishop was formally excommunicated by the Church, however, this was no longer possible.

This was the situation which Pope Benedict XVI inherited. He evidently saw the issuance of his new *motu proprio* as the logical and, indeed, as the necessary, follow-up to the *motu proprio* his predecessor had issued some two decades earlier, with the intention of reconciling those unable to recognize that the Catholic Church had not ceased to be the true Church of Christ all along, even through the very confusing post-conciliar years.

That Pope Benedict XVI envisioned no "return to the past," however, was confirmed by the master of papal liturgical ceremonies, Monsignor Guido Marini, in an interview on Vatican Radio on January 19, 2008. Asked about fears that the pope wanted to abandon the liturgical reforms of the Second Vatican Council, Monsignor Marini replied: "These are certainly incorrect inferences and interpretations." The Vatican liturgist stated that the path of Catholic liturgy is "development in continuity," in which change never loses touch with the Church's living traditions.

Chapter Five
Reactions to Summorum Pontificum

What were the reactions to Pope Benedict XVI's *Summorum Pontificum?* The official reaction by the American bishops was respectful – and factual. A few bishops, such as Cardinal Adam Maida in Detroit and Cardinal Edward Egan in New York issued explanatory statements that were correct but hardly enthusiastic. Warmer statements such as the one issued by Bishop Samuel Aquila of Fargo, North Dakota, were harder to come by.

The chairman of the U.S. Conference of Catholic Bishops' Committee on the Liturgy, Bishop Donald Trautman of Erie, Pennsylvania, credited the pope with being "sensitive to those still clinging to the Tridentine Latin Mass," as he put it, his choice of the word "clinging" here signaling what he probably really thought about the whole business. Bishop Trautman noted that "indult" Tridentine Masses were already permitted in his diocese of Erie, and he indicated that he would be "issuing diocesan norms to help apply and order the specifics of the pope's letter." He announced, for example, that "priests who might want to celebrate the Tridentine Mass will be given a rubrical and Latin exam to comply with the pope's . . . statement." Bishop Trautman was no doubt correct in applying this kind of test, of course, as long as it was not aimed at limiting or excluding the celebration of the Tridentine Mass.

The fact is, though, as one could read between the lines in the case of Bishop Trautman and of some other bishops, most American bishops were, and probably still are, quite opposed to Pope Benedict's revival of the old Mass. According to media reports, Spokane Bishop William Skylstad, the president of the U.S. Conference of Catholic Bishops (USCCB) at the time, had earlier flatly told the pope that the American bishops did not want this revival of the traditional Roman Mass.

This sentiment apparently characterized the reactions of some other bishops besides the American bishops. In November, 2007, the secretary of the Congregation for Divine Worship and the Discipline of the Sacraments, Archbishop Malcolm Ranjith Patabendige Don, was widely quoted in the Catholic press as rather sternly criticizing the fact that in some dioceses "there have been interpretative documents that inexplicably aim to limit the *motu proprio* of the pope." The archbishop even spoke of "rebellion" on the part of some bishops. There were evidently disagreements in some places concerning the characteristics of some of the "stable groups" requesting the traditional Mass and also concerning what knowledge and training a priest should have before celebrating the Mass according to the 1962 Missal. Behind these concerns, the Curia archbishop said, "there hide, on the one hand, ideological prejudices, and, on the other hand, pride, which is one of the most serious sins." He invited everyone to "obey the pope."

However, in America, at any rate, there did not seem to be any actual "disobedience," but only perhaps reluctance. And in any case, opposition by the American bishops almost certainly never equaled that of the bishops of France – where bishops were more starkly confronted with the Lefebvrist phenomenon. According to press reports, prior to the issuance of the *motu proprio*, the French bishops sent more than one delegation to Rome to try to dissuade the pope from carrying out his reported plans to revive the traditional Roman Mass.

Once the *motu proprio* was actually issued, Cardinal Sean O'Malley of Boston, who had been included among a group of some twenty-five or so bishops and cardinals worldwide who attended a preview of the new document, tended to downplay the whole business; he probably reflected the thinking of most American bishops when he said that "this document will not result in a great deal of change for Catholics in the U.S. . . . . The issue of the Latin Mass is not urgent in our country . . . "

This same attitude was reflected in some of the other American reactions to the pope's document. Monsignor M. Francis Mannion, a Utah pastor who is also a liturgical expert in his own right, as well as a weekly columnist for the *Our Sunday Visitor* newspaper, noted that the indult Tridentine Mass earlier authorized in Salt Lake City had had to be cancelled for lack of attendance (but then it was apparently only celebrated *once a month*, which would hardly have encouraged regular attendance!).

Monsignor Mannion added, in his words, that "my own limited research undertaken for an essay I published some years ago is that about one percent of American Catholics want the Tridentine Mass. There is a larger but still relatively small body of American Catholics who think that a Latin Mass 'would be nice' once in awhile. I do not think that these are the people the pope is responding to with his *motu proprio*." This judgment by Monsignor Mannion seemed to be the kind of response that we can probably correctly characterize as "mainstream," at least in the United States.

Among those whom we can loosely categorize as "liberals" in the Church, however, reactions were generally considerably more negative. Often, they were more vehement as well. Liberals strongly tended to oppose and deplore the pope's action, and they also tended to describe it as nothing else but a probable attempt to abandon Vatican II. Some liberal reactions seemed positively alarmist, in fact, and certainly exhibited nothing that could be characterized as liberality or tolerance. A letter in the left-ist *National Catholic Reporter*, for example, declared that:

> Pope Benedict's decision allowing the use of Latin should call for outrage from every intelligent Catholic. This "give me that old-time religion" approach to liturgy is an undoing of the reforms of the Second Vatican Council. That Council never intended to create a structure whereby two forms of the Roman rite would simulta-neously exist . . . Do we really want a liturgy that places emphasis on expiation of sin instead of the paschal mystery emphasizing resurrection? In the Tridentine rite, women are excluded from the sanctuary. The rite can be used for all the sacraments except ordi-nation. In the baptismal rite, the parents say nothing . . . This deci-sion of Pope Benedict will lead to the gradual dismantling of the liturgical reforms of Vatican II . . .

This attitude was not uncommon among Catholic liberals, and was generally in marked contrast to that of most conservatives and traditional-ists, who tended to be more subdued in their reactions. While the latter generally favored the pope's action, some of them at least recognized that it was quite limited in its scope and did not go as far as some of them may have wanted. The world at large, meanwhile, was mostly puzzled by the whole affair and tended to see it as primarily an issue of Latin versus English in the Mass – or perhaps as a question of whether the priest should be celebrating facing the altar or facing the people. None of this was to take in very much of what was really involved. Few commenting on it seemed to have any idea how to put it all into its proper context, or perhaps even to understand what its proper context was and what it really was all about.

The same kind of puzzlement seemed to be the reaction even of some of the supposed "experts" on Catholic affairs, including some of those whom the secular media like to consult and quote in order, they imagined, to get the "real story" behind otherwise mysterious and even incomprehensible happenings within the Catholic Church. For example, the usually glib and confident Jesuit Father Thomas W. Reese of the Woodstock Center, located at Georgetown University, in Washington, D.C., saw the whole affair as mainly "a real pain in the neck for the pastor . . . Where there are groups that want it . . . he's going to be pressed to do it." While this is, of course, a real problem, the cavalier way that Father Reese approached it seemed to make it, for him, just one more instance where he could say "I told you so" about how the pope had, once again in his estimation, badly erred. This rather glib approach to Church developments has long been a specialty of his, and his secular media contacts have apparently not ceased to credit it.

Again, in this case, with equal or perhaps even greater fatuity, Father Reese went on to observe that "if the pope issues a *motu proprio* allowing the use of the Tridentine Mass without the local bishop's permission, he is basically saying that he does not trust the pastoral judgment of the bishop." (Father Reese is the author of books on the Catholic hierarchy as an *institution*; he seems to have little or no regard for what the Church believes and teaches.)

Similarly, Notre Dame theologian Father Richard P. McBrien, another popular TV "expert" on Catholic subjects, thought that *Summorum Pontificum* was a "hot potato" for the Church, undermining the authority of the local bishop over the liturgy and creating, in effect, two separate "Roman rites," in spite of what the pope may have asserted to the contrary. Father McBrien, again, did not seem to be unduly bothered by what the pope had done, as much as he seemed to be bothered by the fact that the pope presumed to do it against what Father McBrien considered to be "enlightened" opinion in the Church.

Few critics on the liberal side seemed to want to credit the pope's stated aim that he was trying to reconcile the disaffected; nor did it seem that they had ever bothered to try to understand what the disaffection was all about. Yet once they had declined to accept the pope's own explanation for his action, these liberal critics were inevitably pretty much at sea in trying to understand what the whole thing really *was* all about.

Again on the liberal side, the most common interpretation was that the pope really was attempting to go back on Vatican Council II. Immediately prior to the official release of the *motu proprio*, for example, Bishop Kieran Comy of Arundel and Brighton in England opined in the press that "it might send out an unfortunate signal that Rome is no longer fully committed to the reforms of the Second Vatican Council."

An Italian bishop, who as a priest had been closely associated with the Consilium which produced the liturgical reforms mandated by the Council, complained quite bitterly in public – and quite emotionally – that the Vatican II liturgical reforms had quite simply now been "cancelled," as he put it. The Most Reverend Luca Brandolini, until recently the bishop of Sora-Aquino-Pontecorvo in Italy, was quoted in an interview with the Italian newspaper, *La Repubblica*, as saying: "This day is for me a day of great grief . . . I am living the saddest day of my life as a priest, as a bishop, and as a man . . . It is a day of grief, not only for me, but for many who lived and worked in the Second Vatican Council. Today a reform for which so many labored at the cost of great sacrifice, animated solely by the wish to renew the Church, has been cancelled . . . " *Cancelled*!

Bishop Brandolini's extreme reaction might have been at least partially understandable on the personal level because he had worked on liturgical matters at the Council; he evidently had a personal stake in them; and, indeed, he had actually been a collaborator of Archbishop Annibale Bugnini, the "architect" of the Vatican II liturgical reforms (whom conservatives in the Church have quite often stigmatized if not demonized for his work). But precisely as a liturgist, Bishop Brandolini should have been able to read the actual language of Pope Benedict XVI's *motu proprio* more carefully and accurately, and hence he should have been able to understand what it plainly said and entailed. Yet, sadly, his mistaken and quite excessive reaction to the *motu proprio* was not untypical of what a good many others on the liberal side in the Church were saying as well.

To cite yet one more example of this kind of reaction, we can turn to Frank K. Flinn, identified as an adjunct professor of religious studies at Washington University in St. Louis. Flinn wrote in the *Boston Globe* that "Pope Benedict XVI's recent decision to encourage wider usage of the traditional Tridentine Mass in Latin is the latest move in the long campaign to undo liberal reforms in Church practices . . . " *Undo!*

Flinn went on to accuse the Holy See of being "inexplicably lenient towards the schismatic Lefebvrists, despite the scorn they continue to heap in the direction of the Vatican itself." "Leniency" is a rather strange concept to invoke here, it would seem, considering that *all* the bishops of the Lefebvrist movement have been *excommunicated*!

Oblivious to such not-so-fine distinctions, Flinn nevertheless went on further to accuse the former Cardinal Ratzinger, personally, of giving the traditionalists "free ammunition." His proof of this was a mention that, "in the preface to a liturgical treatise, [Cardinal Ratzinger] accused modern Masses of being faddish 'showpieces' and 'fabrications.'"

This was apparently a reference to a preface that Cardinal Ratzinger wrote for a 1993 book entitled *The Reform of the Roman Liturgy*. This book was written by the late German liturgist Monsignor Klaus Gamber. In his preface, the cardinal credited Monsignor Gamber with producing a lucid critique of the kind of "fabricated" or "manufactured" liturgy which the cardinal himself had frequently criticized in some of his own copious writings on the subject of the liturgy. Cardinal Ratzinger further saw the late Monsignor Gamber as a possible "father" of a hoped-for new liturgical movement that would work for what has come to be called a "reform of the reform" – a new liturgical movement to correct some of the mistakes made in the course of the liturgical reform and to champion necessary liturgical changes to be carried out in a gradual and "organic" way.

But such words hardly amounted to providing "free ammunition" to the traditionalists, as Flinn contended. Nevertheless, the latter still found himself able to conclude, quite gratuitously, that "by turning back the clock not to the creative multiplicity of the early Christian communities, but to the heyday of the Inquisition and papal monarchism at Trent, Pope Benedict XVI is *abandoning* the principle of collegiality that embraces bishops, all priests, all deacons, and all lay people as the worshipping community of the beloved faithful that says to Vatican II, 'Farewell'" (emphasis added)! *Abandoning!*

This kind of reaction was surely unreal. The pope's action was hardly a repudiation of Vatican II. The term "collegiality" mentioned here by this author is, in reality, a very important theological concept developed at Vatican II, describing the proper relationship of the Catholic bishops comprising the "college" of bishops to each other, and to the head of the college of bishops, the pope. This author, however, seemed to equate it with the idea of a Church as primarily a (horizontal) democratic "community" centered upon itself. This is an idea which did indeed emerge in the post-conciliar era as part of the simplistic mishmash which many liberals still seem to think was the real meaning of Vatican II. But it really had nothing at all to do with what the pope did in issuing *Summorum Pontificum.*

Yet other liberal reactions to the *motu proprio* in the same vein could be cited, though not all of them, perhaps, quite as extreme – or as fatuous – as Flinn's. For example, the reaction of a Benedictine nun long identified with liberal causes in the Church, Sister Joan Chittister, was typical. In her regular column in the leftist *National Catholic Reporter*, she wrote as follows: "It does not make reconciliation easier with women, who are now pointedly left out of the Eucharistic celebration entirely [*sic!*], or with Jews, who find themselves in the Tridentine Good Friday rite again described as 'blind' and as objects of conversion." *Left out!*

But is not the Gospel still supposed to be preached to "the whole creation" (Mk 16:15), including to the Jews? Sister Chittister, however, appeared to take the view, common to many liberals in the Church, that the main point about Vatican Council II is that it somehow supposedly abolished all the beliefs and practices of "the bad old Church," including the practice of preaching the Gospel! Those who hold this view, which amounts to believing that Vatican II somehow created a "new Church" distinct from the Church that has come down to us from apostolic times, can generally be counted upon to come out with such often wildly inappropriate statements, framed in accordance with their own ideological understanding of the Christian faith. But then, whenever the Church, as in the present case, issues a statement indicating that she continues to take seriously what she has in fact not ceased to believe and teach, these people apparently cannot believe or credit the Church's plain words!

In conformity with the theology of the very this-worldly "community" which Vatican II is supposed to have established in place of the Church, Sister Chittister found that "the symbology of a lone celebrant, removed from and independent from the congregation, is clear: ordinary people have no access to God [*sic*]. They are entirely dependent on a special caste of males to contact God for them [*sic*]. They are not 'worthy,' the liturgy says, even to 'receive' the host..."

The liturgy, of course, *does* indeed say that *none of us* is worthy to receive God in the sacrament! But the Church nevertheless teaches that, in his great mercy, God gives himself to us anyway.

One common feature shared by both the "mainstream" and the "liberal" comments made by various Catholics on the pope's *motu proprio* would seem to be a near total misunderstanding of – or at the very least a near total lack of sympathy for – the pope's own generous intention of reconciling disaffected traditionalists with the Church. This point seems to have been largely missed. However, if these reactions by Catholics missed this point, the reactions of some of the Jewish voices that were raised in criticism of the issuance of *Summorum Pontificum* turned out to be *beside the point*.

Chapter Six
Jewish Reactions Beside the Point

Sister Joan Chittister's reference to the supposed exclusion of the Jews by the pontiff's action in *Summorum Pontificum* touched upon an entire additional dimension in the general reaction to the pope's *motu proprio*, namely, the charge that Pope Benedict XVI was reinstating unchanged a rite alleged to have been a source of anti-Semitism among Catholics, which only Vatican II's Declaration on the Relation of the Church to Non-Christian Religions, *Nostra Aetate*, had supposedly done away with. This was a grossly exaggerated charge – not only ill-informed and, indeed, false, but presumptuous as well.

A week before the pope's document was issued, the *Jerusalem Post* published an article with the sensational headline "Pope to Revive 'Anti-Semitic' Mass." This article reported that "the Vatican is expected to publish this week a document authorizing the use of a controversial Latin Mass, parts of which are deemed anti-Semitic." The article went on to state that:

> The 16th-century Tridentine Mass – recited every Good Friday – refers to Jews as "perfidious" and claims they live in "blindness" and "darkness." The Mass prays that God might "take the veil from their hearts" so that Jews can come to acknowledge Jesus Christ.

Unfortunately, this press account is hopelessly garbled as to its facts. It is also more than a little misleading as to what the prayers in the Catholic liturgy at one time did say about the Jews, and what those liturgical prayers continue to say today. It is true that the Good Friday prayers – only recited *once each year*! – at one time did contain a prayer that included the Latin phrase, *perfidies Judaeis*, which in today's typical press reports, such as the one just quoted above, is rendered as "perfidious Jews." The Church's own translation of this Latin expression, however, which I take from a Missal published in 1953, was "faithless Jews," by which was meant that the Jews lacked faith in Jesus Christ the Savior – which, of course, is a simple statement of fact. This old Good Friday prayer pertaining to the Jews read in full as follows:

> Let us pray also for the faithless Jews: that our God and Lord would withdraw the veil from their hearts: that they may acknowl-- edge our Lord Jesus Christ.

This same sequence of Good Friday prayers contains similar prayers for the conversion, among others, of heretics and schismatics, and of pagans (unbelievers), and thus it is not just a prayer for the conversion of the Jews. The Church hopes for and prays for the conversion of *everybody*, of course, and not just the Jews, but it remains true that the Church does hope for and pray for the conversion of the Jews as well – and should.

Contrary to the report in the *Jerusalem Post*, however, Blessed Pope John XXIII, shortly after his accession to the papacy in 1958, had in any case ordered that this particular prayer be *removed* from the Missal. This prayer is *not to be found* in the 1962 Tridentine Missal which has now again been re-authorized for liturgical use; it was removed from the Missal by John XXIII even before Vatican Council II. Already back then, apparently, contemporary sensibilities found the "faithless Jews" language to be a bit strong, especially since the expression was so quickly, and, it seems, virtually automatically, misunderstood, then as now.

Thus, this particular prayer has not been included among the Good Friday prayers since 1959, nearly a half century ago, and there is no way it would ever be used in a revived Tridentine Mass today. In the 1962 edition of the Missal, the only one authorized for the revived Tridentine Mass, the following text pertaining to the Jews appears among the Good Friday prayers:

> Let us pray also for the Jews, that the Lord our God may take the veil from their hearts, and that they may also acknowledge our Lord Jesus Christ.

> Let us pray, almighty and everlasting God, you do not refuse your mercy even to the Jews, hear the prayers which we offer you for the blindness of that people so that they may acknowledge the light of your truth, which is Christ, and be delivered from their darkness.

This is the form of the prayer that was included in the 1962 Tridentine Missal, the only Missal now authorized for the revived Tridentine Mass. Of course, Jews may, and, in fact, some do, object to this language as readily as to the earlier language. Nevertheless, it should not be forgotten that the intention of the Church here is to pray *for* the Jews. The reference to "blindness" is not some kind of invidious singling out of the Jews for special opprobrium. The reference is primarily to the *fact* that the Jews failed to recognize Christ as their own promised Messiah, even though he appeared first among *them,* and, in his own lifetime confined his own ministry also to them, his own people.

It may also be noticed that the language of the "veil" was retained in this prayer as well. But this, again, was not intended to be malicious or invidious language hostile to the Jews. It is actually *scriptural* language. St. Paul writes that:

> . . . Moses . . . put a veil over his face so that the Israelites might not see the end of the fading splendor. But their minds were hardened; for to this day when they read the old covenant, that same veil remains unlifted, because only through Christ is it taken away. Yes, to this day whenever Moses is read, a veil lies over their minds; but when a man turns to the Lord, the veil is removed (II Cor 3: 12–16).

Thus, the language of the veil goes back to the New Testament itself. Regardless of the Church's intention here, though, various Jewish voices have nevertheless strongly objected to this revised prayer for the conversion of the Jews no less than to the earlier one. Rabbi Michael Lerner, the left-leaning editor of the journal *Tikkun*, for example, opined in print that by reviving the Latin Tridentine liturgy, Pope Benedict had taken "a powerful step towards the re-introduction of the of process of demeaning Jews. You cannot respect another religion," he said, "if you teach that those who are part of it must convert to your own religion."

The idea that to pray for the conversion of the Jews is somehow "demeaning" to them was echoed rather widely, as a matter of fact, even among some Christians. Father John Pawlikoski of the International Council of Christians and Jews, for example, wrote prior to the issuance of Benedict's *motu proprio* to Cardinal Walter Kasper, head of the Pontifical Council for Religious Relations with the Jews, to complain about these same Tridentine Mass prayers for the Jews. He called them "profoundly demeaning," not only to Jews but to Muslims and non-Catholic Christians as well. This seemed to be a fairly common reaction among Jews, and perhaps even understandably so, but when Christians also adopt the same outlook, one can only wonder about their understanding of or commitment to their own faith. This is not a Christian-inspired viewpoint in any sense; it is simply the adoption of contemporary "politically correct" language.

For the fact is that the Catholic Church has *always* prayed that the Jews, Christ's own people, will eventually come to believe in him as their promised Messiah. And the Church will without any doubt continue to pray for the Jews – and should.

Nevertheless, Abraham Foxman, the national director of the Jewish Anti-Defamation League, described the pope's action as "a theological set-back in the religious life of Catholics and a body blow to Catholic-Jewish relations." He added that "we are extremely disappointed and deeply offended that nearly 40 years after the Vatican rightly removed anti-Jewish language from the Good Friday liturgy it would permit Catholics to utter such hurtful and insulting words praying for Jews."

Why, again, is it thought to be "hurtful" or "insulting" when the prayers of Christians for the conversion of the Jews are fully intended to be a *benefit* for the latter? Regardless of whether the Jews themselves agree that it would be a benefit, Christians believe it would be, and that is their clear intention of such prayers.

Still, these and other sometimes even stronger expressions of disapproval from Jewish sources made the whole thing sound as if this once-a-year prayer for the conversion of the Jews, was somehow a regular, and perhaps even a daily, "demeaning" feature of the Tridentine Roman liturgy. Rabbi Lerner actually styled it a "central ingredient" in the Latin Mass! But this kind of commentary surely was – beside the point! It is neither insulting or demeaning to anyone that Catholics and the Catholic Church should offer up prayers for them.

In the climate created by such misunderstandings and misstatements, however, the Holy See was nevertheless not inclined to insist that the Tridentine Mass had to be revived with the original Good Friday prayers intact. The Vatican Secretary of State, Cardinal Tarcisio Bertone, speaking at a press conference on July 18, 2007, a little more than a week after the appearance of the pope's *motu proprio*, stated that the Good Friday prayer from the 1970 Missal of Paul VI could perhaps be used instead of the 1962 Tridentine version.

In the event, this would not prove to be the case, although this latter prayer too had already been considerably modified from earlier versions, no doubt in response to objections registered at the time that the new 1970 Missal was published. In this Paul VI Missal, in fact, a prayer for the conversion of the Jews was retained, but only in a very much attenuated form, with the acknowledgment of the hope of redemption in Jesus Christ reduced to a much more general expression to the effect that the Jews might achieve "the fullness of redemption." This is how it read, and how it is currently prayed today by the Catholic faithful on Good Friday, according to the *Novus Ordo*:

> Let us pray for the Jewish people, the first to hear the word of God, that they may continue to grow in the love of his name and in faithfulness to his covenant.

> Almighty and eternal God, long ago you gave your promise to Abraham and his posterity. Listen to your Church as we pray that the people you first made your own *may arrive at the fullness of redemption*. We ask this through Christ our Lord (emphasis added).

From a Christian point of view, of course, "the fullness of redemption" necessarily *means* redemption in Christ, the sole Redeemer. Judging from today's mostly "politically correct" reactions to Benedict XVI's *Summorum Pontificum*, however, not even this language was considered suitable for the Tridentine Mass. A simple return to the prayer language of even a generation ago no longer seemed possible without at least some modifications. In today's charged climate, it had proved inadvisable to do or say many things that earlier generations would have regarded as rather innocuous, if not actually benevolent. In the event, Roman authorities became convinced that the old Good Friday prayer in the Tridentine Missal would have to be modified as a result of contemporary sentiments and opinions. It needed to be modified, however, in a way which would also fit with the original spirit of the Tridentine liturgy.

Accordingly, on February 5, 2008, the Vatican newspaper *L'Osservatore Romano* published the text of the new Latin prayer that would henceforth be included in the 1962 Missal to be prayed on Good Fridays where the Tridentine Mass was being celebrated. A translation of this revised prayer was given as follows:

> Let us pray for the Jews. May the Lord our God enlighten their hearts so that they may acknowledge Jesus Christ, the Savior of all men. Almighty and everlasting God, you who want all men to be saved and to reach the awareness of truth, graciously grant that,

with the fullness of peoples entering into your Church, all Israel
may be saved. Through Christ our Lord. Amen.

Although the Holy See considered this modified prayer to be suitable,
it nevertheless still proved to be inadequate, according to some of the
Jewish voices reacting to it. Rabbi David Rosen, director of interreligious
affairs for the American Jewish Committee, for example, called it "disappointing." While saying that he was pleased that the language considered
offensive had been removed, he objected to the new prayer because it specified that the Jews should find redemption specifically in Christ.

But authentic Christian doctrine specifies that redemption is possible
only in Christ. Leaving out that central point could be considered equivalent to downplaying the doctrine itself, if not abandoning it. But that is
something which Christians ought not to be asked to do. Jewish believers
are not being asked to abandon any article of *their* faith in the interests of
better relations. Cardinal Walter Kasper rightly responded to Rabbi Rosen
by observing that, in interreligious dialogue, "both Christians and Jews
[should] maintain their identities and remain free to express their respective faiths . . . To give witness of our Christian faith, as expressed in the
reformulated prayer, is therefore in no way a return to the language of contempt but is an expression of mutual respect . . . "

Ironically, the idea that Christians should not be praying for the salvation of the Jews in Christ was gainsaid by none other than Rabbi Jacob
Neusner, the same rabbi with whom Pope Benedict XVI "dialogued" so
profitably in the pope's 2007 book, *Jesus of Nazareth*. In an article published in Germany in *Die Tagespost* on February 23, 2008, Rabbi Neusner
observed that:

> Israel prays for the Gentiles. So the other monotheistic religions,
> including the Catholic Church, have the right to do the same thing,
> and no one should feel offended. Any other attitude toward the
> Gentiles would block them from encountering the one God
> revealed to Israel in the Torah.

"This prayer for the conversion of "all of the impious of the earth,"
Rabbi Neusner adds, " . . . is recited not once a year, but *every day*"
(emphasis added). We can surely conclude, along with this outstanding
Jewish rabbi, that the Church's Good Friday prayer for the conversion of
the Jews in the revived Tridentine Mass is *not* offensive to the Jews. The
hullabaloo that was raided about it was surely uncalled for – and, indeed,
beside the point.

Even if agreement on matters of faith is not possible between Christians and Jews, mutual respect between the two faiths *is* possible – and that is the stance that was adopted by the Catholic Church at Vatican II.

Certainly, to pray for the conversion of all men can in no way be considered a form of hatred or contempt for them. Thus, it remained the case that, even while the Catholic Church continued to pray for the Jews, including for their conversion, the Church also firmly and unalterably did not and would not cease to teach that:

> . . . remembering . . . her common heritage with the Jews, and moved not by any political consideration, but solely by the religious motivation of Christian charity, [the Church] deplores all hatreds, persecutions, displays of anti-Semitism leveled at any time or from any source against the Jews" (Vatican Council II, Declaration on the Relation of the Church to Non-Christian Religions, *Nostra Aetate,* 4).

Chapter Seven
But What about the Traditionalists?

Of very great importance in how Benedict XVI's *Summoum Pontificum* will fare in practice in the days to come are surely the reactions of those for whose sake the document was ostensibly issued in the first place, namely, those adhering to the Archbishop Marcel Lefebvre's Society of Saint Pius X (SSPX) and similar traditionalist groups that are currently separated from the Catholic Church and reject her authority.

Yet when we speak of those for whose sake the document was primarily issued, we must not limit ourselves only to those separated from the Church and no longer in communion with her. Pope Benedict XVI, in his letter to the Catholic bishops accompanying his *motu proprio*, spoke rather pointedly also about "many people who clearly accepted the binding character of the Second Vatican Council and were faithful to the pope and bishops [but who] nonetheless also desired to recover the form of the sacred liturgy that was dear to them."

Since it is far from clear whether the pope's new approach will succeed in reconciling many of those who have gone so far as to reject the authority of the Council and the Church, it may be that the greatest effect of *Summorum Pontificum* will in the end turn out to be the effect it has on those tradition-minded Catholics who have stayed with the Church all along, but who also have been deeply dissatisfied with the way some things have gone in the Church since the Council, particularly with regard to the sacred liturgy.

The actual numbers of Catholics in this latter category are neither precisely known nor are these numbers apparently easy to come by; but it is surely *not* an insignificant fact that so many serious and even fervent practicing Catholics (whatever their total number) *have* evidently been dissatisfied with and sometimes even alienated from the Church in various ways as a result of the Vatican-II enactments. One thinks for example of some of the stable orders of monks and nuns, consecrated religious, that have continued to remain attached to the old liturgy, a liturgy which they sometimes see as virtually an integral part of their identity as vowed religious who have dedicated their lives to the regular worship of God.

Similarly, some of the most committed of Catholic activists in various good causes such as the pro-life movement often turn out to be devotees of the "old Mass." I myself know a number of such Catholics, some of whom have not abandoned their parishes. They can often even be seen regularly at daily *Novus Ordo* Masses – but they are nevertheless also happiest when they are able to attend an "indult" Tridentine Mass somewhere on Sundays! A question the leaders of the Church have not much pondered, but perhaps really do need to ponder, is why so many dedicated Catholics have *not* always been completely comfortable with the Vatican II liturgical reforms, even while they have not rejected them outright. (Of course, an equally important question could well be why some serious and dedicated Catholics have not perhaps tried a bit harder to understand and accept the rationale for the solemn recommendations of what, after all, was a general council of the Catholic Church, and thus have not considered it part of their Catholic duty to "get with the program" as far as the Vatican II liturgical reforms are concerned.)

In January 2007, well before Benedict XVI had actually issued his *motu proprio*, a perhaps surprising number of well-known Catholic academics, intellectuals, writers, professionals, and the like in the English-speaking world issued an "Epiphany Declaration" supporting what they called "any papal initiative to allow freer use of the 1962 *Missale Romanum.*" This was at a time when rumors of the coming papal *motu proprio* were rife, but when the document itself had not yet appeared. In their statement, these Catholics recalled that another group of writers and intellectuals had similarly petitioned Pope Paul VI in 1971 to allow the continuation of what the contemporary group was now styling "the classical Roman liturgy." They believed that the old liturgy should continue to be carried on as a "living form of worship in the Church." While most of the signatories of this 2007 Epiphany Declaration could probably be classified as "conservatives," there were certainly some well-known and even distinguished names among them; and their stance was almost certainly not just a matter of mere "conservatism"; nor could the loyalty to the Church of most of these particular signatories be gainsaid. Moreover, they were careful to couch their Epiphany Declaration in terms which made clear that they did *not* reject Vatican II and the reforms it had enacted. Thus, they declared that:

. . . we believe that the presence of the classical form of the Roman liturgy in broader ecclesial and parish life will positively contribute to the on-going efforts to implement the liturgical reforms promulgated by the Second Vatican Council as delineated in *Sacrosanctum Concilium* and as envisioned by the Fathers of the aforesaid Council.

Pope Benedict XVI may have been responding to precisely this kind of thinking when he wrote in his letter to the bishops accompanying his *motu proprio* that:

. . . the two forms of the usage of the Roman rite can be mutually enriching: new saints and some of the new prefaces can and should be inserted in the old Missal. The *Ecclesia Dei* Commission, in contact with various bodies devoted to the *usus antiquior*, will study the practical possibilities in this regard. The celebration of the Mass according to the Missal of Paul VI will be able to demonstrate more powerfully than has been the case hitherto the sacrality that attracts many people to the former usage . . .

It is no doubt true that what the pope calls *sacrality* here is an extremely important issue: some Catholics who treasured this particular quality in the old form have not found it to be present in the new form in the same degree. Why not? It is a question that the leaders of the Church should perhaps have pondered more seriously, and indeed should continue to ponder.

Nevertheless, although Pope Benedict's hope that the two forms might positively influence one another may have some foundation, this hope may still be somewhat exaggerated. Those committed to the old form are very often found to have one way at looking at all this, and those accustomed to the new form another. People do tend to get set in their ways in such cases. Thus, there are those who are simply not disposed to accept the reformed liturgy – just as, at the other end of the spectrum, there are those who almost automatically opt for whatever is "new."

Another area where Pope Benedict XVI may in some ways have been more hopeful than realistic lay in his belief that those in the Church who continued to prefer the Tridentine Mass were also and presumably always necessarily accepting of the "binding" character of the Second Vatican Council. This may well be true of many and perhaps even of the majority of them, but anyone who has sampled some of today's traditionalist-type publications, such as the *Latin Mass* magazine or *The Remnant*, for example, cannot help but realize that there are at least some traditionalists out there – exact numbers again being impossible to estimate – who evidently do *not* necessarily believe in the permanent binding character of Vatican Council II. Some of them, it would seem from some of the opinions that they voice with some regularity, appear to be far from convinced that the Council's enactments are necessarily and strictly "binding" on the faithful, or are even perhaps permanently going to stand as valid Church enactments.

Many of the traditionalists who exhibit this way of thinking appear to believe, rather, that Vatican II was simply a mistake, a mistake which needs to be rectified. How this "rectification" might actually come about is generally not a question that is very concretely addressed with any seriousness by most of them, however. Usually, the attitude of those who tend towards this kind of thinking comes out, precisely, in their call for a revival of the Tridentine Mass. They may not even themselves have thought through very concretely what might come after that. The belief nevertheless does seem to persist among at least some of them that the Council will indeed somehow have to be rolled back or otherwise cancelled out, however that might eventually come about.

Some of these same traditionalist-minded Catholics appear also to believe, regardless of what the pope actually said, that the recent wider authorization of the Tridentine Mass that Benedict XVI has now granted *does* amount to a definite step back towards the pre-conciliar Church which they continue to regard as the norm for what is truly "Catholic."

Many of those of this way of thinking have not necessarily broken with the Church; they may attend *Novus Ordo* Masses in their parishes, at least some of the time, especially if an indult Tridentine Mass has not been easily or frequently available. They may readily agree that the pope and the bishops do indeed possess the authority to regulate the sacred liturgy, as they have done in the case of the reforms called for by the Council. But they nevertheless tend to see all this as really temporary. Does not the Catholic Church think "in centuries," after all? Some of the people with this caste of mind appear to think that the Church will eventually *have* to go back to the Tridentine Mass on a regular basis, and no doubt to other pre-conciliar usages as well, considering how poorly the conciliar reforms, in their view, have turned out. Again, the Council, as they continue to see it, was simply a *mistake*. It may not at all be clear when and how they think that this mistake might actually be rectified, but they still go on thinking what they think.

Moreover, at least some of them are now disposed to view Benedict XVI's *motu proprio*, like John Paul II's indult earlier, as simply another step in what they see as the right and necessary *direction* that the Church needs to follow in order to escape from the ill-effects of the ill-starred Council. We are not necessarily at the end of a road, they think; rather, we may be at the beginning of one. Some of these same traditionalists are almost certainly interpreting Pope Benedict's action not as trying to reconcile the alienated, or finally establishing or settling anything permanently, but merely as the necessary first step in getting out from under what they see as the intolerable burden of the Council.

Interestingly enough, though, Catholic traditionalists of this particular bent usually also tend to regard themselves as *papal loyalists*; they may not actively "fight" the Council in the way that the SSPXers do – or as the "sedevacantists" do, who hold that the popes themselves have not been legitimate since what they believe to be all the "nonsense" about the Council began. These anti-conciliar traditionalists who do still remain within the bosom of the Church, however, largely simply *ignore* the Council in practice, pretty much as if it had never taken place. They seem to profess loyalty instead to a kind of "papal" Church, which they see as the only authentic "Catholic" Church.

Examples of this kind of thinking can certainly be found in some of today's typical traditionalist publications. They can also be found, for example, in the catalogue that the organization called Roman Catholic Books ("Reprinting Catholic Classics for the New Century") regularly sends out to lists of potential Catholic book buyers. This catalogue features many Catholic "classics," but it is even more notable for featuring books that were almost invariably *published prior to Vatican II*. Occasionally a particular isolated book by or about John Paul II or Benedict XVI might be listed; the same thing might be true in the case of some contemporary politically conservative or anti-communist volumes. By and large, however, browsers in this catalogue over the past several years soon come to realize that most of its offerings occupy a rather static time warp that seems to have been closed somewhere near the end of the pontificate of Pope Pius XII in 1958. Such browsers would never know from the pages of this catalogue alone that Popes John XXIII and Paul VI, for example, ever occupied the chair of Peter. Nor for the most part would they ever gather much of an inkling from these pages alone that a Vatican Council II had ever taken place.

Then, suddenly, the Fall 2007 edition of the Roman Catholic Books catalogue arrived in the mail. This edition featured a "Publisher's Letter" up front with a picture of Pope Benedict XVI and an announcement heralding the issuance of the *Summorum Pontificum*, "liberating the Old Mass," as the announcement states. Also announced was the publication of a new *Latin Mass Booklet Missal* by Roman Catholic Books itself (actually a useful service, in view of the issuance of the *motu proprio*; a 1962 altar missal is also helpfully offered in the catalogue). Towards the back of this same edition of the catalogue, however, there then comes one of the rare, if not unique, mentions in this catalogue of the fact that there was indeed a Vatican Council II. This mention comes in the form of an advertisement for a new book entitled *Beyond Vatican II: The Church at a New Crossroads* by the Rev. Claude Barthe. Among other characterizations mentioned, this book describes Vatican II as "a non-council patterned on a council," and speaks of "the few Vatican II texts that can be considered doctrinally definitive." The pitch made in the catalogue lauding the advertised book then declares:

> Forty-three years after Vatican II, there is much disagreement about what can be done to reverse all the collateral damage. This important new book by Rev. Claude Barthe was first published in France shortly before the election of Pope Benedict XVI , and now contains a major new section on how the German pope with his vast experience and learning can "transition" the Church to a period of restoration and genuine renewal "beyond Vatican II."

Beyond Vatican II! Surely it would seem doubtful, merely on the evidence of Benedict XVI's own *motu proprio* and his accompanying letter to the Catholic bishops, that his intention in any of this could possibly have been to "transition" the Church anywhere, much less to go "beyond Vatican II." Such an interpretation of the pope's motive in issuing his *motu proprio* surely leaves out how regularly and how often Pope Benedict XVI, like Pope John Paul II before him, constantly *invokes* the Council, and holds it up as the standard to which all Catholics must rally.

All the popes elected after the Council, in fact, themselves participated actively *at* the Council as one of the great formative events of their personal and priestly lives. This was true of both John Paul II and Benedict XVI (as it was of Paul VI and even of the pope who reigned only one month, John Paul I).

The young Karol Wojtyla, for example, who became archbishop of Cracow before later being elected pope, was among the most active and

influential of the Polish bishops at the Council, and made significant con-
tributions to the Council's Pastoral Constitution on the Church in the
Modern World, *Gaudium et Spes*, among other Council documents. The
young Father Joseph Ratzinger was a *peritus*, or theological expert, for one
of the major figures at the Council, Cardinal Joseph Frings of Cologne,
and himself helped draft significant texts, including having an important
hand in the drafting of the eloquent and beautiful first part of the Council's
Decree on the Church's Missionary Activity, *Ad Gentes.*

Immediately after his election to the chair of Peter, Pope Benedict
XVI, *in his very first message to the cardinals the day after his election*,
immediately called for what he called "an authoritative *re-reading* of the
Second Vatican Council" (emphasis added). He then went on to state that:

> . . . as I prepare myself for the service that is proper to the succes-
> sor of Peter, I also wish to confirm my determination to continue
> *to put the Second Vatican Council into practice*, following in the
> footsteps of my predecessors and in faithful continuity with the
> 2000-year tradition of the Church. This very year [2005] marks the
> 40th anniversary of the conclusion of the Council (8 December,
> 1965). As the years have passed, the conciliar documents have lost
> none of their timeliness; indeed, their teachings are proving partic-
> ularly relevant to the new situation of the Church and the current
> globalized society (Initial Message of Pope Benedict XVI to the
> Cardinals, April 20, 2005; emphasis added).

Nobody who had followed the career of Cardinal Joseph Ratzinger
before his election to the chair of Peter would have been surprised in the
slightest that Pope Benedict XVI should have spoken in this vein.
Similarly, anyone who had paid any attention to the words and actions of
Pope John Paul II in the course of his long pontificate would have to have
realized that he too constantly spoke about nothing else but the Second
Vatican Council, and always in pretty much the same positive terms
employed by Benedict XVI. Pope John Paul II declared, for example,
immediately following *his* election to the papacy in 1978, that:

> . . . we wish to point out the unceasing importance of the Second
> Vatican Ecumenical Council, and we accept the definite duty of
> assiduously *bringing it into effect*. Indeed, is not that universal
> Council a kind of milestone, as it were, an event of the utmost
> importance in the almost two-thousand-year history of the Church,

and, consequently, in the religious and cultural history of the world? (To the Cardinals and to the World, October 17, 1978; emphasis added).

Thus, we see the real convictions of the popes, to whom Catholic traditionalists profess to claim loyalty, even while putting the Council itself out of sight and out of mind. These very same popes, however, instead quite regularly in the course of their papal ministry consistently praised and invoked the Council as the primary guide for Catholics today. The idea of in any way downgrading it or otherwise neglecting it, or claiming to go beyond it, while still professing to be quintessentially "Catholic," would be as incomprehensible to Benedict XVI as it would have been to John Paul II, Paul VI, or, certainly, to Blessed John XXIII.

There is thus, then, quite plainly, some evident "disconnect" here between what some traditionalist Catholic "papal loyalists" apparently feel, and what the popes, on the contrary, assume and take for granted to the contrary, and, indeed, regularly affirm with regard to the Council – even while they also recognize what most Catholics too are certainly aware of as well, namely, that many mistakes, missteps, and disappointments did follow the Council, along with all the positive work that the Council also accomplished for the Church.

At the very least, however, it certainly cannot just be taken for granted that all the traditionalists for whose sake Pope Benedict XVI was primarily motivated when issuing *Summorum Pontificum* necessarily do accept, in the pope's hopeful words, "the binding character of the Second Vatican Council." Nor will these Catholics necessarily be reconciled by the revival of the traditional Mass alone, when it turns out that neither Pope Benedict XVI nor any future pope is really going to "transition" the Church anywhere "beyond Vatican II."

Not all of those who prefer the Tridentine Mass, of course, fall into the category of the kind of "anti-conciliar" Catholics being described here, the kind of Catholics, that is, who tend to act as if the Council never happened, or who, at any rate, seem to be content to allow it simply to go by the board and perhaps, in their view, be mercifully forgotten.

Nevertheless, probably the great majority of the traditionalist Catholics who have stayed with the Church *do*, in fact, understand that the Council took place, however its results might be judged; and that we therefore necessarily do have to go on from there, even while we may still dislike some of the results of the Council. Ecumenical councils, regardless of their outcomes and effects, have been an integral part of the life of the Catholic Church since antiquity, and in no way did that fact change with Vatican II.

The fact that so many Catholics have preferred to hold so firmly to some of the old usages, however, regardless of how much or how little they may have been justified in doing so, is certainly a phenomenon which called for a pastoral response by the Church's leadership. It is a response which Pope Benedict XVI finally – though we may now also surely say, belatedly – did make. Let us hope that it *does* serve to reconcile to the Church many who have been disaffected and alienated from her in any degree.

Chapter Eight
Will the Traditionalists be Reconciled?

Having gone into the traditionalist phenomenon at some length, we are now in a position to assess more accurately some typical traditionalist reactions to *Summorum Pontificum*, and to inquire whether and to what extent the traditionalists, or some of them, might actually be reconciled to the Church by the papal document.

Few developments in the post-conciliar history of the Church have aroused greater interest and expectations, in fact, than Pope Benedict XVI's revival of the old form of the Roman Mass. The buzz and rumors and speculations that proliferated following the election of Cardinal Joseph Ratzinger to the papacy about what this pope was supposedly *going to do* with respect to the traditional liturgy was surely one of the more singular phenomena of the post-conciliar era.

For months on end questions were raised and rumors abounded to the effect that the pope was definitely going to act on the subject of "the Mass." There were those who said, sometimes with great assurance, that, for example, all restrictions on the celebration of the Tridentine Mass would be lifted; that it would be revived on an equal basis with, or might even replace, the *Novus Ordo*; that the excommunications of the bishops illicitly ordained by Archbishop Lefebvre would perhaps now be withdrawn; and that perhaps the vernacular *Novus Ordo* Mass itself might be abolished. It was never really very clear, though, what the pope's action might really turn out to be, nor was the question generally raised as to how a simple papal *motu proprio* might modify or perhaps even reverse the decisions of an ecumenical Council of the Catholic Church that had mandated a reform of the sacred liturgy a generation earlier.

However that may be, the buzz and the rumors continued, and were only intensified with the passage of time. They were accompanied by periodic reports, some of them accurate, to the effect that the pope had met with this or that group of cardinals, bishops, or curial officials, and that the subject of the liturgy, and, especially, of the "old Mass," had been discussed. These reports and speculations often took the form of notices or articles in various publications, particularly those of a traditionalist or conservative bent. From time to time, a prelate who was pretty obviously really in the know – such as a Cardinal Tarciscio Bertone, a Cardinal Jorge Medina Estevez, or a Cardinal Dario Castrillón Hoyos – would confirm that the pope was indeed going to be coming out with something on the traditional Mass. These statements only multiplied the number of rumors that were flying. At times it almost seemed that those awaiting a new ruling on the Tridentine Mass were perhaps expecting nothing less than, say, something like the Second Coming!

Moreover, in the new era of the internet, it should perhaps not have been surprising that the rumors and speculations proliferated to a rather amazing degree *there* as well. On May 4, 2007, two months before the issuance of *Summorum Pontificum,* John L. Allen, Jr., Rome correspondent of the leftist *National Catholic Reporter* – a journal certainly not sympathetic to Catholic traditionalists – wrote that:

> Anyone who has ventured into the Catholic blogosphere recently is aware that speculation about the *motu proprio* has been at a fever pitch for months. One wag has even posted a list of the Top Ten signs that someone is in the grip of "*motu*-mania," including, "You have a calendar with all the likely feast days that the *motu proprio* might be issued marked"; and, "You have written 500 blog posts, and 480 of them have been about the *motu proprio.*"

Allen himself went on to write that "many experts believe that this breathless anticipation will, in the long run, seem excessive in terms of the document's real-world impact." And, indeed, with the issuance of *Summorum Pontificum,* it would seem that some of the hopes apparently invested in the document in some quarters were more than a little exaggerated. As we have seen, although the document does signal a definite change in the Church's "policy" towards those favoring the traditional liturgy, it is nevertheless quite limited both in its scope and in its probable effects.

Yet most of the public statements made by those favoring the Tridentine Mass turned out to be quite positive about what the pope finally decided. For example, Michael Dunnigan, chairman of *Una Voce* America, described in the press as the largest lay organization in America promoting wider access to the traditional Mass, greeted the news of the pope's action with "profound gratitude." He added that the traditional Mass "is a true gem of the Church's heritage, and the Holy Father has taken the most important step towards making it available to many more of the faithful."

The Roman Forum, a traditionalist New York City organization that sponsors public lectures on the history of the Church, described *Summorum Pontificum* as a "victory." The expectation seemed to be that the Tridentine Mass, now that it could be celebrated again on a much wider basis, would surely attract many more adherents to what the Roman Forum described as "the full liturgical splendor of the Roman Catholic Church."

Father Joseph Kramer, a priest stationed at one of the three churches in Rome that had been authorized to celebrate the indult Tridentine Mass, declared that the pope's document "went beyond what we could ever have hoped for." Several press stories described a new and widespread search for old vestments proper to the traditional Mass, including 1962 altar Missals. There were similar reports describing enthusiastic plans in some places to re-introduce the old Latin Mass. It seemed to be well understood, in fact, that both the proper materials and vestments were needed in order to celebrate the old Mass correctly. Proper training for those priests (and acolytes!) who planned to celebrate the old Mass was similarly understood to be an important factor in the revival.

The Our Lady of Guadalupe Seminary of the Priestly Fraternity of Saint Peter (FSSP) in Denton, Nebraska, was prominently mentioned in press stories as a place where proper training was said to be available. The FSSP was an order founded in 1988 expressly to promote the Tridentine Mass following Pope John Paul II's indult allowing it under certain circumstances; thus, the FSSP priests knew it well. Now it seemed that some diocesan priests would be going there to avail themselves of training in the celebration of the old Mass according to the 1962 Missal, as some other priests already had under the initial *Ecclesia Dei* Commission dispensation. It certainly did not appear that traditionally-minded priests were going into this at all casually or carelessly. Rather, on the whole, they were showing themselves to be very respectful of the lines laid down by Pope Benedict XVI in his *motu proprio*.

Catholic conservatives generally were also showing themselves to be generally respectful and willing to remain within the bounds set out by the pope. Conservative journalist (and one-time presidential candidate) Patrick J. Buchanan wrote a widely syndicated article describing the new development as "a triumph for traditionalists." "Many Catholics will respond, 'Alleluia! Alleluia!,'" Buchanan wrote, " . . . the pope has come full circle . . . The Latin Mass, which had fallen into disuse with the introduction of the new rite in 1970, is back. Why? Because the Holy Father knows that the solemnity, mystery, and beauty of the Latin Mass have magnetic appeal, not only for the older faithful, but for the searching young. And he acted to advance a reconciliation with traditionalists out of communion with the Holy See, including the 600,000 followers of the late Archbishop Marcel Lefebvre, excommunicated in 1988 . . . "

In short, whatever the numbers involved may prove to be, Pope Benedict's revival of the Tridentine Mass was hardly just something of antiquarian interest only. It proved to be a very real development for some Catholics, including some of considerable stature in the Church. Whether or not it would serve to reconcile those traditionalists who had unfortunately followed leaders that had effectively led them *out* of the Church, however, was another question. Bishop Bernard Fellay, who had succeeded Archbishop Marcel Lefebvre as head of the Society of Saint Pius X, nevertheless issued a perhaps surprisingly positive initial statement in response to the pope's initiative. He said:

> This is really an historic day. We convey to Pope Benedict XVI our profound gratitude. His document is a gift of grace. It is not just any step. It is a step in the right direction. It is an act of justice, extraordinary supernatural help in a moment of grave ecclesial crisis . . .

Bishop Fellay was no doubt sincere in his praise of the new initiative. For years the SSPX had been saying that the first step towards any prospect of reconciliation of the traditionalists with the Church had to be the recognition on the part of the latter of the "right" of any Catholic priest anywhere to celebrate the traditional Mass. Earlier, in April, 2006, Bishop Fellay had said in an interview with the French publication, *Famille Chrétienne*, that "opening the doors to the old liturgy would probably be the most fruitful way to resolve the crisis in the Church."

And, then, suddenly, lo! the successor of Peter, the vicar of Christ, had perhaps unexpectedly granted nothing else but that very "right"! Any Catholic priest now *could* celebrate the Tridentine Mass! (How such "rights talk," though, ever became a "non-negotiable demand" by an entity such as the SSPX, which had been expressly founded in opposition to the principles of the French Revolution and of "the rights of man" that Archbishop Lefebvre believed had gained entry into the Church via Vatican II, has never been satisfactorily explained.)

In any case, Bishop Fellay did not limit his comments to praising the pope's action. He actually cited the sentence in the pope's letter to the bishops where the Holy Father had stated that it was his intention to seek "an interior reconciliation in the heart of the Church" as proof that the SSPX was *not* in schism! After all, Bishop Fellay thought, if the pope himself was characterizing the whole affair as an *internal* Church matter, then that must mean that the SSPX too was still somehow, somewhere still *in* the Church!

Bishop Fellay also noted, though, and pertinently, that "discussions on doctrinal issues must continue." He stated that, from his standpoint, the *motu proprio* was a "fundamental step which will accelerate the way...we hope to tackle the question of excommunication in a state of calm."

The question of the excommunications was rightly considered a big issue. It cannot be a surprise to anybody that the SSPXers would consider it to be a very sore point. They quite regularly deny, in fact, that they *are* in any way outside the Church, as do some of their adherents and sympathizers. They bitterly resent, for example, that the Church is willing to "dialogue" with the Eastern Orthodox or the Protestants, who by definition disagree with essential Catholic doctrines. Yet the same Church is *unwilling* to dialogue in the same way with *them*, even though they claim to adhere to *all* the authentic doctrines of the Catholic Church. (Of course, high Church officials, including even Pope Paul VI and Pope John Paul II in person, *did* "dialogue" with Archbishop Lefebvre, and did so *for years*, before the latter's illicit ordination of four bishops in the face of numerous solemn warnings finally provoked the excommunications.)

But the difference between ecumenical dialogue with the Protestants and the Orthodox, and dialogue with a rebellious entity such as the SSPX, is that the latter claims that it, rather than the Church herself, represents the true Catholic position. Neither the Protestants nor the Orthodox claim to be propounding the true *Catholic* position while dialoguing with the Church; they claim, rather, that the Catholic position is, according to their traditions, in certain respects mistaken, and they understand that the object of the ecumenical dialogue being carried on with them today is to re-visit issues where the breaks and separations occurred in the past to see whether a better formulation or clearer understanding of these outstanding differences might result in a position that all sides might now agree better represents what Christ has revealed to us.

Also, these non-Catholic communions, long separated from the Church because of decisions made by their ancestors, are not currently being led by bishops who themselves have made conscious personal decisions to reject the legitimate authority of the Catholic Church (to which, in fact, they owed obedience).

Any dialogue with the SSPX cannot avoid the fact that this organization, while claiming to *be* Catholic, nevertheless expressly rejects teachings which the Church considers to be authentic Church teachings, specifically some of the teachings of Vatican Council II. In the very same interview in the same *Famille Chrétienne* article quoted above, Bishop Fellay himself stated that his aim is "to get beyond the Council, looking toward principles that cannot become outdated because they are eternal." We have already encountered, of course, the idea of many traditionalists that the whole point is to get *beyond* the Council! In another letter posted on the SSPX website in February, 2007, Bishop Fellay wrote that "ecumenism, religious liberty, and collegiality remain the points of contention over which we will not budge."

In other words, the SSPX has held, and continues to hold, that in its teachings on ecumenism, religious liberty, and collegiality, among other things, Vatican Council II was simply *wrong*; the Church is wrong, in other words; and hence the SSPXers expect and require that any reconciliation with the Church would have to allow them, at a minimum (as another earlier article on the Church by one of their sympathizers expressed it) "to question the content of some Vatican II documents." This is something that, according to some traditionalists, the Holy See supposedly already did allow in reconciling two other traditionalist groups, the Institute of the Good Shepherd in France, and the Saint John Marie Vianney group in Brazil; these groups were told that they could continue to hold fast to expressions of the Catholic faith that were current prior to the Council. And, of course, Benedict XVI effectively allowed the same thing in approving the revival of the use of the 1962 Missal. At the same time, however, the Holy See, in dealing with these two other traditionalist groups, insisted, as Benedict XVI similarly insisted in his *motu proprio*, that Vatican II must be recognized and affirmed as having been a real and valid ecumenical council of the Catholic Church.

However, judging from statements made by the SSPX over the years, beginning with statements issued by Archbishop Lefebvre himself before his death, it would seem that the SSPX really does believe that Vatican II was wrong in certain of its teachings, and hence by their lights it was not a valid ecumenical council of the Catholic Church, any more than the popes who invoke and follow it today can be considered to be acting in the authentic Catholic tradition when they do so. At its very first General Chapter held in September, 1982, for example, the SSPX declared that:

> We pray for the pope but we refuse to follow him in his errors on religious freedom, ecumenism, socialism, and the application of reforms destructive for the Church. Our apparent disobedience is true obedience to the Church and to the pope as the successor of Peter in the measure that he continues to maintain holy Tradition . . .

We cannot fail to note the qualifier here, namely, that the pope is apparently the successor of Peter *only* "in the measure that he continues to maintain holy Tradition." Meanwhile, the SSPX has arrogated to itself the decision as to what constitutes "holy Tradition." Since the SSPX thus effectively holds that it is the Church that is in error here, it would seem that any reconciliation with the Church could only come about if and when the Church might finally admit to being in error, or at the very least, to being in doubt, on the subjects of "religious freedom, ecumenism, socialism," etc.

But, of course, the Church *cannot* admit this, principally because it is *not true*. For the Church, Vatican Council II was the twenty-first of her general or ecumenical councils. According to the Church's authentic tradition, what ecumenical councils teach, when ratified by a legitimate pope, must not only be accepted by Catholics as true; it has the guarantee of the Holy Spirit. The great Saint Athanasius held that what a Church ecumenical council teaches is nothing less than "the word of the Lord"!

And the Church's contemporary magisterium, or teaching authority, is obliged to affirm and insist on this. Not only can the Church never formally allow any element within her communion to hold or teach anything contrary to what her official magisterium has declared to be the truth; the Church cannot allow it even to be "questioned" by any element within her communion. In any reconciliation with heretical or schismatic groups, the Church *has* to require them to accept this – in the present case, at a minimum, to accept the validity of Vatican Council II and to agree to study disputed questions with a positive and open mind. While, of course, freely allowing traditionalists to "hold fast to expressions of the Catholic faith made prior to the Council" – the *Church herself* holds fast to these! – the Church cannot allow at the same time that any of her faithful might be allowed to question, for example, "the content of some of the Vatican II documents."

For, as one of the very documents questioned by the SSPX, Vatican II's Declaration on Religious Freedom, *Dignitatis Humanae*, teaches:

> . . . the Catholic Church is by the will of Christ the *teacher of truth*. It is her duty to proclaim and teach with authority the truth which is Christ and, at the same time, to declare and confirm by her authority the principle of the moral order which spring from human nature itself . . . in forming their consciences, the faithful must pay careful attention to the *sacred and certain teaching of the Church* (DH 14; emphasis added).

The Church is "the teacher of truth," then, and she is definitely not going to go back on this teaching of one of her general councils. Historically, Church councils have been among the means by which the Church teaches the truth that she does, in fact, teach. Vatican II was no exception to this. Anyone who has studied the history of the Church knows that this is her firm and unalterable *tradition*. To speak of any supposed "Catholic tradition" apart from this, as some traditionalists appear to do, is to speak inaccurately and incorrectly.

Although no one can predict the future or foresee possible changes of heart or mind, it is hard to imagine at present how Bishop Fellay and his fellow SSPX bishops, given their announced positions, could ever accept the conditions that it would seem the Church would *have* to require of them. Pope Benedict XVI has surely pretty much already granted all that the Church *can* grant in this regard.

Of course, in the new climate of respect for traditionalists brought about in the Church by Benedict's *motu proprio*, it may be that some or even many of the individual members of the SSPX or followers of the Tridentinist line generally will see their way to return to communion with the Church. This is surely to be hoped for. The new situation created by the pope may also remove some of the reasons why anyone might ever still be tempted to join a Tridentinist group or sect. Nevertheless, it still seems likely, as things stand today, that the SSPX and some similar traditionalist groups will *not* be able to come to any kind of reconciliation with the Church.

The kind of self-assured and obstinate intransigence exhibited up to now by the SSPX has, unfortunately, been encountered before in the history of the Church. It was the hallmark of such heretical groups as, for example, the "holier than thou" ancient Donatists who believed that they *were* the Church – the real Church had simply failed to measure up to their standards! This is a sad and disappointing reality to contemplate, and it would not be surprising if some Roman officials, including perhaps even Pope Benedict XVI himself, draw back somewhat almost reflexively from fully recognizing what it is they are really dealing with in the case of the SSPX and similar groups.

The head of the *Ecclesia Dei* Commission, Cardinal Dario Castrillón Hoyos, for example, was almost lavish in welcoming the traditionalists back. In an interview published the day after the issuance of the pope's document, he was quoted as saying that "with this *motu proprio* the door is widely opened (*si spalanca la porta*) for a return of the Society of St. Pius X to full communion. If, after this act, the return does not take place, I truly will not be able to comprehend . . . " The Colombian cardinal nevertheless actively continued in his efforts to effect a reconciliation with the SSPX, launching yet another initiative in the summer of 2008. There were no signs, however, that the SSPX was prepared to respond positively in kind.

Cardinal Castrillón Hoyos was apparently unable to take in or comprehend what was perhaps necessarily and inevitably entailed in any position that was based on a genuine and obstinate belief that Vatican Council II was *wrong*, that a general council of the Catholic Church *could be* wrong.

But the saga of the SSPX nevertheless went on, and there were surprises still to come. On January 24, 2009, Pope Benedict XVI unexpectedly lifted the formal excommunications of the four bishops who had been illicitly ordained by Archbishop Lefebvre in 1988. Besides Bishop Bernard Fellay, there were Bishops Bernard Tissier de Mallerais, Alfonso del Gallereta, and Richard Williamson. The canceling of these formal excommunications had been one of the conditions – like granting to all Catholic priests the "right" to celebrate the Tridentine Mass – which the SSPX had long called for as supposedly showing the Church's good faith. And it truly seemed that Pope Benedict XVI, for his part, *was* aiming to show precisely that, good faith, while removing yet one more obstacle or excuse in the way of a possible SSPX acceptance of the Church's necessary terms.

For the revocation of these four personal excommunications did not in any way regularize the SSPX's obviously very irregular situation vis-à-vis the Church. A Vatican spokesman explicitly noted this at the time: "The revocation of the excommunications does not yet mean full communion...[It] does not conclude a sorrowful situation like that of the Lefebvrist schism. With it the pope merely removes pretexts for infinite polemics, directly confronting the authentic problem: the full acceptance of the magisterium, obviously including Vatican II."

Yet in a generally positive and even effusive letter praising the pope's action, Bishop Bernard Fellay nevertheless reaffirmed the SSPX position of having "reservations" about Vatican Council II. While claiming "acceptance" of the Church's teaching, and even specifically mentioning acceptance of "the primacy of Peter," Bishop Fellay nevertheless also – significantly – employed the expression "the magisterium of all time." Apparently, this "magisterium of all time" was distinct from (opposed to?) the actual authentic magisterium of the Catholic Church currently exercised by Pope Benedict XVI in union with the bishops of the Catholic Church worldwide. Was Bishop Fellay thereby signaling a continuing SSPX intransigence, in spite of the lifting of the excommunications? This was not clear. Whether the latest generous gesture of Pope Benedict XVI would succeed in bringing the schism to an end still remained to be seen.

Meanwhile, the whole situation became greatly exacerbated as soon as the pope's decision was announced. It appeared that one of the SSPX bishops, Richard Williamson, was known to be a denier of Hitler's Holocaust against the Jews. No more volatile a consideration – extraneous though it might be to the question of the schism – could be imagined. Bishop Williamson had reportedly stated on Swedish television that he did not believe there had been any Nazi gas chambers or that some six million Jews could ever have been exterminated by Hitler. These statements quickly became prominently reported and repeated in the press and media, and a new and sensational *cause célèbre* then immediately blew up that threatened the improved Catholic-Jewish relations which the Church, especially the Holy See, had labored so hard to cultivate ever since the end of Vatican II.

It did not matter that a Vatican spokesman quickly and pointedly reiterated that the Church's position on the Jews and on anti-semitism had obviously not been changed in the slightest because of a papal decree dealing with the ecclesiastical status of four illicitly ordained Catholic bishops. Anti-semitism remained and would remain a serious sin in the eyes of the Church; this was plain. But again, it did not matter that the head of the Catholic Church's Commission for Religious Relations with the Jews, the German Cardinal Walter Kasper, labeled the Williamson divagations as "foolish" and as "gibberish." It did not matter that the SSPX itself promptly repudiated Bishop Williamson's opinion and declared itself firmly opposed to any kind of anti-semitism; Bishop Fellay, in fact, immediately *silenced* Bishop Williamson and prohibited him from taking any public positions on political or historical questions. He also apologized directly to the pope.

But the damage was done. As in the case of the Good Friday prayers, Jewish leaders roundly denounced the pope's decree. The *Jerusalem Post* called for suspending official relations between Jewish groups and the Vatican. An announced papal visit to Jerusalem was called into question. The Chief Rabbinate of Israel cancelled a scheduled meeting with the Pontifical Commission for Religious Relations with the Jews "until a response comes from the Vatican that is satisfactory to enable us to resume our relationship as before."

No doubt Pope Benedict's action in deciding to revoke the excommunication of the SSPX bishops was not really concerned with any such questions as these, but instead indicated a rather narrow papal focus on what was considered to be an internal Church matter, namely, bringing to an end the one single schism in the Church that has issued from Vatican Council II. It is hard to believe, however, that neither the Holy Father, nor his advisors, could have been unaware of the furor that would almost certainly result from any hint or suggestion that the Church might be anything but foursquare in her condemnation of anti-semitism. The Church *is* foursquare in that regard, as a matter of fact, and, moreover, she condemns in principle any discrimination on racial or religious grounds as well. Still, the pope should obviously have been concerned with the appearances that would inevitably arise once the subject of Hitler's Holocaust against the Jews got raised.

Belatedly, Benedict XVI seems to have realized this. Once the controversy had become a regrettable reality, he took the extraordinary step of issuing a special personal statement explaining why he had decided to lift the excommunications of the SSPX bishops (including, unhappily, a Holocaust denier!). The pope said: "I undertook this act of paternal mercy because these prelates had repeatedly manifested to me their deep pain at the situation in which they had come to find themselves." It is surely typical of Benedict that he would take such a controversial step for such a compassionate *personal* reason! The pope added: "I hope my gesture is followed by the hoped for commitment on their part to take the further steps necessary to realize full communion with the Church, thus witnessing true fidelity and true recognition of the magisterium and the authority of the pope and of the Second Vatican Council." He insisted that trying to achieve full unity in the Church was one of his primary pastoral tasks.

In another address the day after the Chief Rabbinate of Israel had broken off ties with the Vatican, at least for the moment, the pope explicitly renewed his "full and unquestionable solidarity" with the world's Jews, and condemned all ignorance, denial and downplaying of the brutal slaughter of millions of Jewish people during the Holocaust. He said he hoped "the memory of the Holocaust will persuade humanity to reflect on the unpredictable power of evil when it conquers the heart of man." He declared that the Jews were "innocent victims of a blind racist and religious hatred."

It was not clear what else the pope of Rome could do or say. It was to be hoped that his honest motives for lifting the excommunications of four schismatic bishops would be honored, just as his equally sincere concern for the fate of the Jewish victims of the Holocaust would be believed and credited. Otherwise it would seem to be a very high price for the Church to have to pay for what, very probably, would not turn out to be anything but a very doubtful benefit as far as ending the Lefebvrist schism was concerned.

However, the furor did not subside immediately. Some Jewish leaders continued to criticize the pope, as did some other public figures, including the German chancellor! Some fifty Catholic members of the U.S. Congress wrote to the pope to urge him to disavow the position of Bishop Williamson (as if he had not already done so). A good deal of this criticism was based on ignorance of the Church's firm and well-established position against anti-Semitism as well as of what was really involved in the pope's lifting of the excommunications of Bishop Williamson and the other SSPX bishops. Still, the Holy See found it necessary to issue further disclaimers. The papal secretary of state publicly stated that the pope had not been aware of Bishop Williamson's denial of the Holocaust, and it was also announced that the SSPX bishop would be obliged to recant and repudiate his position in a public manner before he could be fully reconciled to the Church. Pope Benedict himself met with sixty American Jewish leaders and told them that the denial, or even the minimization, of the Holocaust was unacceptable. The pope strongly reiterated that the Church remains "profoundly and irrevocably committed to reject all anti-Semitism."

Chapter Nine
What about the New Liturgy Then?

If the convinced, hard-core traditionalists in the SSPX and similar groups seem likely to remain separated from the Church, in spite of Pope Benedict XVI's generous and sincere effort to achieve reconciliation with them – at the cost, it should be pointed out, of no little discontent and criticism of *him* in various quarters! – what are the prospects for those who have remained in the Church, meanwhile continuing to prefer the Church's former primary form of worship, which the Council decreed needed to be reformed?

It is hard not to conclude that Pope Benedict XVI has granted to these lovers of the Tridentine Mass pretty much everything that he *could* grant to them, under the circumstances. Among other things, he has made it possible for them to be *respectable* again. They are free to try to attract as many Catholics to their Tridentine Masses and to draw them into their own ranks as they are able to do. This is all to the good. Only time will tell how many Catholics will be drawn to the traditional liturgy. Still, it never was in the cards that a pope would undertake on behalf of the traditionalists to reject, or even seriously to modify, the decisions of a Church general Council. The Church's reformed liturgy is perforce going to continue in possession of the field, and the great majority of Catholics, probably by far, are surely going to continue to celebrate the sacred liturgy in that mode.

Even if it were granted that Vatican II's decision to reform the liturgy was a mistake – as some of the ways in which the reform was carried out, unfortunately, *were* mistaken in certain respects – the reform was nevertheless legitimately and properly decided upon and carried out by the Holy See and by the Catholic bishops of the world. Any continuing dissatisfaction with the reformed liturgy must therefore find remedies in some version of a "reform of the reform." There is no going back. As Cardinal Joseph Ratzinger himself wrote in his 1985 *Ratzinger Report*:

. . . there is no going back, nor is it possible to go back. Hence
there is no "restoration" in this sense. But if by *restoration* we
understand the search for a new balance after all the exaggerations
of an indiscriminate opening to the world, after the overly positive
interpretations of an agnostic and atheistic world, well, then a
restoration in this sense (a newly found balance of orientations
and values within the Catholic totality) is altogether desirable and
is already in operation in the Church. In this sense, it can be said
that the first phase after Vatican II has come to a close.

There is no way, in other words, in which the Church could or would
ever act as if Vatican II had *not* taken place. In any case, it cannot be seriously maintained that the Vatican II liturgical reforms were, purely and
simply, a mistake. No doubt some things were downgraded or lost with the
immense changeover that was entailed in a complete revision of the
Church's liturgy – not to speak of the changeover that was entailed in the
switch from Latin to the vernacular! Pope Benedict himself has admitted
that an important measure of *sacrality* was lost. But not a few things were
gained as well. In an address to the Brazilian bishops on the occasion of
their *ad limina* visit to Rome in the spring of 1990, Pope John Paul II quite
eloquently described some of the benefits of the new liturgy, and it is worth
being reminded of what he said on this occasion – which was only one of
a number of occasions on which he spoke on this same subject:

> What did the renewal envisioned by *Sacrosanctum Concilium*
> bring to the Church? It brought her above all a *new concept of
> liturgy*. Previously people had an idea of the liturgy which regular-
> ly did not go beyond external aspects: ceremonies, rubrics, and
> norms for properly carrying out liturgical actions. While those
> actions are also worthy of respect, the Constitution told us that the
> liturgy is something more. In it we find the very action of Christ
> the priest, an action in which he associates his very self with the
> Church. That is, the action of the Head and members (SC, no. 7).
> To celebrate the Mass, the Sacraments, and the Liturgy of the
> Hours is to make present and actual the action of Jesus Christ the
> Priest brought about in his *Paschal mystery* . . .
>
> Placing the liturgy in the context of *salvation history made
> present in the Church*, the Council not only recognizes its eminent
> role in the life of the Church, but also appeals to the responsibility
> of Christians; all of them are called to integrate the liturgical

actions into their lives. Throughout the entire Constitution the *Leitmotif* is *participation*. Liturgy is not assisting at an action which others carry out; it is celebrating something, or, better, Someone. And in that celebration all are and must be involved . . .

This new concept of liturgy brought many fruits to the life of the post-conciliar Church . . . it helped to overcome formalism, and reduced the distance between clergy and people during the celebrations – encouraging initiatives in favor of active and personal participation, freeing the Christian from the role of mere "spectator" and leading the Christian forward towards God and his brothers and sisters (cf. SC, no.26). Persons who, previously, were content with merely fulfilling their Sunday Mass obligation felt themselves included in the new style of celebration through its words and actions and they discovered that they, too, ultimately have a role to play in the Christian community (cf. SC, no. 26).

This is only one of a number of instances where the popes have gone out of their way to extol the results of the liturgical renewal. It represents, again, one of those themes where the popes have constantly invoked the Council. Nor, in speaking of some of the benefits of the new liturgy, were the popes merely attempting to cover up some of the mistakes that were also made. In the very same address to the bishops of Brazil that has just been quoted, Pope John Paul II also candidly recognized the downside of the liturgical reform when he granted that "in applying *Sacrosanctum Concilium*, there certainly have been *deficiencies, hesitations,* and *abuses*. But it cannot be denied that where communities were prepared for it through proper information and catechesis, the results were positive" (emphasis in the original).

Without attempting any kind of enumeration of all the virtues of the reformed liturgy (or even a bare outline of such an enumeration), we can at least briefly list some of the advantages of the path Vatican II took in enacting its Constitution on the Sacred Liturgy, *Sacrosanctum Concilium*. They should not be passed over or forgotten. Benedict XVI has not forgotten them, even while he also considered it important and necessary as well to reach out to those less convinced of the value and benefits of the liturgical reforms. But the value and benefits of the new liturgy remain. They include:

1) The new three-year cycle of Scripture readings from both the Old and New Testaments that replaced the old one-year cycle of New Testament readings only, most of which were from the single Gospel of

Matthew only. The sacred Scriptures are the Word of God, and the enrichment of the Church's liturgy and worship by and through them was long overdue. The people need to *hear* the Word of God!

2) The use of the vernacular which enables the faithful to understand and follow the priest at the altar in the prayers surrounding the sacrificial action of Christ in the Mass. The knowledge and study of Latin in our society had been declining for many decades up to the time of the Council, and this decline has scarcely abated since. Latin is *not* widely known any longer by people today. The all-Latin liturgy had become unintelligible for many of the faithful, especially where bi-lingual Missals were lacking.

3) The restoration of the ancient practice of the people joining in active responses to the prayers of the priest, especially in the General Intercessions, or Prayers of the Faithful.

4) The vocal confession of sins by the people in the Penitential Rite; and the reciting or singing of the Creed, the Our Father, and the Responsorial Psalms by the people.

5) The recital or singing of other fixed parts of the Mass: the *Kyrie*, *Gloria*, *Sanctus*, *Benedictus*, and *Agnus Dei* (rarely do the votaries of the traditional Mass, by the way, remark on the fact that all these key prayers are *exactly the same* in the old and new forms of the Mass!).

6) Congregational singing of hymns which represents a revival of both Christian and Jewish ancient worship – which, however, had become diminished and truncated in the Tridentine era, with only a few exceptions, the one hymn generally known by all Catholics, for example, being, "Holy God, We Praise Thy Name"!

7) The multiple Eucharistic Prayers which, together, have added significant prayers from both East and West to the Roman rite.

These are only a few of the virtues or benefits of the new liturgy. More could be adduced. Even lovers of Latin and of the traditional Mass should be able to appreciate them. In any case, if it were just a matter of Latin, the *Novus Ordo* can be celebrated in Latin, and when it is, especially in the case of a sung Mass, few can even distinguish it from the Tridentine Mass. It is thus not hard to agree with Pope John Paul II, who wrote as follows in his *Vincesimus Quintus Annus* of December 8, 1988, on the 25th Anniversary of the Constitution on the Sacred Liturgy:

> The vast majority of the pastors and the Christian people have accepted the liturgical reform in a spirit of obedience and indeed joyful fervor. For this we should give thanks that the table of the

Word of God is now abundantly furnished for all; for the immense effort undertaken throughout the world to provide the Christian people with translations of the Bible, the Missal, and other liturgical books; for the increased participation of the faithful by prayer and song, gesture, and silence, in the Eucharist and other sacraments; for the ministries exercised by lay people and the responsibilities that they have assumed in virtue of the common priesthood into which they have been initiated through baptism and confirmation; for the radiant vitality of so many Christian communities, a vitality drawn from the well spring of the liturgy. These are all reasons for holding fast to the teaching of the Constitution *Sacrosanctum Concilium* and to the reforms which it has made possible (VQA 12).

Chapter Ten
The Liturgy Is Not the Only Problem

Mention of the virtues or benefits of the reformed liturgy should remind us that the problems of the Church in the post-conciliar era do not by any means reside uniquely in the liturgy. It can even be argued that many serious Catholics committed to the full Creed and practice of the Church may sometimes have focused too exclusively on the liturgy in trying to deal with the confusion and turmoil that have in so many ways marked the post-conciliar era. Invoking as they often did the ancient maxim, *lex orandi, lex credendi*, the law of prayer dictates the law of belief – just as, in fact, the pope himself invokes the same maxim in *Summorum Pontificum*! – many serious Catholics tended to ascribe most of the troubles in the post-conciliar era to "the changes in the Mass."

Indeed, Cardinal Joseph Ratzinger himself actually stated in his brief book of memoirs entitled *Milestones* (1998) that: "I am convinced that the crisis in the Church that we are experiencing today is to a large extent due to the disintegration of the liturgy." Yes, that is undoubtedly true in a very important sense, and we have surely experienced ample proof that drastic changes in the *lex orandi* can have, and have had, major effects on the *lex credendi*, on what Catholics continue to believe and practice today. We certainly have abundantly witnessed not a few such effects in the post-conciliar era, and we have taken cognizance of many of them in these pages.

At the same time, though, it is also true that if we cease to believe on whatever grounds, we are not going to pray properly either. It works the other way around too: *lex credendi* dictates *lex orandi*. What we actually believe, or come to believe, is necessarily reflected in how we then pray. And the fact is that the immediate post-Vatican-II period in the Church coincided with the revolutionary 1960s in society at large, when not a few of society's beliefs, convictions, and practices were rather widely and abruptly tossed overboard nearly everywhere. The same thing held true in some ways in the case of the Catholic Church; she was not the only institution that was thrown into turmoil during and following the 1960s! Much of what had been the received ideas or the conventional wisdom of society suddenly became subject to skepticism and doubt and denial on a simply massive scale. "That's not where things are today," or "we don't do that anymore," became watchwords nearly everywhere. Few were unaffected by these trends, including Catholics – including Catholic leaders!

For Catholics in particular, the year 1968 saw an absolutely unprecedented and near universal rebellion against the teaching authority of the Church, going against what had been established Catholic teaching for centuries. This occurred when Pope Paul VI issued his encyclical *Humanae Vitae* reaffirming the Church's belief that each and every marriage act must remain open to the transmission of life, that is to say, continuing the Church's moral condemnation of the use of contraception. This teaching had been the consistent and undeviating teaching of the Church since apostolic times. No authoritative Christian writer prior to modern times ever judged intentional birth prevention, while continuing to engage in marital intercourse, whatever the means employed to bring it about, to be anything but an evil.

In the modern era, however – especially following the Church of England's Lambeth Conference in 1930, when that communion caved in and became the first Christian body to concede that birth control just might sometimes be morally permissible in hard cases – contraception very quickly found moral acceptance nearly everywhere in modern society. By the 1960s, it had come almost universally to be considered no longer an evil, but rather an unalloyed moral and social *good*. Hardly anybody any longer saw anything wrong with it. To oppose it was simply incomprehensible – like opposing, say, automobile or air travel, telephonic communication, or air conditioning. It was no longer even seen as a moral question. For the modern mind there could simply be no rational justification for opposing contraception. It had become a self-evident good.

But when Pope Paul VI in his encyclical *Humanae Vitae* nevertheless formally continued to insist that contraception *was* morally wrong, the most typical reaction to the pope's words was usually incredulity at best, but more often it was flat and outright rejection of them, and it occurred almost instantaneously nearly everywhere. Going against the grain, the pope might continue to teach the contrary in the name of the Catholic Church as the authentic word of God, but the typical reaction of most Catholics was simply to repudiate the teaching; they ceased to believe what the Church was teaching. This was also, of course, the reaction of the public at large. The pope could not possibly be right, most people thought;

it seemed self-evident to almost everybody that the Church could not possibly be anything but very seriously mistaken about this anti-contraception teaching.

What this rejection meant, however, was that, literally from one day to the next, a large majority of Catholics came to believe, whether they consciously or explicitly formulated this to themselves or not, that the Catholic Church was *no longer* "the teacher of truth," as Vatican II had taught. She couldn't be. If the Church's magisterium could be so wrong about contraception – as it now seemed to virtually the whole world, including most Catholics, that the Church's magisterium *was* wrong about this – then the Church's magisterium could obviously be wrong about other things as well. This was only logical. And what this meant in turn was that, almost from one day to the next, the Church's formerly firm teachings suddenly became henceforth open to question and up for grabs, subject to the individual "private judgment" of everybody (up to then, "private judgment" was thought to be a characteristic of *Protestantism*!).

This is the situation that substantially still obtains for the Catholic Church today: not just the world at large but aparently most Catholics too simply *do not believe* that what the Church teaches is necessarily true. This is undeniably the case if we are to credit today's polls on the elevated percentages of Catholics who quite frankly and expressly say that they reject the teaching of *Humanae Vitae*. Various polls consistently show a figure of well over 80 percent of Catholics today who do *not* accept the teaching of the Church on birth control – which is to say, that they no longer necessarily believe in other things that the Church teaches, either; they no longer accept, in other words, that the Church *is* "the teacher of truth."

Again, if the Church can be so wrong about birth control, she can be wrong about other things as well, and various polls in fact do show an elevated number of Catholics who do reject the Church's teaching on not a few of the other moral issues of the day. And it has certainly become the prevailing opinion today that believing what the Church teaches is no longer a requirement for being a "good Catholic." This is precisely the prevailing attitude, of course, among today's pro-abortion politicians and other public figures, who believe and act on the premise that the Church's teaching no longer has to count for anything with them; *they* decide for themselves what they have to believe; and they are not only certain of, but even self-righteous in, their conviction that they can publicly go against and set at naught the Church's known teachings, and yet, in their view, they still remain no less "Catholic" for all of that.

Meanwhile, the Catholic bishops, the leaders of the Church, seemingly have no idea how to go about possibly remedying the public scandal of so many prominent members of their flocks publicly disregarding and setting at naught the Church's known and acknowledged teachings. This has been a prominent feature of the Church's life throughout the post-conciliar period.

While all this no doubt shows that the salt has to a great extent lost its savor among the contemporary Catholic people today, at least for the moment, this loss was almost certainly not brought about because of anything having to do with the changes in the Mass or the liturgy. Nor was it brought about by anything that Vatican Council II did or decided. It came about because, in the well known and well documented *Humanae Vitae* imbroglio, the Catholic people massively *ceased to believe* in the Church's teachings!

Just because these Catholics ceased to believe in the Church's teaching, however, does not mean that they thereby necessarily left the Church – although some did. Others, however, stayed around. They didn't necessarily dislike the Church, which still remained in their eyes one of the world's greatest social and charitable organizations. They thus continued to "practice" the faith and attend Mass even while they adopted the typical historical "Protestant" position that *they*, not the Church, would decide what they were going to believe or not believe. They became, in other words, the "cultural" Catholics that a priest-sociologist such as Father Andrew Greeley openly touts and celebrates. Of course, the statistics on normal Catholic observance and practice in such things as Mass attendance, recourse to the sacrament of penance, contracting an authentic Catholic marriage, and the like were also bound to go down sharply in such a situation of massive skepticism and disbelief – and they did go down.

But if this situation reflects the true state of Catholic *belief* today, namely, that in the view of a majority of Catholics the Church's teaching need not be necessarily accepted and followed, then a good many of the aberrations, abuses, dissidences, frivolities, and the like that we have witnessed in the post-conciliar era – including some of those in the liturgy, though not only in the liturgy – become much more readily, even though sadly, explicable. If we do not believe properly, then we are *not* going to pray properly either! *Lex credendi* manifestly *does* dictate *lex orandi* in a very important sense. What Pope Benedict XVI called "deformations" in the liturgy in his letter to the bishops, then, might well stem, to a greater extent than most people have thought or imagined, from the current, very deficient state of Catholic *belief* today – one which has obtained virtually throughout the entire post-conciliar period. And it came about not so much because of Vatican II and the "changes" in the Church and the Mass, but principally on account of the initial massive rejection of *Humanae Vitae* nearly everywhere, which very quickly got extended to other areas of Catholic belief and practice as well.

For if the Church is *not* "the teacher of truth," then perhaps she is not "the body of Christ" either. Perhaps we *are* all just a "community" of "nice," modern people getting together at church to congratulate ourselves on how nice in fact we are – "I'm okay, and you're okay"! And maybe that is all that the liturgy is supposed to be about too. Maybe the whole bill of goods that the Church tried to sell for so long – and actually succeeded in doing so for quite a while before the scales finally dropped from people's eyes – is really nothing more than what the modern world has contended all along: namely, man-made ritual, which we can change to suit our liking.

If this is the case – and, again, various polls and studies tend to show that it cannot be very far from the truth – then perhaps some of the liturgical disorders we have witnessed over the past generation also simply reflect this new secularized state of mind. What the former Cardinal Ratzinger styled "the disintegration of the liturgy," among other things, was almost bound to come about, in fact, if most Catholics no longer really believed – believed, that is, in Newman's "real" sense and not just in some mere "notional" sense – that the Catholic Church truly was "the teacher of truth" and the "body of Christ," that she possessed the power to bring Christ down upon her altars and insure the sanctification and salvation of her communicants.

The main point here is that the real *causes* of Pope Benedict's "deformations" which have brought about such widespread discontent on the part of so many serious Catholics today, so much of which has been directed principally at the liturgical reforms decreed by the Second Vatican Council – these causes almost certainly extend far beyond the liturgical sphere itself and pertain to current Catholic life and belief generally. It is almost a truism that the liturgical reforms were badly managed and imperfectly carried out, particularly in the beginning. Nobody knew *how* to effect a complete renewal of the Church's entire liturgy, after all; the results were almost bound to be mixed at best. Back in the good old days of Pope Pius XII before the Council, however, almost all Catholics still *believed* in the Church and in her sacred actions, and hence the Mass of that day was indeed a solemn occasion that was regularly celebrated with the reverence and awe – and the sacrality – that unfortunately became so often lacking later on.

Take, the so-called folk Mass, for example! Its putative popularity surely stems as much from defective belief as from any changes instituted by liberal liturgists – for the fact of the matter is that *their* ideas stem from the same kind of defective belief as well!

When, in addition to all the official changes that were being made to carry out the reform mandated by the Council, the authorities of the Church also proved either unwilling or unable to correct many of the other mistakes and missteps that were occurring – they were not always so stellar in how they upheld the Church's doctrinal and moral *teachings*, after all, any more than they were always prepared to correct abuses in the liturgy! – the unsatisfactory results that then came about were almost inevitable. Only fairly recently have things – thankfully – become more stabilized, holding out the prospect that we might now finally be able to realize some of the hopes that the Council Fathers so ardently wished for when they called for the reforms they wanted to see implemented. This was surely the hope of Pope Benedict XVI as well in issuing *Summorum Pontificum.*

For the fact remains that a general Council of the Catholic Church *did* call for the reform and renewal of the sacred liturgy. Even if this reform was not carried out as well as it should have been; even if some of its results partook too much of the kind of liturgy "fabricated" by "experts" which Cardinal Joseph Ratzinger, among others, had himself so often and so aptly criticized – nevertheless the fact that this new liturgy was authorized and was duly put in place by the authority of the Catholic Church – all this surely called for a greater degree of acceptance from serious, loyal, and "orthodox" Catholics than the *Novus Ordo* has sometimes received in at least some quarters of the Church.

Similarly, the rather considerable literature that has been produced in the course of the post-conciliar era extolling the "traditional Mass" at the expense of the *Novus Ordo* has never been very helpful in the practical order. For one thing, it has focused unduly on the negative in a way that has helped to take away some of the joy that should always come from the practice of the faith. For another thing, the Catholic bishops – upon whom the prospects for any real liturgical improvement usually rested – tended to see this Tridentinist literature simply as negative criticism, and perhaps even as rejection, of the Second Vatican Council itself (which it not infrequently was). However, since the bishops correctly saw themselves as strictly obliged to carry out the mandates of the Council, they were very little disposed to heed criticisms which seemed to call the Council itself into question. Any "dialogue" on these questions – and there *was* hardly any – was almost bound to be a dialogue of the deaf.

It may not perhaps even be too much to suggest as well that the tenor of much of the drum beat of criticism on liturgical matters that so often harkened back to Tridentine models contributed to keeping the bishops firmly lodged in the camp of the liberal liturgical reformers – unwilling, perhaps, even to consider that "mistakes were made."

All these things have formed part of the "Mass misunderstandings" that have unhappily proliferated in the Catholic Church virtually since the end of Vatican Council II. In one very important sense, of course, it seems clear that "an enemy has done this" (Mt 13:28). In another sense, it is really quite amazing that these misunderstandings have come about and have persisted in the way that they have. The Council Fathers would not even remotely have imagined such an outcome. As Cardinal Ratzinger, again, recorded in his book of memoirs entitled *Milestones* that has been quoted previously:

> The reform of the liturgy in the spirit of the liturgical movement was not a priority for the majority of the Fathers, and for many not even a consideration. Thus, for example, in his outline of themes after the beginning of the Council, Cardinal Montini – who as Paul VI would be the real pope of the Council – said quite clearly that he did not see the reform of the liturgy as a substantial task in the Council. The liturgy and its reform had, since the end of World War I, become a pressing question only in France and Germany, and indeed above all from the perspective of the purest possible restoration of the ancient Roman liturgy, to which belonged the active involvement of the people in the liturgical event. These two countries, which at that time enjoyed theological leadership in the Church (and we must of course add Belgium and the Netherlands), had during the preparation phase succeeded in putting through a *schema* on the sacred liturgy, which quite naturally found its place in the general theme of the Church. The fact that this text became the first subject for the Council's discussions really had nothing to do with the majority of the Fathers having an intense interest in the liturgical question. Quite simply, no great disagreements were expected in this area, and the undertaking

was viewed as a kind of practical exercise to learn and test the method of conciliar work . . .

If this is at all an accurate account of how the Vatican II liturgical reforms actually got started and carried forward – and there certainly cannot be any doubt that the young Father Joseph Ratzinger was *there*! – then the subsequent history of these liturgical reforms, along with the Mass misunderstandings that have stemmed from them and have persisted since, have to be considered all the more amazing. Surely it is necessary to go back to the Council itself in order to acquire even a glimmer of understanding of what really happened, and why it happened, and what the consequences of it are for us today.

PART TWO

VATICAN COUNCIL II AND THE
REFORM OF THE SACRED LITURGY

Chapter Eleven
Vatican Council II and Its Aftermath

The Second Vatican Council of the years 1962–1965 was by any reckoning one of the most important religious events of the twentieth century. While the Council was still going on, the great World War II leader, General Charles De Gaulle, who by then had become president of France – as reported by the noted Vatican-II *peritus* ("expert") and French theologian, Father Yves M.-J. Congar, O.P., in the book *Vatican II Revisited* – once declared that Vatican Council II was the most important event *of any kind* in the twentieth century!

This was surely a remarkable, indeed, at first hearing, a startling judgment. Catholics in the years following the Council certainly became only too aware of the constant references that never ceased to be made to and about the Council, yet its importance rarely loomed as large as this in the minds of most of them, even those who considered themselves to be strong supporters of the Council (or what they deemed the Council to have been); but it was hardly thought by many – or even any – to be "the most important event in the twentieth century."

Yet why not? If the Catholic Church consists of the embodiment in history of God's salvific plan for mankind, why would a historic "summit meeting" of her leaders *not* be one of the most important events of the closing century of the Second Millennium of Christianity? If the Catholic Church truly represents the extension of Jesus Christ, the Redeemer of mankind, in human history, and if the salvation of mankind is in a true though perhaps often very mysterious sense somehow linked to this unique institution, as the Church herself has not ceased to teach and proclaim, then surely a solemn assembly of all the more than 2500 Catholic bishops in the world at the time – today there are more than 4000 Catholic bishops around the world – would surely have to qualify as a very important gathering by any standard.

The Catholic Church today is the world's *largest* organized body of human beings, with more than a billion members; she is also the most *widely extended* organized body in the world today, with "branches" on all five continents, and, indeed, virtually everywhere; and she is also the *oldest* continuously existing human organization in the world, her bishops going back in an unbroken line to the apostles of Jesus Christ.

How could an official meeting of all the bishops of this Church, convened under the authority of her head bishop, the bishop of Rome, the pope, in sessions extending for a three-month period every year over a four-year period in order to discuss in depth and authoritatively decide about most of today's outstanding questions related to the teachings, practices, and discipline of the Church – how could such a meeting, again, *not* be of enormous, incalculable importance?

French President De Gaulle, himself a practicing Catholic, with the perspicacity which marked his entire public career, was probably looking ahead and thinking about what the world too would finally witness with the collapse of Communism and the Soviet Union in the late 1980s – long after the end of the Council and after the death of Charles De Gaulle himself. At the time, though, in the 1960s, atheistic and monolithic Communism in power was still seen and feared as perhaps the greatest single enemy of the Catholic Church, as well as one of the greatest single obstacles to the success of her religious mission or any religious mission.

Hence, in at least one large sense, the decline and fall of Communism could be seen as a special triumph of the Church – while the Council could be seen as renewing and fortifying the Church in the face of a continuing Communist threat which, in the end, did not turn out to be nearly as great, or last as long, as had once been thought and feared. Certainly the Catholic Church in Communist lands – especially following the election of the Polish Pope John Paul II in 1978 – did turn out to be a major factor in the eventual fall of Communism.

It is now well over forty years since the Second Vatican Council was first convened, and De Gaulle's judgment seems to be an especially surprising one today because the period which in the Catholic lexicon is now styled the "post-conciliar" period (or era, or years) – that is, the period following the Council – has scarcely seemed to be a period of great flowering or advancement for the Catholic Church or for the Christian faith generally, particularly in those areas of the world, principally the Western world, once known as "Christendom."

Of course, the Church in these same years has grown and is growing rapidly in regions such as Africa and Asia, where she was never as strong before. In his book *The Next Christendom: The Coming of Global*

Christianity, Pennsylvania State University scholar Philip Jenkins cites the case of Africa, for example:

> Catholic growth has been particularly dramatic in Africa, usually in former French and Belgian territories. As recently as 1955, the Church claimed a mere 16 million Catholics in the whole of Africa. . . . Today [2002] there are 120 million African Catholics, and the number is growing daily: there could be 230 million by 2025, which would represent one-sixth of Catholics worldwide. . . . Tanzania offers a good example. The number of Catholics there has grown 419 percent since 1961. . . . By the 1990s Tanzania had four provinces incorporating 29 dioceses. . . . By 1996, local men headed all these dioceses . . .

And quite apart from and in addition to such spectacular current growth in certain areas, the Catholic Church worldwide also still remains, and by far, the largest single communion of Christians as well. Yet in the countries of Europe and North and South America that once constituted the greater part of Christendom, the Catholic Church in the post-conciliar years nevertheless seemed rather to have entered into a period of serious disarray and *decline*. Some even ascribe that decline, at least in part, *to* the Council, as some Church leaders have had occasion to note.

Writing about the results of Vatican Council II only ten years after its close, in 1975, for example, the future Pope Benedict XVI, the German Cardinal Joseph Ratzinger, former archbishop of Munich beginning in 1977, and then later prefect of the Congregation for the Doctrine of the Faith in Rome from 1981 on until his election to the chair of Peter in 2005, judged that:

> Vatican II today stands in a twilight. For a long time it has been regarded by the so-called progressive wing as completely surpassed and, consequently, as a thing of the past, no longer relevant to the present. By the opposite side, the "conservative" wing, it is, conversely, viewed as the cause of the present decadence of the Catholic Church, and even judged as an apostasy from Vatican I and the Council of Trent. Consequently, demands have been made for its retraction or for a revision that would be tantamount to a retraction.

Nearly ten years after that, in 1985, the above passage was deliberately reprinted in Cardinal Ratzinger's book, *The Ratzinger Report*; and the

German cardinal then went on to add, from the perspective of the by then nearly twenty years after the Council itself, that further developments had been "decidedly unfavorable for the Catholic Church." He wrote:

> Developments since the Council seem to be in striking contrast to the expectations of all, beginning with those of John XXIII and Paul VI...What the popes and the Council fathers were expecting was a new Catholic unity, and instead one has encountered a dissension which – to use the words of Paul VI – seems to have passed over from self-criticism to self-destruction. There had been the expectation of a new enthusiasm, and, instead, too often it has ended in boredom and discouragement. There had been expectations of a step forward, and instead one found oneself facing a progressive process of decadence that to a large measure has been unfolding under the sign of a summons to a presumed "spirit of the Council," and by so doing has actually and increasingly discredited it...

Thus, according to the then Cardinal Ratzinger, writing some ten and then again some twenty years after the end of the Council, Vatican II stood "in twilight," and references to it as causative of or responsible for what followed it strongly contributed to *discrediting* it. Nor in the subsequent years up to the present time, now more than forty years after the Council, have there been any developments that would now require any substantial change in the cardinal's judgment concerning the results of the Council.

The Ratzinger Report, in fact, caused a sensation when it was published in 1985, not only because of the prominence of its author, but also because of the book's candid portrait of the confusions, disarray, and decadence in the Church that had followed the Council – and all this issuing from a man who had once been considered an outstanding "progressive" theologian. He himself had been a *peritus* at the Council, working as theological advisor for the still vigorous Cardinal Joseph Frings of Cologne, who had been one of the undisputed movers and shakers among the Council Fathers at Vatican II.

Cardinal Ratzinger's mention of Pope Paul VI's own use of the term "self-destruction" is equally indicative of what occurred and how it seemed to some observers at the time: the very same pope who had presided over the last three sessions of the Council, and ratified virtually all of its official acts, was himself suddenly talking about the Church's "self-destruction," and this had come as early as 1968, only three years after the end of the Council (as reported in *L'Osservatore Romano* of December 8, 1968). Of course, the earthquake following the issuance of the same pope's anti-birth control encyclical, *Humanae Vitae*, along with the worldwide protests, dissensions, and turmoil which then followed, had occurred in July of 1968; and this, of course, helps explain why the Holy Father himself was talking about the Church's "self-destruction" by the end of 1968.

A few years later, in 1972, on the Feast of Saints Peter and Paul (June 29), Paul VI dramatically cried out, in an anguished statement that was very widely reported and commented upon at the time, that "by means of some fissure the smoke of Satan has entered the temple of God... It was believed that after the Council there would be a day of sunshine in the history of the Church. There came instead a day of clouds, and darkness, of uncertainty..."

Pope Paul VI's "smoke of Satan" metaphor thus even went beyond Cardinal Ratzinger's negative characterization of the developments in the post-conciliar period. Again, this pontiff was not the only one to notice what was happening. The first Synod of Bishops – an advisory body of bishops established by Vatican II's Decree on the Pastoral Office of Bishops in the Church, *Christus Dominus* (5) – meeting in 1967, just two years after the end of the Council, properly took note of the "opportune and fruitful renewal" that was in the course of being carried out. But the Synod also noted that the changes in "many seemingly permanent customs and ways of thinking" had also "aroused difficulty and even uncertainty."

Many Catholics, including especially many priests and theologians, according to the 1967 Synod of Bishops report entitled "On Dangerous Opinions and on Atheism" (*Ratione Habita*, 28/10/67), were going beyond "legitimate efforts to adapt the expression of traditional doctrine to new needs and new ways of modern human culture"; and were instead embracing "unwarranted innovations, false opinions, and even errors in the faith" (RH 1). The Synod Fathers recommended that "those who are rash or imprudent should be warned; those who are pertinacious should be removed from office" (RH 3).

In the event, of course, few dissenters from Catholic teaching in the post-conciliar era ever were removed for their dissent; nor were many of them warned, either. By the time the huge wave of dissent from Pope Paul VI's *Humanae Vitae* came crashing into shore, neither most Catholic pastors in their parishes, most Catholic bishops around the world in their respective dioceses, nor the officials of the Roman Curia itself, seemed any longer to have any idea *what* to do in the face of such unprecedented, massive defections from Catholic teaching and discipline. Consequently, what most of them too often ended up doing about the aberrations and dissensions that were increasingly encountered all around them was – little or nothing at all! They remained mostly passive in the face of the new Age of Dissent and Do-Your-Own-Thing that had arrived with such clamor. And this largely remained the case throughout the subsequent post-conciliar period up to the present day.

Still, early on, there was no lack of official recognition at the highest levels of the Church that all was not perhaps entirely well with the implementation of Vatican Council II. However, the difficulties being encountered did not all stem *from* Vatican II. There were many forces and factors at work. The post-conciliar period certainly was, for example, one of widespread and rapid secularization in the world generally. The period witnessed the abandonment of religious practice by large numbers of people, not just Catholics (though including many of them too). In most of the countries formerly constituting Christendom, religion in general, and the Catholic Church in particular, had probably never declined so rapidly, nor become more marginalized and less respected in society, than they suddenly found themselves, and still mostly find themselves today.

In the first years of what he had often touted as the new hopeful Third Millennium of Christianity, for example, Pope John Paul II found himself instead urging in vain that some reference to Europe's Christian heritage should be included in the new "constitution" being drafted for the European Union. But drafters of the constitution fundamentally did not agree with the pontiff, and as things turned out, there would be no mention of Europe's Christian heritage in the document. Even when the document itself failed to be ratified by the voters of France and the Netherlands, and hence was effectively dropped for the moment, this was not because of its failure to recognize Europe's Christian heritage; it was because that heritage truly no longer counted. Pope John Paul II himself considered his failure to secure recognition for that heritage to be one of the great failures of his pontificate. Former Christendom had entered into a post-Christian era with a vengeance, it turned out, and this was not a phenomenon that was confined to the Catholic Church.

The post-conciliar years thus witnessed not merely "secularization" in general in what had formerly been a Christian society. They also saw the successful rise and acceptance by society at large of such radically anti-Christian developments as the widespread legalization of abortion and, in some places, assisted suicide and euthanasia, as well as so-called "same-sex marriage." The drive for this last aberration had gathered momentum throughout most of former Christendom shortly after the turn of the new century. What Pope John Paul II sadly but quite correctly called "the culture of death," in fact, seemed to be the veritable new *program* of what had once been a vibrant Christian civilization!

At the same time, former Christendom also seemed to be embarked upon a relentless program of depopulating itself, with the birth rate of almost all European countries quickly falling below replacement level. For the most part, the United States only resisted this same depopulation trend – and only temporarily, it would seem – because of the continued high rate of immigration here, especially from Latin America. Little had the confident dissenters from the encyclical *Humanae Vitae* ever anticipated *this* kind of outcome, namely, the slow racial suicide of Christian Europe, when they rejected the Catholic Church's ancient wisdom on such a massive scale!

This same culture of death broadly characterized the veritable Brave New World into which the former Christian civilization seemed determined to enter. It featured, for example, the rapid development of bio-technologies which expressly repudiated the Catholic idea of the dignity of the human person; these bio-technologies included such things as genetic engineering, in-vitro fertilization, embryonic stem-cell research, and even human cloning. One strains to imagine such things coming in and getting established back in the pre-Vatican-II days, when the Church was both believed and followed by her members and respected by the powers that be.

Then there was the growth of such aggressively anti-religious movements as radical feminism, radical environmentalism, and the homosexual "rights" movement – not to speak of such contemporary social phenomena as today's widespread family break-up, no-fault divorce, co-habitation by the unmarried, teen-age pregnancy, out-of-wedlock childbirth, and "fatherless children." So-called "same-sex marriage" (or "civil unions" of homosexuals) was only the latest in this long string of what truly had to be considered the disastrous results of the so-called Sexual Revolution, another one of the revolutionary phenomena of the 1960s.

Indeed, this now near ubiquitous Sexual Revolution must be counted, at least in the West, as one of the most radical and destructive of all the modern anti-Christian developments. No one can deny that the institution of "no fault" sexual conduct has caught on in modern society. And this development occurred precisely in the years during and following the Second Vatican Council. The moral code that had once pertained to sexual behavior suddenly seemed simply to have been dropped down George

Orwell's "memory hole" by just about everybody. This was never debated; it simply came about. People generally came to believe that they can and should do whatever they want with their "sexuality," without regard to any such thing as traditional morality; the pertinence, if not the very existence, of which came to be almost universally denied. The only remaining moral requirement related to sexual activity was seemingly that the "partners" must "consent." To dare to oppose this radical permissiveness came to mean nothing more than quite illegitimately to attempt to "impose" one's (or the Church's) morality on others!

Nor has Christian, or, specifically, Catholic, witness against or opposition to all these un-Christian and sometimes even radically anti-Christian developments in modern society either been very notable or proved very effective. The popes, of course, have generally spoken out, bravely and accurately; they help to prove thereby what they say they are, namely, the "spokesmen" for Jesus Christ. Some of the bishops' conferences too have pertinently and pointedly spoken out against today's widespread and drastic moral decline. Nevertheless, Christian resistance to, or witness against, the contemporary secularization and paganization of Western society has been both relatively ineffectual and, sometimes, seemingly not even founded on very great conviction.

Meanwhile, those who accept and favor the new moral and social trends often decisively and even vociferously reject the very idea that Christianity or the Catholic Church could or should ever have anything to do or say about the direction in which so much of the world is now so obviously and even quite relentlessly moving. Politicians, judges, journalists, media moguls, academics, intellectuals, and other "opinion leaders" and "decision makers" in today's secular society also tend to go along quite unapologetically with all these radically secular contemporary developments. What was once almost universally accepted as "the moral law" is today forgotten as if it never existed.

Of course, we should no doubt not exaggerate, either. In spite of the hostile climate in which she is currently obliged to live and try to function, the Church herself today is hardly on her last legs, nor even close to them; nor is she about to fade away or disappear. On the contrary, as we have noted, she continues to grow all the time. With a membership of more than sixty-five million in the United States alone, she still gains thousands of new converts every year. Though she is far from having the kind of influence on society and culture that she has had in some other historical eras, she is far from being entirely without influence, either.

In past centuries, the Church very often substantially *created* the culture that surrounded her. Today she often seems reduced and even sometimes eclipsed by the powerful secular culture by which she currently finds herself surrounded. And, too often, her own children no longer follow her lead. Rather, they follow the lead of the surrounding decadent secular culture instead, paying little attention to the Church's teachings in the process, or even disregarding them. The phenomenon of Catholic "faithful" who are *not* faithful seems to have grown exponentially since Vatican II. What happened in the Church after the Council was not entirely attributable to the Council alone, but to many other converging factors.

Thus, in examining one of the specific products of the Second Vatican Council, that is, the reform of the sacred liturgy which the Council mandated, we cannot lose sight of the effect of all these other factors separate from the Council, but nevertheless related to what happened in its wake. The reform of the Church's liturgy did not take place in a vacuum, but turned out to be in many ways very much a product of the times. These were "revolutionary" times in the world at large, and in certain respects they proved to be "revolutionary" times within the Church as well. This does not mean, however, that the Council was not justified in calling for a reform of the liturgy. Nor, certainly, does it mean that no reform of the liturgy was ever really needed. Nor can we judge the validity of such a need merely by pointing out how poorly in some ways it was met.

Rather, we have to evaluate both the Council and its aftermath not only on their own terms, but also in terms of what came about not always as a result of the Council's own decisions and actions, but rather on account of factors external to the Council which nevertheless had an enormous influence on how everything did turn out. We have to look at this broader picture if we are going to be able to have any idea of where the Church needs to go from here. Above all, we have to remember that the difficulties, and even the failures, that followed the Council do not necessarily invalidate what the Council itself decided and did.

Chapter Twelve
The Reform of the Liturgy

In the more than forty years since the end of the Second Vatican Council, nothing produced by the Council has affected Catholics more profoundly than its Constitution on the Sacred Liturgy, *Sacrosanctum Concilium.* The liturgy was the first major subject to be taken up by the Council. Although this had not been anticipated, it turned out that there was enormous interest in the subject; many interventions were made by bishops from all around the world; the debate was lively and intense, and, at times, even sharp and contentious; and, finally, on December 4, 1963, near the end of the second session of the Council, *Sacrosanctum Concilium* became the first of the sixteen documents of Vatican II to be approved.

This Constitution on the Sacred Liturgy passed by a lopsided margin of 2147 votes in favor and only four against. It was immediately promulgated by Pope Paul VI – a full two years before the end of the Council itself. By the time the Council wound up, in fact, some of the effects of the conciliar decisions embodied in this liturgy Constitution were already beginning to be experienced in the life of the Church.

One of the reasons why the debate on the liturgy at the Council was so lively and intense – and why this particular Constitution on the Sacred Liturgy was destined to have such an immediate, tangible, and even dramatic effect on the average Catholic – was that liturgy inescapably affects everybody in the Church. The bishops at the Council, like all Catholics, tended to have strong opinions on the subject. Liturgy is where all believing and practicing Catholics experience a regular communal and public encounter with the thrice-holy God who created and redeemed us. The liturgy, *Sacrosanctum Concilium* declares, "is principally the worship of the divine majesty" (SC 33). More than that, the document says, it is "the summit towards which the activity of the Church is directed; it is also the fount from which all her power flows" (SC 10). Or again, the liturgy, the document declares:

...is rightly seen as an exercise of the priestly office of Jesus Christ. It involves the presentation of man's sanctification under the guise of signs perceptible by the senses and its accomplishment in ways appropriate to each of these signs. In it full public worship is performed by the Mystical Body of Jesus Christ, that is, by the head and his members.

From this it follows that every liturgical celebration, because it is an action of Christ the Priest and of his Body, which is the Church, is a sacred action surpassing all others (SC 7).

It is through participation in the liturgy – especially the Mass and the other sacraments – that we most directly live the life of the Church – that to say, the life of Christ – with a reality and an intensity that occur nowhere else in our lives. Again, *Sacrosanctum Concilium* says:

For it is the liturgy through which, especially in the divine sacrifice of the Eucharist, the work of our redemption is accomplished, and it is through the liturgy, especially, that the faithful are enabled to express in their lives and manifest to others the mystery of Christ and the real nature of the true Church . . . The liturgy daily builds up those who are in the Church, making of them a holy temple of the Lord, a dwelling place for God in the Spirit, to the mature measure of the fullness of Christ (SC 1).

Although the "regulation of the sacred liturgy depends solely on the authority of the Church" (SC 22), and although the Church has a responsibility to regulate and even reform her liturgy when necessary, it is quite probable that few of the fathers of the Second Vatican Council had any idea how far-reaching the effects would be of their decision to reform the entire liturgy of the Church. In retrospect, and in the light of the effects on the Church and on the faith of the Council's decision to carry out such a comprehensive liturgical reform, it seems clear that the whole enterprise should have been much more carefully thought through and much more slowly – and gradually – carried out.

In particular, the reforms should have been accompanied by a much more thorough catechesis of the faithful at all levels on the fundamental meaning of the sacred liturgy, as well as on the nature of the changes being made and the reasons for making them. If the pastors had been obliged to explain the changes they were making as they went along, perhaps they would not have been quite so quick to make them!

As things turned out, the implementation of the liturgical reform decided upon by the Council brought about years of confusion and even turmoil. Changes were introduced both wholesale and piecemeal, often by priests who themselves seemed to have little or no understanding of what the changes were all about or what the rationale for them was. They were "implementers" who were simply "following orders." Rarely were explanations provided to average Catholics in the pews. Probably most of the pastors and priests of the day were incapable of furnishing such explanations anyway, lacking as they did the special training and orientation which should have been provided before the changes were actually made.

Then, in addition to all of the officially decreed changes, there were the many liturgical *abuses* that took place. In the new, official era of "change" decreed by Church authority, it proved easier both to introduce liturgical abuses, and to get away with them. Unfortunately, the liturgy even became a kind of proving ground for self-appointed enthusiasts (who were sometimes, unfortunately, the same people as the officially appointed implementers!). Varied phenomena such as banners, balloons, dance troupes, rock or folk groups, even clowns and performers sometimes made their appearances in the sanctuary; nor were improvisations at Mass by the celebrant and variant readings, not necessarily from Scripture, entirely unheard of. On the contrary!

Or, again: if the faithful were not, for example, invited to come up and cluster around the altar with the priest, then perhaps the priest himself might well descend deep into the congregation proffering enthusiastic handshakes at the time of "the kiss of peace."

Some of the more egregious of these kinds of things have thankfully abated somewhat in recent years, although more than traces of some of them still do remain in some places. One apparently permanent "legacy" of the liturgical reform, visible nearly everywhere in the Church today, for example, seems to be the presence in the sanctuary of swarms of "extraordinary ministers" deputed to lead the music, recite the prayers of the faithful, read the Scriptures, and give out Communion, sometimes while the actual celebrant (or celebrants) remains idle. The fact is, though, that anyone actually ordained who is present at a liturgical service is supposed to perform these required functions ahead of any "extraordinary ministers," who, by definition, are supposed to be "extraordinary." But as most Catholics know by now, today's "extraordinary ministers" are for the most part no longer extraordinary!

Whatever one may think of these developments, it has to be conceded that these extraordinary ministers *were* for the most part duly authorized, at least in principle, by legitimate Church authority in the course of the official liturgical reforms. Pope Paul VI issued express Instructions in 1971 and 1972 abolishing the former "minor orders" of sub-deacon, acolyte, exorcist, lector, and porter, while providing that lay people, as well as candidates for the diaconate and the priesthood, might be "installed" (rather than ordained) in new "ministries" (rather than "orders").

And there definitely was also a certain logic in such new developments. It has unfortunately been typical of much of what the liturgical reform came to represent, however, that often what was first only permitted, as "extraordinary," often quickly become "ordinary," at least in practice. The "extraordinary" often quickly become the norm, in fact.

This whole phenomenon of "extraordinary ministers" figured so prominently in the post-conciliar period, however, that the Holy See felt obliged, on November 13, 1997, to issue a special instructional document on the subject. The document in question was developed by no less than *eight* separate Vatican dicasteries, or departments, including the Congregations for Bishops, the Clergy, the Doctrine of the Faith, the Evangelization of Peoples, and Divine Worship and the Discipline of the Sacraments, along with the Institutes of Consecrated Life and Societies of Apostolic Life, as well as the Pontifical Councils for the Laity and for the Interpretation of Legislative Texts. This joint document, entitled "Collaboration of Non-ordained Faithful in Priests' Sacred Ministry," with the Latin title *Ecclesiae de Mysterio,* attempted to define and, in important respects, to regulate and limit, the post-Vatican-II proliferation of "lay ministers."

The joint instructional document states at the outset: "It is necessary that all who are in any way involved in (ministerial) collaboration exercise particular care to safeguard the nature and mission of sacred (ordained) ministry, and the vocation and secular character of the lay faithful. It must be remembered that *collaboration with* does not mean *substitute for,*" the document emphasizes. The ministerial priesthood, in the Church of Christ, is different in kind and not just in degree from the priesthood of all the faithful; and thus priests are necessarily "set apart" for certain purposes. "Only in some...functions, and to a limited extent," the joint document specifies, "may the non-ordained faithful cooperate with their pastors should they be called to do so by lawful authority." This joint document from the various departments of the Holy See was surely, and quite obviously, addressing a very real problem in the post-conciliar Church, and it was a problem that stemmed directly from the liturgical reform that had been mandated by the Council.

The document goes on to specify, among other things, that:

* Temporary deputation for liturgical purposes...does not confer any special or permanent title on the non-ordained faithful.

* It is unlawful for the non-ordained faithful to assume titles such as pastor, chaplain, coordinator, moderator, or other such similar titles which can confuse their role and that of the pastor, who is always a bishop or a priest.

* The homily must be reserved to the sacred minister, priest or deacon.

* In liturgical celebrations, non-ordained lay persons...may not pronounce prayers, use gestures, or wear vestments reserved to the celebrant [priest].

* Extraordinary ministers of the Eucharist may not give Communion to themselves or receive Communion apart from the other faithful, as though they were celebrants.

In an article published in *L'Osservatore Romano*, on March 11, 1998, Cardinal Joseph Ratzinger, then prefect of the Congregation for the Doctrine of the Faith, and probably little imagining at the time that he would one day be the pope, wrote that these Vatican prescriptions were necessary, both in order to afford a better understanding of the variety of roles within the Church, and, at the same time, to avoid a "de-valuation of the ordained ministry." "Clarity," the then cardinal wrote, was needed in order to avoid falling into what he called "a Protestantization of the concepts of ministry and of the Church"; it was also needed to avoid the clericalization of the laity, he thought. He noted that, in some parts of the world, "a loss of the meaning of the sacrament of Holy Orders, and the growth of a parallel ministry by so-called 'pastoral assistants,' was leading to confusion about the special identity of ordained priests."

That the Holy See continued to be concerned about the phenomenon of extraordinary ministers blurring the lines between ordained and non-ordained persons was further indicated when a revised new *General Instruction on the Roman Missal* (GIRM) was approved by Pope John Paul II during the Jubilee Year 2000. Among other provisions, the revised new GIRM specified that only ordained ministers could distribute Hosts (or Precious Blood) into other vessels; and that the priest himself must hand sacred vessels to extraordinary ministers. The faithful are not permitted to take up the sacred vessels or the sacred species themselves.

All these prescriptions and comments on the question of extraordinary ministers tended to illustrate how the typical Vatican II reforms, legitimate as they may have been when they were first prescribed or allowed, nevertheless tended to slide into the category of abuses, especially given how things developed in the post-Vatican-II atmosphere that so quickly came to prevail. The multiplication of so many "lay ministers," and the resulting not so subtle downgrading of those ordained to the priesthood or the diaconate, was only one of the many consequences of the liturgical reforms. Moreover, the same kind of thing became manifest in many other aspects of the liturgical reform as well, at least, as the reform was actually carried out. Actual abuses such as Communion-in-the-hand, for example, came to be practiced so often and so widely that they later had to be justified as "customs" and legalized after the fact. Communion-in-the-hand was legalized in precisely this way in the United States in 1977 (it had been approved in Belgium as early as 1969).

We shall encounter more of these same kinds of things as we look at other aspects of the Church's liturgical reform. What is remarkable about phenomena such as these, though, is that many of them were never either mandated or even apparently desired by Vatican II. Anyone acquainted with *Sacrosanctum Concilium,* and with the subsequent liturgical directives from the Holy See stemming from it, will find that some of the most salient things experienced by the faithful as jarring and disconcerting "changes" in the liturgy were not only not necessarily mandated, but were sometimes even expressly *excluded*, by these applicable Church directives.

To take another example, *Sacrosanctum Concilium*, declares that the musical instruments employed in divine worship must be "suitable...for sacred use [and must] accord with the dignity of the temple and...truly contribute to the edification of the faithful" (SC 120). Yet among the earliest results of the liturgical reform was the introduction of *guitars,* along with their distinctly non-sacral folk music, which quickly became almost universal in the United States for awhile, and are still in wide liturgical use.

Anyone who bothers to study the Church's actual liturgical documents will find no warrant for changes such as the guitar "folk" Mass (or the rinky-dink piano Mass!). For the most part, the official liturgical documents are eminently sensible, in fact; often they are even edifying and inspiring. And viewed from the standpoint of the Council's intentions rather than from that of how things actually played out in the churches, the liturgical reform in the beginning *practically consisted of documents*! There was a veritable blizzard of them: over a hundred liturgical documents issued from the Holy See alone in the first decade following the Council; and, in addition to these Roman documents, there was an equal or greater number from national or diocesan liturgical commissions during the same period.

These documents covered everything from the manner of distributing Communion to the manner of integrating sacred music into the liturgy, from the question of who might serve at Mass to the question of the language of the liturgy. Among the Roman documents in particular, in addition to a new Roman Missal, there were extensively revised "rites" for all of the seven sacraments, as well as similar "rites" for events such as consecrations, weddings, funerals, and the like. There was also a completely revised Liturgical Calendar; and a completely revised Liturgy of the Hours. Over the years, the Holy See also issued no less than five lengthy separate Instructions on the Proper Implementation of the Constitution on the Sacred Liturgy. The most recent one of these – on the use of vernacular languages in the Roman rite – dates from as recently as April 2001.

The Council's liturgical reform is still going on, in other words. The Holy See has been more steadily occupied over the last forty years with liturgical questions than with almost any other questions at all.

Vatican II's primary aim in decreeing a thorough reform of the liturgy – "the aim," in the Council's own words, "to be considered before all else" – was to restore what the Council called "the full and active participation by all the people" in the sacred liturgy. "Mother Church earnestly desires," *Sacrosanctum Concilium* specifies, "that all the faithful should be led to the full, conscious, and active participation in liturgical celebration which is demanded by the very nature of the liturgy" (SC 14). "Full, conscious, and active participation," in fact, is the single phrase that best expresses the principal aim of the Council in decreeing a reform of the liturgy.

"The liturgy," the document continues, "is made up of unchangeable elements divinely instituted, and of elements subject to change. These latter not only may be changed, but ought to be changed with the passage of time if they have suffered from the intrusion of anything out of harmony with the inner nature of the liturgy or have become less suitable" (SC 21). Changes properly decided by Church authority, then, were deemed not only legitimate, but sometimes necessary.

However, *Sacrosanctum Concilium* goes on immediately to say that "no other person, not even a priest, may add, remove, or change anything in the liturgy on his own authority" (SC 22) – thus excluding at the outset the kinds of improvisations that unfortunately became quite common in the post-conciliar era anyway, in spite of this plain prohibition of them. The document further declares that "there must be no innovations unless the good of the Church genuinely and certainly requires them, and care must be taken that any new forms adopted should in some way grow organically from forms already existing" (SC 23).

Thus, if we look only at the text of the Constitution on the Sacred Liturgy itself, it seems to envision well-prepared and legitimate changes, and only those. In general, it seems to be an eminently sound and sane document in practically everything that it says, as a matter of fact. The same thing is true of most of the implementing documents on the liturgy subsequently issued by the Holy See. On the basis of these documents alone, it is hard to see how or why the reform of the liturgy went wrong in so many ways. Of course, the actual reform entailed much more than only what was written in the documents. Among other things, it obviously entailed *interpretation* of what was written in the documents – not to speak of the tendency (or temptation) to proceed ahead with one's own idea of what needed to be changed in the liturgy, *regardless* of what might be written in the documents themselves! Nevertheless, we still must look more closely at some of these documents before going on to consider how the actual reform of the liturgy was carried out.

Chapter Thirteen
Some Positive Features of the Church's Liturgical Documents

Vatican Council II's Constitution on the Sacred Liturgy, *Sacrosanctum Concilium*, as well as most of the many subsequent implementing documents issued by the Holy See, actually read quite well, as we have already noted. They are really quite consistent in this respect, in fact. Reading them, it is hard to imagine that the Church's liturgical reform turned out the way it did – particularly from the point of view of traditional or "orthodox" Catholics. These official documents are *not* generally documents crafted by "liberals"!

Sacrosanctum Concilium, for example, in no way excludes popular devotions – although one of the ways in which many of the faithful most directly experienced the liturgical reforms was through efforts to downgrade or "ban" popular devotions such as the Angelus, the Rosary, or Benediction. Some "liturgists" proved to be veritable tigers about these kinds of things, in fact; for them, nothing could more quickly mark one as hopelessly backward and "pre-Vatican-II," for example, than a continuing devotion to the Rosary. *Sacrosanctum Concilium* itself, however, very plainly states that "popular devotions of the Christian people, provided they conform to the laws and norms of the Church, are to be highly recommended" (SC 13).

And as recently as April 9, 2002, the Congregation for Divine Worship and the Discipline of the Sacraments, making reference to that same Section 13 of the Vatican II liturgy Constitution, actually issued a *Directory on Popular Piety and the Liturgy*, containing chapters on the history, theology, and magisterial treatment of popular piety and the liturgy, as well as chapters on the liturgical year, veneration of the Blessed Mother and the saints, suffrage for the dead, and shrines and pilgrimages. On the occasion of the issuance of this *Directory*, Pope John Paul II declared that "popular religious practice...when it is genuine, has faith as its source and therefore must be valued and fostered.... [It] prepares the faithful for the celebration of the sacred mysteries."

Later on in the same year, on October 16, 2002, Pope John Paul II, always known as a Marian pope in any case, issued an apostolic letter on the Rosary of the Virgin Mary, *Rosarium Virginis Mariae,* in which he promulgated a new set of mysteries to be prayed between the traditional Joyful Mysteries devoted to the Blessed Virgin and the Christ Child, and the traditional Sorrowful Mysteries devoted to the Passion and Crucifixion of Our Lord Jesus Christ.

The new mysteries to be meditated upon while praying the Rosary beads were styled "Luminous Mysteries," or "Mysteries of Light," and they include events in the public life of Our Lord neglected up to now in the praying of the Rosary; these are: 1) the Baptism of the Lord in the Jordan (Mt 3:13:17; Mk 1:9–11; Lk 3:21–22); 2) the Wedding at Cana, with the first miracle (Jn 2:1–11); 3) the Proclamation of the Kingdom (Mt 4:23; Mk 1:14–15); 4) the Transfiguration of Jesus (Mt 17:1–13; Mk 9:2–13; Lk 9:28–36); and 5) the Institution of the Eucharist at the Last Supper (Mt 26:26–29; Mk 14:22–24; Lk 22:14–20).

Thus, more than four hundred years after the Rosary became fixed in its traditional form of fifteen decades of prayers, Pope John Paul II considered this popular devotion to be important enough to add these five new Luminous Mysteries to the traditional Joyful, Sorrowful, and Glorious Mysteries (these last devoted to the Resurrection of Christ and after). In this the pontiff was in no way acting contrary to Vatican II's principles of liturgical reform, but rather he was acting very much in harmony with them.

For the Council, contrary to the popular idea which has grown up about it, was eminently respectful of the Church's traditions of prayer, devotion, and formal liturgy. The Council believed, however, that the revised rites "should be distinguished by a noble simplicity. They should be short, clear, and free from useless repetitions. They should be within the people's powers of comprehension" (SC 34). In particular, "a more ample, more varied, and more suitable reading from sacred Scripture" was also thought to be desirable (SC 35).

Most Catholics today, in fact, will probably agree that the rich and varied new three-year Sunday cycle of scriptural readings at Mass prepared in response to this particular directive has been among the more successful of Vatican II's liturgical reforms. The Word of God in Scripture possesses its own inherent power, and the faithful cannot get too much of this particular good thing.

Similarly, the Council's directive that the priest's sermon "should draw its content mainly from scriptural and liturgical sources" (SC 35) was probably an important corrective for preaching – although some preachers have occasionally used this new emphasis on Scripture and the readings as an excuse *not* to preach about some of today's controversial moral issues, such as co-habitation, contraception, abortion, or so-called "gay rights," since such things are allegedly not directly covered in Scripture.

Among other reforms specifically mandated by the basic *Sacrosanctum Concilium* document itself must be mentioned: the revival of the Prayer of the Faithful after the Gospel and the homily, the authorization of Communion under both kinds under certain circumstances, and the revival of the celebration of Mass by more than one priest (concelebration). Also – what may surprise those whose experience of Catholic worship is confined to the vernacular Masses of the post-conciliar years – Vatican II's Constitution on the Sacred Liturgy specifically, and in more than one place, decreed that Latin was to be "preserved" as the language of the liturgy in what the Council itself referred to as "the Latin rites" (SC 36.1). The term "Roman rite," of course, is more commonly used to refer to the Western Church, as well as to distinguish it from the Oriental, or Eastern, rites that together make up "the Catholic Church" (*Not* "the Roman Catholic Church," by the way, for Christ's Church extends quite significantly beyond the "Roman rite," however predominant the latter may be within the total life of the Church).

Since, contrary to SC 36.1, Latin quite obviously has *not* been preserved in this way as the language of the liturgy in the Roman rite, however – since, in fact, a vernacular liturgy quickly became well nigh universal in the Roman rite in the post-conciliar period – we shall need to look more carefully at this particular question below. There was, as it happens, a perfectly legitimate "chain of authority" that resulted in the adoption of the vernacular liturgy nearly everywhere following the Council. However, in view of the plain words of the conciliar Constitution stating that Latin was to be preserved, further examination and explanation of this question are surely called for.

The same thing is true of the vexed question of liturgical translations; once a vernacular liturgy was approved, the question of translations naturally came to the fore; and so we shall have to devote yet another special chapter to that topic as well, after we have covered such important topics of kneeling, the placement of the tabernacle, and Latin in the liturgy.

It should be clear from what has been said up to this point, however, that *Sacrosanctum Concilium*, Vatican II's Constitution on the Sacred

Liturgy, is itself in no way a revolutionary or a radical document. It is, on the contrary, quite a traditional document – as it is also, indisputably, a thoroughly *Catholic* document, in spite of what has sometimes been falsely claimed about it in many of the disputes that have accompanied or followed the reform of the liturgy in the post-conciliar era.

In many ways, this liturgy Constitution is even an eloquent and inspiring document. It quite specifically *says,* for example, that "in order that sound tradition be retained, and yet the way be open to legitimate progress, a careful investigation – theological, historical, and pastoral – should always be made into each part of the liturgy which is to be revised" (SC 23). What else could anybody have asked for? In the event, careful studies into the parts of the liturgy to be revised *were* made, as the Council had directed – and as witness the plethora of liturgical documents that have been issued in the post-conciliar years, and are still being issued!

It may legitimately be asked, therefore, that if the Council's foundational document on the liturgy is itself so basically sound, and if the procedures for the liturgical reform it envisaged were both prudent and responsible, as a careful reading will also generally show, then why did so many things go so wrong in so many ways with the Church's reform of the liturgy? We will mostly be engaged in trying to throw some light precisely this question in the course of the rest of this book.

Meanwhile, even while seeking an answer to the question of why the Vatican-II reform of the liturgy went so wrong in so many respects, we must, first of all, not exaggerate: not everything in the liturgical reform *did* go wrong. Where the reformed liturgy is properly and reverently celebrated according to the directives of the Church that are currently in place – as has increasingly been the case in recent years in many, if not most, parishes in the United States today – then we definitely do have finally something probably not too different from what the fathers of Vatican II wanted and provided for in the document they issued with such prudence and such care. Moreover, the *Novus Ordo* instituted in response to the mandate of Vatican II is a rite which *does* do suitable honor to God, and does bring worshippers closer to him, especially in the solemn sung Masses celebrated on important feast days.

And today we truly *can* find this basically sound kind of liturgy in many, many dioceses and parishes in the United States today, and this *in spite of* all of the confusion and even turmoil that too often accompanied putting in place the reformed liturgy. At the same time, many of the abuses which at first too often accompanied the reform of the liturgy have become much less common today. Things have fortunately become more stabilized since the Vatican II liturgical "changes" were first introduced.

Nevertheless, there is probably no single or easy answer to the overall question of why the things that went wrong did go wrong. We have already adverted to some of these reasons: an imperfect understanding of the Council's intentions; the abrupt and seemingly unplanned way that so many things were changed, often in no particular order and without many explanations being provided; and the fact that most priests did not really understand what was happening and why. There was also a fairly general failure on the part of Church authorities to understand that *any* change, even a needed and legitimate change, in people's deep-seated habits of prayer and worship, was bound to have consequences. These consequences should have been anticipated and taken into account. Nor was it just a matter of not disturbing people's habits: constant changes too easily *do* accustom us to regard the Mass and the sacraments as malleable things, as things that *we* can devise and control, rather than things coming to us by the will of Christ in the Church.

To all these reasons there must be added yet another one, namely: the undue influence of modern "liturgists," that is, liturgical experts too often intent upon their own in-group ideas rather than upon the needs and sensibilities of the faithful. Reliance on "experts" and "professionals," rather than upon reason and common sense, has in many ways been the bane of the post-conciliar period generally.

Then, of course, there was the too frequent and marked impatience and sometimes even the arrogance of some of those in authority, relying uncritically upon their experts, and prone to dig in their heels when faced with perceived resistance to, or criticism of, many of the changes that were being made.

And yet again, in a much more general sense, it should also have been more clearly recognized by Church authority that concepts such as "noble simplicity" and "full, conscious, and active participation" in liturgical celebrations, although consciously and honestly launched by the Council itself, were almost inevitably going to be interpreted in different ways by different people. For some, "noble simplicity" can apparently mean denuding churches of statues and stations of the cross, or dismantling decorative altar rails or screens – just as "full, conscious, and active participation" can mean requiring the proliferation of the various lay "ministries" that have in fact proliferated in the post-conciliar era – or trying, perhaps, to require standing rather than kneeling because that supposedly means that we are all standing together as a symbol of our sacred communion (and, meanwhile, the priest, deacon, and other servers are, after all, still standing too!).

Beyond that, "full, conscious, and active participation" for many meant insisting upon the dialogue Mass with the priest facing the people and with numerous responses from the congregation (even though *Sacrosanctum Concilium* specifically also decrees (SC 30) that "at the proper time a reverent *silence* should be observed"!).

These are only some of the ways in which what began as the perfectly honest and legitimate decisions of Vatican Council II with respect to the reform of the sacred liturgy, set forth in *Sacrosanctum Concilium* and the post-conciliar implementing documents from the Holy See on the liturgy which followed it, nevertheless could be, as they definitely were, subject to misinterpretation, misapplication, and even abuse.

The very comprehensiveness and complexity of what was entailed in the decision of the Second Vatican Council to reform the entire liturgy of the Catholic Church were almost bound in the nature of things to result in many missteps and even conflicting instructions in actually carrying out of the conciliar reforms. Nobody *knew*, or could have known, in advance, how to implement the liturgical reforms, or how they were going to work out. And sometimes the particular reforms themselves were not decreed in response to any specific mandate of the Council or felt need of the faithful. Rather, too often, as we have suggested, they just seem to have been put in place following various theories of some of our contemporary professional "liturgists."

In one important sense, perhaps, this should not surprise us. We live in an age of professional expertise, after all, and it would have been unusual if the Catholic bishops had *not* tended to rely on professional experts, as do leaders in so many areas of our society. The trouble came, it seems, when Church leaders continued to rely *uncritically* on these experts, even after it became increasingly clear that the experts in question were departing significantly, and sometimes even radically, not only from the spirit but sometimes even from the letter of *Sacrosanctum Concilium* and the actual post-conciliar liturgical directives from the Holy See. Sometimes they were departing from the canons of common sense as well, not to speak of the habits and preferences of the faithful!

We might have hoped, for example, for an occasional salutary pause in the pace of the reform, and perhaps even for a reconsideration of what was being put in place, *when* it turned out that the faithful, or even just some of them, were reacting strongly and negatively to what was being done to their cherished habits and practices with regard to the worship of the divine Majesty.

Alas, these negative reactions occurred in all too many cases; and among the results of them, there came instead not accommodation but rather the seemingly never-ending liturgical disputes that ensued, some of which have lasted up to the present day. We may take, as one example, a dispute that has endured into the new century and up to the present day. It concerns one of those things that has most often disturbed devoted Catholics in the post-conciliar years, namely, the whole question of kneeling, both during the Eucharistic Prayer and at the reception of Holy Communion.

In the next two chapters, we need to look at the rules concerning kneeling and standing, and at how these rules have been applied in the United States. In the chapter after that, we shall then look at another question which has disturbed many of the faithful today, namely, the placement of the tabernacle in which the Blessed Sacrament of Our Lord Jesus Christ is reserved.

Chapter Fourteen
Kneeling or Standing?

The whole question of when, if ever, we should kneel during the celebration of Mass and when receiving Holy Communion is illustrative both of how the Vatican II liturgical reforms were often put in place, and how they sometimes went wrong. The pattern was that Rome would first issue an instruction containing new liturgical regulations. These often seemed to be both reasonable and well-intentioned, but they did not always exhibit any awareness or understanding either of how the new regulations would impact upon the faithful, or how the faithful would understand and react to them.

Meanwhile, the local Church authorities responsible for the implementation of the liturgical reforms sometimes had an understanding different from that of Rome about what the new regulations entailed or were supposed to accomplish – if they did not sometimes actually have a different agenda entirely for liturgical reform than that laid out in the Church's official documents. This kind of pattern repeated itself not a few times in the course of the implementations of the Vatican II liturgical reforms.

With regard to the question of kneeling or standing at Mass and when receiving Communion, this whole question was already one of the long-disputed questions that got reopened when John Paul II promulgated the new, revised edition of the *General Instruction on the Roman Missal* (GIRM) in the Jubilee Year 2000, some thirty years after the original 1970 post-Vatican-II GIRM. Many liturgists today believe that kneeling is alien to modern culture and that it is an unsuitable posture for modern "democratic" man, even when worshipping. Standing, they say, is the "resurrection posture." Also, the congregation should supposedly stand in order to express greater unity, participation, and respect for everyone in the community. Hence many liturgists have long aimed at getting the faithful to stand, whether during the canon of the Mass, or for the reception of Holy Communion. The idea seems to have been to establish a "custom" of standing, following which the practice could then be enshrined in the actual Church regulations governing the liturgy.

In point of fact, persistent professional liturgist influence can be said to have succeeded in getting the reception of Communion standing established as the "normal" way to receive in the United States – a fact which was not formally codified until the publication of the new, revised Jubilee Year 2000 GIRM (actually issued on March 18, 2001). Among the approved "American Adaptations" to this new revised GIRM, there is one which specifies that "the norm for reception of Holy Communion is standing"; the text goes on immediately to say, however, that "communicants should not be *denied* Holy Communion because they kneel" (GIRM 162.3; emphasis added). Still, the official new *rule* for the reception of Communion in the United States is: standing. The liturgists could thus be said to have won this particular round; for their idea on standing for the reception of Communion did become enacted into Church law for the United States, as set forth in the new GIRM.

The influence of the liturgists was not nearly as successful in getting kneeling abolished during the celebration of Mass itself, however – even though in some places liturgical zealots have sternly demanded that all stand, and some pastors have even gone so far as to have the kneelers removed from Church pews in some places in order to *prevent* kneeling during the celebration! We still hear of incidents of this kind occurring in one place or another – although we also now hear of some cases where kneelers that were earlier removed are now being put back in. This latter action accords with the new official Church rules that were put in place by the new GIRM.

For this revised new *General Instruction on the Roman Missal* specifies that in the United States "people should kneel beginning after the singing or recitation of the *Sanctus* ["Holy, Holy, Holy"] until after the Amen of the Eucharistic Prayer. The faithful [also] kneel at the *Ecce Agnus Dei* ["Lamb of God"] unless the diocesan bishop decides otherwise" (GIRM 43.3). What this last clause means, of course, is that a diocesan bishop *can* decree standing at and after the *Agnus Dei*, though not during the Eucharistic Prayer itself. Also, the fact that the bishop is specifically given discretion in this one case would seem to mean that he does *not* have discretion to change any of the other GIRM rules (e.g., to require standing throughout the Mass).

After the end of the Council and the introduction of the New Order of the Mass, American Catholics, in continuity with their established practice of kneeling during the canon of the pre-Vatican-II "Tridentine Mass," kept on following the – authentic! – custom of kneeling at the *Sanctus* and again after the *Agnus Dei,* as well as again following the reception of Holy Communion. The new, revised GIRM codified this long-standing custom. The liturgists, notably, did *not* win this round, in other words. In this case, the more traditional practice prevailed.

All the time, though, many liturgists kept saying that standing ought to be the regular posture at Mass, as is the case in the Eastern Orthodox Church and some other communions. Arguments for this included claims that standing, not kneeling, was the practice in the early Church; that kneeling only came about in medieval times in imitation of vassals kneeling before their feudal lords; and that standing more readily allowed the "full, conscious, and active participation" in the sacred liturgy that we have seen is called for by *Sacrosanctum Concilium* 14.

A further argument that has regularly been made is that standing in no way necessarily implies irreverence or disrespect towards God, since we stand as a mark of respect when the Gospel is read, just as we pray the Our Father standing, and just as we also stand to profess the Creed and the Prayers of the Faithful at Mass.

Thus, the liturgists are no doubt correct in holding that standing as such implies no irreverence or disrespect for the divine Majesty. Their other argument, though, that kneeling was not practiced in the early Church would seem to fail in the face of such Scripture passages as Luke 22:41 describing the action of Jesus himself in the Garden of Gethsemane: "And he withdrew from them about a stone's throw, and knelt down and prayed." Acts 20:36 similarly describes kneeling as the common practice in the early Church: "And when [Paul] had spoken thus, he knelt down and prayed with them all." St. Paul even specifies in Philippians 2:10 that: "At the name of Jesus every knee should bow, in heaven and on earth and under the earth."

Many other similar passages could be cited from Scripture. Kneeling is frequently mentioned in connection with the worship of God in both the Old and the New Testaments. Psalm 95:6–7 expressly says: "O come, let us worship and bow down, let us kneel before the Lord, our Maker! For he is our God, and we are the people of his pasture, and the sheep of this hand."

Similarly, the argument that kneeling only goes back to the practice of kneeling before one's feudal lord in medieval times, besides not being accurate, fails to come to grips with the fact that legitimate Church customs and traditions may arise in any age. The early Church is not the only model for the Church today. The medieval Church too can and does and should serve as a valid model for certain traditions. The Middle Ages were a great age of faith, after all. In any case, as the former Cardinal Joseph Ratzinger pointed out in his excellent book, *The Spirit of the Liturgy*, kneeling is a most appropriate devotional posture and *fits* with Christian worship. The cardinal wrote as follows:

> It may well be that kneeling is alien to modern culture...for this culture has turned away from the faith and no longer knows the One before whom kneeling is the right, indeed the intrinsically necessary, gesture. The man who learns to believe learns also to kneel, and a faith or a liturgy no longer familiar with kneeling would be sick at the core. Where it has been lost, *kneeling must be rediscovered*, so that, in our prayer, we remain in fellowship with the apostles and martyrs, in fellowship with the whole cosmos, indeed in union with Jesus Christ Himself (emphasis added).

Kneeling at Mass, then, whatever its origin and development – which very probably did become strongly solidified in medieval times, especially as a result of the adoration of the reserved Blessed Sacrament – kneeling at Mass surely does constitute true worship, and it also quite aptly corresponds to a genuine need for adoration on the part of the believing faithful. It has served the Church well for many centuries. The notion that it should now just be abolished in conformity with the theories of some modern liturgists concerning "community Masses" is an exceedingly shallow notion, as is the other idea of some liturgists that the faithful are somehow *not* fully, consciously, and actively "participating" in the liturgy when they are kneeling.

Fortunately, Church authority made the sensible decision to continue in the United States the practice of kneeling during those parts of the Mass that continued to be customary here even after Vatican II. It is worth quoting the exact new rule in this regard contained in the revised new *General Instruction on the Roman Missal*:

> In the dioceses of the United States of America, [the faithful] should kneel beginning after the singing or the recitation of the *Sanctus* until after the *Amen* of the Eucharistic Prayer, except when prevented on occasion by reasons of health, lack of space, the large number of people present, or some other good reason. Those who do not kneel ought to make a profound bow when the priest genuflects after the consecration. The faithful kneel after the

Agnus Dei unless the diocesan bishop determines otherwise (GIRM 43.3).

Kneeling during these customary parts of the Mass will thus be continued in the United States. Kneeling to receive Communion, however, although still desired by many of the faithful, did not fare as well in the new rules for the celebration of Mass. One of the reasons for this is that standing and going up in a line to receive Communion really already *had* become pretty much established as the standard practice or custom in the United States in the post-Vatican-II era. As things stand today, there would probably have been another major disruption, which nobody should want, if the GIRM had attempted to restore across the board kneeling to receive Communion. This is the way the rule for the United States now reads in full in the new revised GIRM:

> The norm for reception of Holy Communion in the dioceses of the United States is standing. *Communicants should not be denied Holy Communion because they kneel.* Rather, such instances should be addressed pastorally, by providing the faithful with proper catechesis on the reasons for the norm (GIRM 160.2; emphasis added).

What this rule does is to codify what the custom for receiving Communion had now become in the United States in the post-conciliar years. This particular norm amounted to a change from pre-Vatican-II days, though, when the more prevalent custom was to receive Communion kneeling at the altar rail (and on the tongue!). Moreover, the change to standing did not come about without opposition, sometimes contentious, from some of the faithful, many of whom preferred to continue to receive kneeling. But this preference was effectively eliminated for them in many cases by the simple expedient of removing the altar rails. In any case, there were strong pressures in most parishes to conform to the new usage. Eventually, nearly all of the faithful did conform, and this was reflected in the rule that got codified to this effect in the new GIRM.

Even after accepting the practice of coming up in line and receiving Communion, however, many of the faithful still preferred to genuflect before receiving. This too sometimes became a bone of contention, just as kneeling had, since the recommended sign of reverence was now supposed to be a bow of the head. The new revised GIRM rule clearly now prescribes the latter, as follows:

...when receiving Holy Communion...the communicant bows his
or her head before the sacrament as a gesture of reverence and
receives the Body of the Lord from the minister. The consecrated
host may be received either on the tongue or in the hand at the discretion of each communicant. When Holy Communion is received
under both kinds, the sign of reverence is also made before receiving the Precious Blood (GIRM 160.2).

The new requirement for bowing the head as a sign of reverence before
receiving Communion appears to be a genuinely new one; and it was perhaps even a bit of a surprise to see it instituted, since bowing in this fashion before receiving Communion was never a particularly widespread custom in the United States. Nor do there seem to have been any noteworthy
instructions or programs of catechesis concerning this kind of bowing. The
new bowing requirement seems to be something that the liturgists, again,
thought up and then were able to slip in – perhaps to forestall kneeling or
genuflecting. For *if* the new rule was to receive standing, as was the case,
then it is true that kneeling or genuflecting *can* impede the process of the
faithful coming up in a line to receive (but then so can bowing, at least to
some extent).

However that may be, nobody could argue that the new rule was unreasonable. There can surely be no doubt that a bow *is* a sign of reverence. By
the fact of enshrining this new rule in its new, revised GIRM, the legitimate
authority of the Church plainly endorsed bowing and thereby indicated to
the faithful that a bow is indeed a suitable and adequate sign of reverence
before the divine Majesty present in the Blessed Sacrament.

All of these things together, then, constituted the official new rules for
the United States concerning when we stand and when we kneel at Mass
and while receiving Communion: we are to kneel in the pews at the designated times during the celebration of the Mass, but we are to receive the
Body of Christ standing. The exception in the new GIRM regulations providing that those who wish to continue to kneel – or genuflect – to receive
should not be refused, but rather should be accommodated, reflecting a
salutary pastoral recognition on the part of the Church that some of the
devout faithful continued to believe that they *must* kneel to receive
Communion. The fact that those people who preferred to kneel were supposed to be "catechized" to adopt the new rule, however – as the GIRM text
very clearly states – would seem to confirm that standing *was* the new rule,
which the Church wished to see applied universally in the United States.

Chapter Fifteen
Putting the New Rules into Practice

The reactions to the new rules on kneeling and standing in the new GIRM were not untypical of how the Vatican II liturgical reforms were too often received. The rule providing for kneeling at the designated times during the Mass quickly became very widely if not almost universally observed. Most of the faithful seemed quite comfortable with this long-standing custom, now finally codified as a formal rule. There also seemed to be fewer and fewer cases where zealot pastors tried to impose standing throughout the Mass, whether or not by actually removing the kneelers from the pews. Indeed there was hope that the encoding of the new GIRM rule would eliminate this abuse entirely.

Similarly, standing to receive Communion also seemed to be generally accepted; it had already pretty much also become the norm. The same thing did not seem to be true of the required bow of the head, however. One's admittedly unscientific impression was that few people were bowing their heads before the GIRM rule came out; and although more began to do so as they became aware of the new rule, the practice still seemed far from universal. The American bishops surely needed to institute a serious nationwide catechesis designed to inform people about the new rule and the reasons for it and to seek their compliance with it. One conjectures that the American bishops were probably the ones who got Rome to sign off on the new bowing rule in the first place, as one of the American "adaptations" in the new GIRM; but it was not untypical of too many of the Vatican II liturgical reforms generally that one saw few signs of the bishops attempting to see that the faithful were properly instructed in the matter after the new rule was issued.

In this regard, priests needed to *announce* at Mass that the people coming up to Communion were expected to bow as a sign of reverence to the Blessed Sacrament. As had pretty much been the practice for a long time, many communicants were making no sign of reverence at all as they came forward in the line; a fair number of them were accustomed to genuflect, however, and a few to make the sign of the cross.

There was no uniformity, however. Only a very few, it would seem, continued to insist on kneeling. In the case of those few, however, there were sometimes instances where the priests *denied Communion to them*; and there were yet other instances where the priests lectured or chastised those who continued to genuflect or kneel.

Such behavior, by any definition, certainly constituted a serious abuse on the part of the priests in question. I personally know of a case where a prominent public figure and recent convert to the Church was denied Communion at a Holy Day Mass at the cathedral because he wished to kneel to receive. After the Mass, outside, the convert tried to explain his action to the cathedral rector: "I kneel in the presence of Jesus Christ," he said. Instead of providing the "proper catechesis on the reasons" for giving out Communion to the faithful standing, as the GIRM rule requires, the cathedral rector called him a vulgar name.

Unhappily, similar incidents have not been entirely rare in the course of arriving at the Church's new rules in the matter. Nor does it seem that such incidents completely ceased once the promulgation of the new GIRM finally set forth the applicable rules. On the contrary, further strife and contention seemed in the offing as a result of misplaced zeal on both sides: on one side, there was the conviction on the part of some of those in authority that there was no longer any excuse for not following the rule; and on the other side, there persisted the belief that one *must* kneel (or that one had a *right* to kneel!). These convictions on both sides even seem to have hardened in some cases. It did not help, however, that the Roman instructions were not entirely clear in the matter.

The new Roman rules were first clearly laid out for the United States in a letter dated April 25, 2002, from the prefect of the Congregation for Divine Worship and the Discipline of the Sacraments to the president of the USCCB. Shortly afterwards, the July, 2002, issue of the Newsletter of the U.S. Bishops' Committee on the Liturgy (BCL) stated that kneeling "is not a licit posture for receiving holy Communion in the dioceses of the United States unless the bishop of a particular diocese has derogated from this norm in an individual and extraordinary circumstance."

Not *licit!* Although the new Roman rules undeniably did call for the reception of Communion standing, they also allowed for an exception in the case of those insisting on kneeling or genuflecting; and while these latter may indeed be in need of catechesis regarding the new rules – as the GIRM also plainly says they are – they should not, meanwhile, be denied Communion. What was disturbing about the BCL Newsletter statement was the attitude that any violation of the new rules – rules that many Catholic had never even heard about (owing, again, to a *lack* of any serious catechesis or instructions on the subject in most places!) – constituted a serious disciplinary breach, and perhaps even called for some kind of a "crackdown" on those whose behavior was no longer considered "licit."

Would that the BCL had shown even a fraction of such concern for some of the liturgical abuses that the faithful have had to put up with for a rather long time! The Church in the United States may have tolerated all kinds of dissent and disobedience and abuses throughout most of the post-conciliar period – and, in fact, these things *have* been widely tolerated. If the BCL had anything to say about it now, however, the Church in America was certainly no longer going to tolerate anyone receiving Communion kneeling or genuflecting!

Unfortunately, this harsh attitude evinced in the BCL Newsletter was perhaps not all that uncommon among some of those with responsibilities for the liturgy. Some bishops, for example, spoke of "dissent" or "disobedience" on the part of those still kneeling or genuflecting when receiving Communion. One bishop in Indiana, for example, wrote in his diocesan newspaper – as *The National Catholic Register* reported (10/5/02) – that

> ...a person is not to genuflect before receiving . . . The sign of reverence has now been clearly determined for the United States. It is a bow of the head...Should a person insist on kneeling for the reception of holy Communion, Communion will not be denied, but they clearly will be demonstrating dissent from the mind of the Church. Rather than reverence, the emphasis will be on refusal to embrace particular law approved by the Vatican for the United States...

Thus an American bishop. Nor was he the only bishop who publicly adopted the line that the faithful who continued to genuflect or kneel were into "dissent" and "disobedience." That *this* should have been the issue on which some American bishops were apparently prepared, finally, to take a stand against dissent and disobedience was more than a little ironic. The American bishops, as is only too well known and documented, have rarely found themselves able to speak out anywhere near this strongly about the dissent and disobediences still widely found "on the left." Nor have they consistently rebuked or corrected many of those engaged in actual liturgical abuses – of which the refusal of Communion to those kneeling or genuflecting has certainly been one. By all that was good and holy, though, some of these same bishops now suddenly seemed grimly determined to invoke their authority against communicants piously wishing to kneel or genuflect when receiving Communion!

Such a sudden rash of episcopal zeal against those who insisted on kneeling, however, seemed both misplaced and excessive; and it certainly indicated a rather faulty set of episcopal priorities. The whole renewed controversy over kneeling amounted to a sad but probably typical example of how and why liturgical reforms too often went wrong in the post-conciliar era. It often worked this way: the bishops, or even Rome, would put out new rules which were hardly ever really explained to anybody – but then they would be surprised when the result turned out to be more liturgical confusion.

Bishops and liturgists and even priests tend to be aware of the pertinent background of liturgical changes in the course of their work, namely, that, in this case, the *General Instruction on the Roman Missal* was being revised after many years, and some new rules were being promulgated. The faithful, however, generally do not follow such things; and so when, suddenly, seemingly arbitrary new rules are again announced without any particular explanation, they seem to come out of the blue. Many of the faithful, not surprisingly, can become both baffled and disoriented, and sometimes even angry, in this kind of situation. When the new rules in question are accompanied by episcopal strictures declaring that anyone who continues, say, to genuflect before receiving Communion is "disobedient" – especially when so little instruction has meanwhile been provided in the matter – there can be little wonder that Vatican II's vaunted liturgical reform will once again be perceived to have missed the mark and to have "failed" in the eyes of not a few of the faithful.

Rome, it seems, was not quite as concerned as the BCL and some of the bishops that the faithful were not yet fully compliant with the new norms. At the very time in July, 2002, that the BCL Newsletter was complaining that kneeling was no longer a "licit posture" for receiving Holy Communion in the United States, the prefect for the Congregation for Divine Worship and the Discipline of the Sacraments, Chilean Cardinal Jorge Arturo Medina Estevez, was writing a rather strong admonitory letter dated July 1, 2002, to a bishop in the United States in whose diocese members of the faithful had been refused Communion while kneeling. In his letter, Cardinal Medina stated, among other things, that:

> The Congregation…is concerned at the number of similar complaints that it has received in recent months from various places,

and considers any refusal of Holy Communion to a member of the faithful on the basis of his or her kneeling posture to be a grave violation of one of the most basic rights of the Christian faithful, namely that of being assisted by the Pastors by means of the Sacraments (*Codex Iuris Canonici*, Canon 213). In view of the law that "sacred ministers may not deny the sacraments to those who opportunely ask for them, are properly disposed, and are not prohibited by law from receiving them" (Canon 843.1), there should be no such refusal to *any* Catholic who presents himself for Holy Communion at Mass, except in cases presenting a danger of grave scandal to other believers arising out of the person's unrepented public sin or obstinate heresy or schism, publicly professed or declared. Even where the Congregation has approved of legislation denoting standing as the posture for Holy Communion, in accordance with the adaptations permitted to the Conferences of Bishops by the *Institutio Generalis Missalis Romani* (GIRM 160.2), it has done so with the stipulation that communicants who choose to kneel are not to be denied Holy Communion on these grounds.

This is pretty strong language. Cardinal Medina actually speaks about " . . . one of the most basic *rights* of the Christian faithful," and he specifies that "ministers may not *deny* [Communion] . . . even where the Congregation has approved of legislation denoting standing . . . " (emphasis added).

In the same letter, emphasizing that those who would deny Communion to kneeling communicants would be the ones out of line, Cardinal Medina went on to refer to his then colleague – once again the former Cardinal Joseph Ratzinger! "As His Eminence Cardinal Joseph Ratzinger has recently emphasized," Cardinal Medina wrote, "the practice of kneeling for Holy Communion has in its favor a centuries-old tradition, and it is a particularly expressive sign of adoration, completely appropriate in light of the true, real, and substantial presence of Our Lord Jesus Christ under the consecrated species."

The faithful who are moved to kneel in the Real Presence of the Lord should thus not in any way be *penalized*! This was the firm, considered judgment of the Church's highest authority in liturgical matters. What is surprising is how any such thing could ever have become controversial or considered to be a matter of possible "disobedience," especially when so many other kinds of disobedience were going uncorrected, and, too often, even apparently unremarked, in the Church.

In yet another letter dated February 26, 2003, over the signature of the undersecretary of the Congregation for Divine Worship and the Discipline of the Sacraments, Mario Marini, it was further made clear that not only should the faithful not be denied Communion because they choose to kneel or genuflect, but that they "should not be imposed upon *nor accused of disobedience and of acting illicitly when they kneel to receive Holy Communion*" (emphasis added). So much for the strictures of the Bishops' Committee on the Liturgy and the bishop in Indiana (among others). Even while approving new rules calling for receiving Holy Communion standing (following a bow of the head in reverence), the Holy See at the same time clearly did not want those faithful who believed that they should genuflect or kneel to be harassed or chastised. Undoubtedly, this was precisely the sane pastoral approach that was called for.

So what, in the end, should be the reaction of the average Catholic to all this? Catholics ought to be willing to follow the rules as they are now codified, namely, kneeling for the greater part of the service during Mass, combined with standing (while bowing) to receive Communion. These are in no way unreasonable rules. Nevertheless, they do go against what some devout Catholics continue to believe with regard to the reverence owed to the Holy Eucharist, and so the Holy See wisely also decreed that these communicants may not be refused when they kneel or genuflect. Bishops and priests, in turn, should respect the consciences of the communicants in these cases. The Holy See has now clearly judged that their consciences in this matter should take precedence over any desired uniformity in the liturgy.

Of course, none of this represents either a neat or perhaps even a completely logical solution to this particular problem arising out of the still ongoing Vatican II liturgical reforms in this regard. The Congregation for Divine Worship and the Discipline of the Sacraments is here quite deliberately sanctioning exceptions to a rule that it has itself approved and promulgated. What we have here, then, is a case where the American bishops and the liturgical establishment probably lobbied to get the standing for Communion rule into the new GIRM among the "American Adaptations." The Congregation for Divine Worship may even have been less than enthusiastic about this, though it usually makes it a practice to accommodate the conferences of bishops where it finds that it can. The whole business of a bow as a sign of reverence for the Eucharist was probably added when the

Holy See perhaps raised the question about the need for such a sign, if kneeling (or genuflecting) was no longer to be practiced. But the fact of the matter was, however, that hardly anybody in America had ever heard of such a bow before. It was certainly not a widely established custom.

After the new GIRM rule was approved, though, it turned out that some of the faithful – whom the bishops and the liturgical establishment have certainly never been accustomed to consult in such matters – persisted in the custom of genuflecting or kneeling. When the Congregation for Divine Worship and the Discipline of the Sacraments began receiving letters from members of the faithful being denied Communion, or being harassed when trying to receive it kneeling or genuflecting, Rome's uneasy compromise requiring that they had to be allowed to do so surely became inevitable.

However, the whole confused business of standing versus kneeling at Mass and in the reception of Communion sadly represents a not untypical example of how many of the Vatican II liturgical reforms actually did get introduced and carried forward in the post-conciliar years. It would have been a positive and helpful step in this case, as in many other cases, if the American bishops had simply undertaken a more serious and sustained program of catechesis on this and other disputed liturgical questions in advance of the changes being made. This should regularly have been done from the time of the first liturgical reforms, as a matter of fact. One sometimes gets the impression that the Church leadership generally somehow thinks or imagines that it *was* done, but the experience of at least many of the faithful in many places who lived through all the changes would suggest that, whatever the intentions of the Church leadership may have been, what was in fact done was *not* adequate. The actual record pertaining to most of the liturgical reforms put in place does *not* indicate that Church leaders ever really understood very well what was needed; nor do all of them always appear to understand this very well yet. The problem is ongoing.

And concerning the continuing vexed question of standing or kneeling, perhaps another straw in the ⌄ ind indicating where things might be going came when the master ⌐ papal liturgical ceremonies, Msgr. Guido Marini, in an interview in *L'Osservatore Romano* on June 26, 2008, announced that reception of Communion at papal Masses would henceforth take place with communicants kneeling before the Holy Father and receiving the host on the tongue. This new (though eminently traditional) papal practice began on May 22, 2008, at a Mass in the Basilica of St. John

Lateran, when two ushers placed a kneeler in front of the altar and the communicants then all knelt and received on the tongue. In his interview explaining what was now the new papal norm, Msgr. Marini remarked that "it is necessary not to forget that the distribution of Communion in the hand from a juridical standpoint remains up to now an indult," or exception to the general rule, which the Holy See granted to the bishops' conferences which requested it. The master of papal liturgical ceremonies added that Pope Benedict's adoption of the traditional practice of kneeling and receiving Communion on the tongue aimed "to highlight the force of the valid norm for the whole Church."

Chapter Sixteen
The Tabernacle of the Blessed Sacrament

Another one of the major bones of contention after Vatican Council II instituted its reform of the sacred liturgy has been the placement of the tabernacle in which the Blessed Sacrament is reserved in our churches and chapels. As the reforms proceeded, and as such things as the remodeling of churches and sanctuaries began to be carried out, many complaints began to be voiced by the devout laity that the Blessed Sacrament was being irreverently *downgraded* when the tabernacle containing it was moved, say, from a main altar in the center of the Church to a side altar or to a Blessed Sacrament chapel.

Amid other instances of post-conciliar confusion, alert members of the faithful were sometimes given no small reason to doubt the entirely wholehearted Eucharistic devotion of some of the liturgists and theologians prominently engaged in "implementing the Council." There was a new theology abroad, after all – one which persists in the Church down to the present day. This theology holds that the presence of Christ is chiefly and most importantly to be found in what its votaries like to style "the gathered assembly," that is, in the people, rather than in the reserved consecrated sacred species. And then, rather suddenly and disconcertingly, just as intimations of this new people-centered theology began to register in people's minds, the faithful *also* began seeing tabernacles being displaced as an integral part of what were said to be required Vatican II liturgical reforms.

What did Vatican II say about this particular subject? Did the Council decree that reverence to the Blessed Sacrament in the tabernacle should be de-emphasized? In point of fact, the Council said nothing at all about this subject. *Sacrosanctum Concilium* never mentions the subject in any way. However, the Holy See's First Instruction on the Proper Implementation of the Sacred Liturgy, *Inter Oecumenici,* issued by the Sacred Congregation for Rites on September 26, 1964 – that is, more than a year before the end of the Council itself – this First Instruction provided that 1) there could only be one tabernacle with the reserved Blessed Sacrament in each church or chapel; 2) this tabernacle could be placed in a Blessed Sacrament chapel to encourage the private devotion of the faithful; or 3) it could be placed "in the middle of the main altar or on a side altar." Whether it was in a special chapel or on a main altar – or on a side altar! – the tabernacle was always supposed to be in a "prominent place" (IO 95).

Such were the provisions regarding the placement of the tabernacle found in the Holy See's First Instruction on the Proper Implementation of the Sacred Liturgy. These provisions were repeated more or less verbatim in the Sacred Congregation for Rites' later Instruction on the Worship of the Eucharistic Mystery, *Eucharisticum Mysterium*, issued on May 25, 1967. In order to understand some of the typical kind of thinking that went into the liturgical reforms, it is worth quoting from this latter Instruction the entire text subtitled "Where the Blessed Sacrament Is to be Reserved":

A. The Tabernacle

Where reservation of the Blessed Sacrament is permitted according to the provision of [canon] law, it may be reserved permanently or regularly only on one altar or in one place in the church. Therefore, as a rule, each church should have only one tabernacle, and this tabernacle must be safe and inviolable.

B. The Blessed Sacrament Chapel

The place in a church or oratory where the Blessed Sacrament is reserved in the tabernacle should be truly prominent. It ought to be suitable for private prayer so that the faithful may easily and fruitfully, by private devotion also, continue to honor Our Lord in this sacrament. It is therefore recommended that, as far as possible, the tabernacle be placed in a chapel distinct from the middle or central part of the church, above all in those churches where marriages and funerals take place frequently, and in places which are much visited for their artistic or historical treasures.

C. The Tabernacle in the Middle of the Altar or in Some Other Part of the Church

"The Blessed Sacrament should be reserved in a solid, inviolable tabernacle in the middle of the main altar or on a side altar, but in a truly prominent place. Alternatively, according to legitimate customs, and in individual cases to be decided by the local ordinary, it may be placed in some other part of the church which is really worthy and properly equipped.

"Mass may be celebrated facing the people even though there is a tabernacle on the altar, provided this is small yet adequate." (These last two paragraphs here are placed between quotation marks since they are direct quotations from the First Instruction *Inter Oecumenici* 95 quoted above.)

So what do we have here with regard to the placement of the tabernacle in a church or chapel, according to the official Instructions from the Holy See? The main point in the above Instruction would seem to be that, wherever it might be placed, the tabernacle should be "prominent." So there does not seem to have been any effort here to downgrade or diminish the importance of the reserved Blessed Sacrament.

Otherwise, though, it would seem that the tabernacle can licitly be placed virtually *anywhere*: that is, in a Blessed Sacrament chapel, in the middle of the main altar, in the middle of a side altar, *or* "in some other part of the church" (with the approval of the bishop). At one point the Instruction even seems to say that, at least in frequently visited churches, it probably *should* be in a Blessed Sacrament chapel ("as far as possible") rather than on a regular altar – but then the Instruction goes right on to discuss its placement on a main or on a side altar anyway!

Thus, referring to the Church's own official Instructions in the matter does not appear to help much in cases where the complaint is that the Blessed Sacrament is being downgraded by being moved, say, from the center of the main altar. *Is* it being "downgraded"? Is it a case of adhering to a questionable theology holding that Christ resides principally in the people at Mass rather than in the reserved species? Or are there other perfectly legitimate reasons that might dictate that this avowed Body of Christ needs to be placed elsewhere? There seems to be no way that people generally could answer these questions on the sole basis of the existing official Church Instructions in the matter, since these Instructions themselves give no explanation at the same time as they offer so many options.

The unresolved ambiguity on this particular topic was simply perpetuated in subsequent Roman instructions. The original *General Instruction on the Roman Missal* (GIRM), published on March 26, 1970, for example, provided that:

> It is strongly recommended that the Blessed Sacrament be reserved in a *special chapel* well suited for private prayer, *apart from the nave*. But if the plan of the Church or legitimate local custom impedes this, then the Sacrament should be kept on *an* altar or

elsewhere in the church in a place of honor suitably adorned
(GIRM, 276; emphasis added throughout).

In other words, again, it is necessary to put the tabernacle – virtually
anywhere! The acute anxiety of some of the faithful about this – that perhaps the belief of the Church in the Real Presence of Jesus in the sacrament of the altar was being downgraded by the way some of the official
changes of Vatican II were being implemented – specifically, by the way
the tabernacle was being moved from the central altar – this kind of anxiety was simply not recognized or credited – or even imagined, apparently
– by the highest Church authorities as they issued their successive
Instructions on the matter.

This remains true today. In the revised new *General Instruction on the
Roman Missal (Institutio Generalis Missalis Romani),* the full text of
which was finally presented to Pope John Paul II on March 18, 2002, as we
have noted above, it is specified that the tabernacle:

> ...should be placed according to the judgment of the diocesan bish-
> op: a) either in the sanctuary, apart from the altar of celebration, in
> the most suitable form and place, not excluding on an altar which
> is no longer used for celebrations; b) or in another chapel suitable
> for adoration and the private prayer of the faithful, and which is
> integrally connected to the Church, and is conspicuous to the
> faithful (GIRM 315).

Not all of the liturgical directives contained in the hundreds of pages
of Roman liturgical documents issued in the post-conciliar years are as
indefinite, and, indeed, as confusing, as these directives on the placement
of the tabernacle with the reserved Sacrament. On the contrary, most of the
Roman directives are quite clear and definite; and the problems concerning them, if any, have typically involved abuses stemming from *not* following them, not from any defect or ambiguity in the directives themselves.
Still, this tabernacle question nevertheless does illustrate one important
point about the liturgical reform which has been quite consistent in the
years since Vatican II.

The point is this: by and large Church authorities have simply gone on
with the reforms as originally conceived with little or no regard for how
any reforms may have played out when implemented in practice – or may
have been received by the faithful – or may have been misunderstood by
the faithful. There seems to have been little or no recognition that perhaps

not all of the reforms put in place made sense, have actually worked very well, or have been received by the faithful. Specifically, in the case of the placement of the tabernacle, complaints quickly arose when tabernacles began to be moved; these complaints were that the Church's faith in the reserved sacred species was not being respected: it was Christ himself, after all, who was being shunted off to a side altar or sequestered in a chapel apart from the main church. This was how many of the faithful saw the matter.

However, none of this seems to have registered at any point or in any way with Church authorities, including the Roman authorities. As is apparent from the above quotations, they simply went on repeating their original directives in successive Instructions as if there were no problem at all. The same thing was surely true farther down the line: at no level in the Church, apparently, did anyone ever bother to clarify, modify, or even explain why tabernacles were suddenly being moved. If and when the faithful inquired, they were usually ignored or rebuffed; they were thought to have no competence in the matter, nor any reason to have any interest in it.

There was never any way, in other words, for the concerns of the faithful to be conveyed to the authorities responsible for the liturgical changes – to which these authorities might then have responded with clarifications, modifications, or explanations as appropriate. There was no system at all, in other words, for what today we call "feedback" built into the post-Vatican-II liturgical reforms. The liturgists and pastors tranquilly proceeded with their plans, as directed by the bishops, who themselves seemed oblivious to the problems being experienced by the faithful in the pews. Those faithful simply had to put up with whatever the results turned out to be. The fact that many of the faithful were distressed by this way of proceeding, and in this particular case, for example, sincerely *believed*, whether rightly or wrongly, that the intention *was* to downgrade the status of the reserved Blessed Sacrament, generally just did not seem to register with the pastors and the bishops at all. On an official level, few in authority apparently ever saw anything at all possibly amiss in what was being done when moving tabernacles – or if they saw it, they didn't admit it!

This, unhappily, turned out, too often, to be the case with the liturgical reforms as a whole. They were not considered to be the business of the laity; the laity were not supposed to have an opinion about them; they were apparently just supposed to accept *whatever* was put in place. All this helped to create enormous confusion, disaffection, and sometimes worse among the faithful. Many liturgical reforms may have made perfectly good sense – many of them *did* make perfectly good sense – but unless this happened to be immediately evident, which was not always the case, there was little or no way the faithful were ever going to find it out from the way many of these same reforms were presented and put in place.

And, as we have now seen in the case of the successive Roman Instructions provided for the placement of the tabernacle, the Church authorities themselves seem never to have arrived at a clear or coherent idea of just where and how the tabernacle should be placed. Certainly they never provided any *explanation* of what had been decided. On this subject, as on a number of others, we simply continue to go on living today with official "instructions" that remain unclear.

And if this could be true of many well-meant and often even very legitimate reforms, what can be said about the changes that were *not* so legitimate? The case has indeed been far worse for some of the things brought forward for implementation, not by any true mandate from the Council, but by those with their own particular "agendas." The bishops and priests in the immediate post-conciliar years sometimes had a very imperfect idea of what the Council had really intended and ruled. This did not prevent them, since they *were* the official implementers of the Council, after all, from implementing it in accordance with their own defective understanding of the Council's actual enactments. Many of them were able with a perfectly clear conscience to implement *their* ideas of what they thought the liturgical reform should, regardless of what the official documents actually said.

It is unhappily true that some of the things that have been saddled upon the faithful in the name of the conciliar reforms were probably never even remotely imagined by the Fathers of Vatican II, let alone mandated by them. We need think, for example, only of such things as churches without kneelers, or, for that matter, of the once nearly ubiquitous "guitar Masses," which, thankfully, seem to have receded somewhat in recent years. But the idea that there could ever actually have been a question or controversy over where the tabernacle of the Blessed Sacrament ought to be placed in the church would surely never have crossed the minds of the Fathers of Vatican Council II!

Chapter Seventeen
Service at the Altar

When we speak of changes brought forward in accordance with particular "agendas" in the name of Vatican II (or in the name of the famous "spirit of the Council"), we are touching upon one of the most significant and all-pervasive factors of the whole post-conciliar period. Those who had their own agendas for what they thought ought to be changed in the Church, including, in particular, liturgists and other experts, often seized upon the Council's officially inaugurated period of change to introduce not necessarily what the Council had decreed, but rather their ideas of what they thought the Council *should* have decreed.

We could point to not a few examples of this phenomenon in the post-conciliar period. It was encountered fairly often in the course of the implementation of the liturgical reforms. Among the various examples of it that we might choose to illustrate this point, we shall mention here the question of service at the altar, and, in particular, *female* service at the altar, assisting the priest, that is, "altar girls."

Among the more salient phenomena in contemporary society coinciding almost exactly with the post-conciliar years has been the rise of radical feminism. Almost all of the institutions of our society have been enormously influenced by feminist assumptions and not infrequently by outright pressure from the organized radical feminist movement. The Catholic Church has not been spared in this regard. God may have created them "male and female" (Gen 1:27) all right, but modern radical feminists firmly believe that women got much the worst of the deal, and nothing will now do for them but to achieve complete "equality" – if not "uniformity" – with men in all things (some feminists even claim "superiority" over men).

This feminist drive for what they demand must be complete equality with men is probably most dramatically seen in the modern feminist insistence upon a woman's supposed right to have an abortion – women should not have to bear children if men don't! Besides viewing childbirth as nothing but a burden, this idea seems to leave out the obvious fact that men *cannot* bear children; but it nevertheless seems to be one of the few remaining moral absolutes in the world of today, at least for some, in an otherwise morally relativistic world. How believing Catholics could succumb to this kind of radical feminist ideology is hard to understand; but, on the evidence, many Catholics *have* succumbed to it, and have become fellow travelers with the feminists, if they have not themselves become feminists *tout court*.

Within the Catholic Church, the immemorial tradition that only men can be ordained to the sacred priesthood inevitably came to be called into question by typical feminist thinking. The exclusion of women from ordination was seen as yet one more injustice perpetrated against women by male domination, in this case, by the all-male Church hierarchy, which very soon came to be viewed as an oppressive "patriarchy." It is ironic, of course, that patriarchy, of all things, should have come to be so hated by those feminists still calling themselves Christians – considering that it was nothing else but the institution of a patriarchy which God employed when he first called Abraham "our father in faith" in order to set in motion his ages-long divine work for the sake of our salvation!

Once the question of female ordination got raised, though, probably a majority of modern American Catholics, influenced as they are by the predominant received ideas of the secular culture in which they live, really seem to have had no great objections to it. Few could see any point in opposing it. Few could any longer grasp the symbolism of the male priest standing in for the male Christ. It had become increasingly accepted in other social institutions, and in other areas of modern life, that women should not be denied anything that was available to men. So why not the priesthood? Why couldn't women be ordained as well? An affirmative answer to this question seemed to be self-evident, what people today call a "no-brainer."

Nevertheless, the tradition of the Church remained solidly against the ordination of women. Christ himself chose only men to be his apostles, men who were sent out to "preach the Gospel to the whole creation" (Mk 16:15); and the Church has consistently maintained the tradition of a male-only ordained priesthood in both East and West. This has remained true down to our own day.

Agitation to try to undermine and break down this tradition, however, soon became an important goal of the feminist movement. Pro-feminist convictions turned out to be particularly strong among some of the members of female religious orders, although such convictions were by no means limited to them. Similar convictions could even sometimes be found among not a few members of the hierarchy. Feminists soon made such inroads in the normal thinking of Catholics, in fact, that the Holy See eventually felt obliged to reiterate and restate the Church's unbroken tradition in the matter of female non-ordination.

Thus, on October 15, 1976, the Sacred Congregation for the Doctrine of the Faith issued a Declaration on the Admission of Women to the Ministerial Priesthood, *Inter Insigniores,* which concluded that the unbroken tradition of the Church in ordaining only males to the priesthood was based primarily on the necessity for what the document called a "natural resemblance" between the one acting *in persona Christi,* "in the person of Christ," as a priest does, and Christ himself, who became incarnate as a man, not as a woman.

The Church's position in not ordaining women was thus based not just on prejudice or custom or a desire to keep women in their place, but on serious anthropological and theological reasons. Undoubtedly it was the correct position too, if the practice of Christ himself, and the Church's responsibility to follow Christ's practice, mean anything. Indeed, upon serious reflection, it seems to be the only possible position. At the same time, though, the document *Inter Insigniores* made very clear the Church's teaching that women were in no way of any lesser *human dignity* than men, even though they could not properly stand *in persona Christi* as priests. Women were nevertheless also created in the image of God along with men and, like men, they were equally saved by Christ; and, every bit as much as men, they enjoyed the dignity to which their full humanity entitled them; they simply had, in the Church's understanding, following Christ, different complementary roles and functions from those of men.

While affirming the equality of the two sexes in terms of human dignity, then, the Church has nevertheless consistently stressed their complementarity (rather than a false uniformity). As with so many post-conciliar Church decisions, however, *Inter Insigniores* failed either to compel assent or to convince many of those influenced by modern feminist ideas. Feminist agitation for female ordination, if anything, became intensified following the issuance of this document. It was derided as showing how ill-founded the Church's prohibition of female ordination supposedly was.

Nearly two decades later, on May 22, 1994, in part at least because few apparently had been convinced by *Inter Insigniores,* Pope John Paul II felt obliged to issue yet another clarification of the Church's constant teaching. This time it was a *motu proprio* of the pope's entitled *Ordinatio*

Sacerdotalis, in which John Paul II solemnly judged that "the Church has no authority whatever to confer priestly ordination on women." Speaking authoritatively as the supreme teacher in the Church of Christ, the pope added that this judgment of his barring female ordination to the sacred priesthood was "to be definitively held by all the faithful."

Even this strong – and one would have thought indeed definitive – intervention on the part of John Paul II, however, failed to close down the on-going debate on the matter. Regardless of the contrary judgment of Church authority, many Catholics went right on believing anyway that female ordination was not only possible and desirable, but indeed was inevitable. So much had the old saying, *Roma locuta, causa finita* ("Rome has spoken, the case is decided") become eroded in the minds of many contemporary Catholics, that the issuance of such a "definitive" judgment by the supreme teaching authority in the Church not only failed to settle the question but inspired renewed opposition to Church authority in the matter. In the minds of the unconvinced, it was simply taken for granted that a subsequent pope would have to reverse the supposed erroneous decisions of Pope Paul VI and Pope John Paul II (as if a later pope *could* reverse the "definitive" decision of an earlier pope!).

Thus, in spite of a seemingly definitive contrary judgment of Church authority, sentiment in favor of female ordination has persisted very strongly in the Church up to the present day. And one of the ways in which the feminists and their sympathizers and fellow travelers in the Church have tried to continue to promote the idea of female ordination has been through encouraging *service at the altar* by women. This kind of encouragement, in particular, has included promoting young girls as altar servers. Girls have been told that they must come forward and demand their equal "rights" to serve the priests at the altar, just as boys traditionally have done. Proponents have strongly promoted altar girls as at least a step in the right direction towards eventual female ordination, while in some cases drawing back from direct agitation for female ordination on the theory that direct promotion of the latter might be counterproductive, at least for the moment, in view of the fact that the popes have so strongly pronounced against it.

This actually seemed to be the position of the American bishops at the 1987 Synod of Bishops in Rome. Led by Archbishop Rembert Weakland of Milwaukee – whose resignation, some fifteen years later, had to be accepted after it was revealed in the course of the clerical sex abuse scandals of 2002 that as a bishop he had "paid off" a huge, nearly half-million-dollar sum in what amounted to blackmail to a former homosexual lover – the American bishops' delegation in 1987 Synod knew that they could not openly and directly advocate female ordination (which some of them quite evidently wanted). The next best thing, as they saw it, was to promote female altar service as a stage on the road towards eventual female ordination. This effort failed at that time, however, owing especially to the opposition of the African bishops at the Synod of Bishops, who had been alerted to the plan. This did not mean, however, that efforts to secure approval of female altar service would not re-surface in other ways, however, as we shall presently see.

Of course, like ordination itself, until very recently, female altar service too was forbidden, both by tradition and by positive Church regulations. The tradition of male only altar service was related to and had paralleled that of male only ordination. In the eighteenth century, in re-iterating the Church's traditional prohibition of female altar servers, Pope Benedict XIV, in an encyclical entitled *Allatae Sunt*, dated July 26, 1755, had summed up the Church's long tradition in the matter, citing precedents as far back as Pope Gelasius I (492–496), who condemned the practice of female altar service when it occurred in his day in Lucania in Southern Italy. Benedict XIV, however, an eighteenth-century pope in the age of the Enlightenment, had also quoted a medieval pope, Innocent IV (1243–1254), who wrote that "women should not dare to serve at the altar; they should altogether be refused this ministry." Such was the traditional practice, however well or badly it had ever been articulated or perhaps even understood.

In the post-conciliar years, the Sacred Congregation for Divine Worship's Third Instruction on the Correct Implementation of the Constitution on the Sacred Liturgy, *Liturgiae Instaurationes,* dated September 5, 1970, accurately stated what the Church's tradition concerning female altar service had been. It affirmed this tradition and laid down the rule that "the traditional liturgical norms of the Church *prohibit* women (young girls, married women, religious) from serving the priest at the altar, even in women's chapels, houses, convents, schools, and institutes" (emphasis added).

Liturgiae Instaurationes did, however, specifically allow women at Mass to serve as lectors, to lead the prayers of the faithful, to lead congregational singing, and to provide explanatory comments concerning a given service. None of these things was traditional for women up to that point, however, and the fact that they were now specifically permitted by the

Third Instruction to carry out these functions indicated a significant degree of official liberalization of the Church's practices in favor of women, even though altar service as such, at that point, still remained expressly prohibited for women.

The new, somewhat liberalized positions now accepted for women had been foreshadowed, however, although only tentatively, in the original post-Vatican-II *General Instruction on the Roman Missal.* This GIRM had been issued just a few months before the Third Instruction, on March 26, 1970. This original GIRM specified that "the bishops' conference may *permit* a woman to read those Scripture passages which precede the Gospel"; and it also allowed that "those ministries which are performed *outside the sanctuary* may be entrusted to women if this be judged prudent by the priest in charge..." (GIRM 66 & 70; emphasis added).

The idea that women should not even be permitted in the sanctuary at all, in fact, was quite traditional in the Church before Vatican II, as this writer learned in Italy in the late 1950s. A little later on, while helping to organize a memorial Mass for the assassinated President John F. Kennedy in 1963 in Libya, where I was then stationed at the American Embassy, I ran into adamant opposition from the local Italian clergy to the idea that the lady organist for our American Catholic community could ever be allowed inside the sanctuary (where the organ happened to be located in the Tripoli cathedral). That this "tradition" was soon destined to go by the board, though, became quite evident once women were able to lead the prayers of the faithful, to be cantors or song leaders, and to be lectors or extraordinary ministers. In performing these functions – now called "ministries" – they often, and necessarily, had to be allowed into the sanctuary.

Nevertheless, the Church was still attempting to draw the line by continuing to prohibit actual female service assisting the priest at the altar itself. This position made sense if it was true that the priestly sacrificial celebration at the altar itself was different in kind from the other ministries related to the prayers, the readings, and the distribution of Holy Communion.

And however that may be, the Church did continue to try to hold this line. This was indicated in the Sacred Congregation for the Sacraments and Divine Worship's Instruction on Certain Norms concerning the Worship of the Eucharistic Mystery, *Inaestimabile Donum*, dated April 3, 1980 – nearly a full decade after the Third Instruction. On the subject of women in the liturgy, *Inaestimabile Donum* stated that "there are, of course, various roles that women can perform in the liturgical assembly: these include reading the word of God and proclaiming the intentions of the prayer of the faithful. Women are not, however, permitted to act as altar servers" (ID 20). Thus was this traditional prohibition authoritatively decreed – again! As we have seen, though, this represented no real change in the rule, but was merely a brief re-iteration of, what women were already permitted to do by the Third Instruction.

How, then, in spite of both the Church's strong tradition against, and her actual repeated positive regulations prohibiting, female service at the altar, did those with their own pro-feminist agendas for the Church nevertheless succeed in getting female altar service approved? For, getting a bit ahead of ourselves for a moment, female altar service *did* ultimately get approved in spite of these regulations prohibiting it which we have just been citing. How did this come about? This is a very interesting question which we shall take up in the next chapter.

Chapter Eighteen
How "Altar Girls" Got Approved

We have seen that the traditional Catholic practice – one dating back many centuries, indeed, back to the beginnings of Christianity – was to exclude women from direct service to the priests celebrating at the altar. This practice was not based on any idea that women were somehow "inferior" to men – a typical contemporary notion – but rather it stemmed from the Church's belief that women lacked a natural resemblance to Christ the priest, a belief that Christ himself had fostered when selecting only men to be his apostles, even as he honored and respected women in other ways.

It is true that some of the Fathers of the Church, reflecting the ideas of the ancient societies and cultures in which they lived, sometimes wrote in a way which suggested that *they* considered women to be an inferior sex. This was not, however, a teaching of the Church. Indeed, it must be stated that Christianity in general, beginning with the attitudes and practices of Christ himself, consistently affirmed the equal human dignity of women with men, and this precisely because women were believed to be made in the image of God and to have immortal souls. Christianity in history was in point of fact a major factor in enhancing the status of women in human society.

But this Christian belief in the equal human dignity of women did not entail either priestly ordination or service at the altar. The Church's ancient "deaconesses," for example, were never ordained; nor was it their function to serve at the altar. Their major function was to assist in such tasks as the baptism of adult female converts, a task which was thought to violate female modesty if performed by a priest alone. This was especially true of the Church in the East. So much was female non-ordination and non-service at the altar taken for granted in most places in the history of the Church that the question was scarcely ever even seriously raised until modern times.

This exclusion of women from direct altar service continued to be embodied in official Church regulations, even after such ministries as lectoring, leading the singing, giving out Holy Communion, and the like were opened up to women. Thus, it was thought by many that, since women were barred from ordination by a "definitive" decision of the supreme pontiff – solemnly reiterated, as we have noted, as recently as 1994 – women would also continue to be excluded from direct service at the altar, since that service was so closely related to the action of the priest acting *in persona Christi capitis*, "in the person of Christ the head."

However, this turned out not to be the case. Female service at the altar got approved after all. And the answer to the question of *how* female altar service came to be approved provides an almost classic example of how traditional and legitimate Church principles and procedures sometimes got successfully manipulated by those promoting their own agendas in the Church, in this case, the feminists and their sympathizers.

The route that was followed to secure pontifical approval for female service at the altar, in spite of the Church's long tradition prohibiting it, was to secure a favorable opinion – or, rather, an interpretation – from the Pontifical Council for the Interpretation of Legislative Texts (PCILT). This interpretation made by the PCILT was based upon its reading of a sub-canon in the 1983 Code of Canon Law concerned with "other functions" in the liturgy at which *lay people* are allowed to assist. The first and principal part of the canon in question (Canon 230.1) specifies that only lay *men (viri laici)* can be "installed" permanently in the Church ministries of lector and acolyte (altar server); but then the next sub-canon (Canon 230.2) says that lay *persons (laici)* – not just lay men – can fulfill these functions "by temporary deputation." Thus, it seems, females are not *explicitly excluded* from fulfilling these functions by the Code of Canon Law, even if they cannot be officially *installed* in them as such.

Once the question was framed in this way, even Pope John Paul II was apparently persuaded that canon law did not explicitly *exclude* women from performing "by deputation" those liturgical functions not requiring ordination. But if these liturgical functions were not excluded, then they must be permitted. This was the logic to which the pope, rather passively, it would seem, acceded. Nor was this the first time that Pope John Paul II showed himself to be a stickler for what canon law actually says. He himself had presided over the revision of the 1983 Code of Canon Law, after all; it was one of the great accomplishments of his pontificate.

The upshot of the new interpretation of canon law was that women are still not permitted to be permanently "installed" in the ministries of lector or acolyte; they may merely "temporarily" perform the functions of these ministries by deputation – contrary to the published regulations that had obtained up to then, which still did explicitly continue to deny them the ability to serve the priest at the altar itself. But the fact remained that, temporarily or not, women were now not understood to be *excluded* from direct service at the altar any longer by the Code of Canon Law.

What was clearly a new – indeed an entirely historically novel – policy of allowing female altar servers, then, even if under limited conditions, was announced to the bishops of the world in a Circular Letter dated March 15, 1994, which stated that the PCILT had made its decision two years earlier, on June 30, 1992. Why this decision was not immediately announced at the time it was made is not publicly known; it is another one of those famous Roman "mysteries." Perhaps some time may have been required to persuade Pope John Paul II to sign off on this new – and indeed novel – interpretation of canon law.

Although women may still not be appointed to or installed as acolytes, or servers at the altar, then, they now are permitted to fulfill the "functions" of acolytes – just as, earlier, they were allowed to fulfill the functions of lectors, leaders of the prayers, and extraordinary ministers. All this may still not have pleased the feminists very much, since women as such are still not permitted to enter upon these *ministries* in the full sense of the word. Women still remain, in the radical feminist perspective, "second-class citizens" in the Church, allowed only to perform the "functions" of the ministries in question, not to be installed in those ministries themselves.

However, even the feminists and feminist-sympathizers in the Church were apparently willing to accept this half loaf as better than nothing, at least for the moment. There were no protests from feminist supporters concerning the new interpretation of canon law. Nevertheless, it is not likely women will be permanently appeased by the PCILT's "compromise" solution. They are surely going to continue pressing for full feminine "equality," including ordination itself – for in their view if men can be ordained, how in justice can women be excluded?

What Rome did grant in this case, though, was apparently enough for the American bishops. They rushed with unseemly haste to allow "altar girls" in nearly every diocese of the United States, with the exceptions only of Lincoln, Nebraska, and Arlington, Virginia, and, subsequently, even Arlington now allows them at the discretion of the pastor at the time of this writing.

This, however, was surely a serious mistake by the American bishops, although it is hard to imagine how they could have acted otherwise in the present climate. Pope John Paul II too, it must be said, also made a serious mistake in permitting this new interpretation of canon law to be applied. That he apparently approved it just two months before issuing his *Ordinatio Sacerdotalis* definitively excluding female ordination is so mystifying that it truly boggles the mind. While trying to close the door permanently to female ordination, in other words, he opened, in effect, another door to further agitation on the same subject by those who see direct female altar service as a stage on the road to eventual female ordination. Was the pope perhaps trying to give women some kind of a "consolation prize" *because* he intended to close off the priesthood to them definitively? Nobody knows. But it seems evident that the pontiff simply did not see or credit the connection between female altar service and continued agitation for female ordination.

Even while recognizing that canon law, as currently written, technically does not exclude this temporary female altar service, the pope could nevertheless have quite legally decided that, as supreme pontiff, *he* was going to continue to exclude it anyway, if for no other reason than to discourage continued feminist agitation for the ordination of women.

For the goal of the radical feminists remains female ordination. Even though the pope has now declared "definitively" that this is excluded, those who demand female ordination anyway are not deterred and are simply going to wait for the next pope, as they see it – or for the next pope after that. Allowing female altar service only encourages them in this. After all, *that* was once banned as completely as female ordination has regularly been banned throughout all of the Church's long history. And yet it has now been allowed.

Even so, complaints by the faithful have perhaps caused the Holy See to back off a bit from its blanket approval. In a letter dated July 7, 2001, the Congregation for Divine Worship, under Cardinal Jorge Arturo Medina Estevez, stated that only a diocesan bishop could decide whether to permit female altar servers in his diocese; that no priest is *obliged* to have female servers, even in dioceses that permit them; that no one has a "right" to serve at the altar; and that the use of altar boys should be encouraged in order to encourage priestly vocations.

Still, in the present confused and ambiguous climate, who is going to dare to say that female ordination too will *not* come about in its own due time? Thus do the radical feminists and their fellow travelers continue to reason and claim. After all, so much that was formerly prohibited for women has now been granted – why not the priesthood too? Only those who are well versed in the history of doctrine understand that female ordination has already been *permanently excluded* by the supreme authority in the Church. It has been excluded in such a way and at such a magisterial level that it is exceedingly difficult, if not impossible, to see how it could ever be altered.

In point of fact, though, now that female altar service is allowed, agitation for the ordination of women, at least as deacons, continues to go on as yet another wedge issue, and this is fairly widely credited in more than a few quarters. So active has the drive for female ordination to the diaconate become, in fact, that on September 17, 2001, three Roman congregations – the Congregations for the Doctrine of the Faith, for the Clergy, and for Divine Worship and the Discipline of the Sacraments – felt obliged to issue a joint statement declaring that "it is not licit to undertake initiatives which in some way aim at preparing female candidates for diaconal ordination...The authentic promotion of women in the Church," the statement said, "opens other ample prospects for service and collaboration"; but to create possible expectations that women somehow *might* be able to be ordained deaconesses lacked what the joint statement called "solid doctrinal soundness" and could lead to "pastoral disorientation."

Ordination of women to the diaconate is not going to happen, in other words. It is not going to happen any more than ordination of women to the priesthood is going to happen. Both prospects have clearly and definitively been excluded by the Church's magisterium. To understand some of the reasons why they have been excluded, readers may be referred to the definitive study contained in the book *Deaconesses* by Aimé-Georges Martimort, translated by the present writer, and published by Ignatius Press in San Francisco, in 1986. There is no real chance at all that women might somehow be ordained to Holy Orders some day at any level. In the words of Vatican II, "the Lord...appointed certain *men* as ministers in order that they might be united in one body in which 'all members have not the same function'" (Rom 12:4) (Decree on the Ministry and Life of Priests, *Presbyterorum Ordinis*, 2; emphasis added).

Nevertheless, as long as female altar service continues to be allowed, many people are nevertheless going to go on believing that ordination, perhaps to the diaconate first, and then only later to the priesthood, remains a possible and for them the only fair and just outcome.

Experience since female altar service was first allowed in 1994 suggests, however, that because women are neither eligible for ordination *nor* for anything but temporary, "deputed" or "delegated" service at the altar, it is actually a *disservice* to them to allow them to go on serving at the altar in this fashion. Certainly it is a disservice to young girls, who are thereby allowed to think that they just might possibly be ordained to the priesthood some day. Just as service at the altar encourages priestly vocations in boys, so it can encourage the (false) hope of possible ordination in the minds of some girls. Anyone who has talked to some of these altar girls (or, especially, to their parents!) knows that many of them do think precisely this, that they might be able to be priests some day.

For those who understand the level of magisterial authority at which the pope excluded the possibility of female ordination with his *motu proprio* in 1994, however, it is clear that this is something the Church *cannot* go back on as long as she remains the Church. The teaching is irrevocable. This should be evident not only to someone who in faith accepts the Church's definitive judgments as coming from Christ; it should be evident also to anyone who has studied the actual history of the Church's magisterial pronouncements and knows that the Church *never* goes back on teachings issued in such a way as firm magisterial decisions. Popes do not go back on what previous popes have "definitively" decided with regard to doctrine. Those who continue to imagine that Pope John Paul II's judgment definitively excluding female ordination might still somehow be altered or revoked by a successor pope know little or nothing at all about how the Church's magisterial teachings have been consistently maintained by the Church's hierarchy down through history. This record constitutes one of the major convincing proofs that the Catholic Church is what she says she is.

Meanwhile, we already have an entire generation and more of feminist-influenced women, many of whom are currently disillusioned with the Church on more than one count. Too many of the women who work for the Church in various capacities, including in bishops' chanceries, for example, continue to reflect this state of mind; the same thing is true of some of the religious sisters in some of the older and now dying female religious orders; they are disaffected Catholics who harbor typical feminist-type grievances against the Church. Why would anyone want to perpetuate such an unhappy situation by continuing to allow girls and women to believe that they just might, some day, after all, be declared eligible to be ordained?

Much better and healthier for girls would be to learn at an early age that their role in the Church – as in life! – is complementary to, but *different* from, that of boys and men, though no less equal in dignity. Just as a man who is ordained to the priesthood bears a natural resemblance to Christ the priest, so all girls and women bear a natural resemblance to the one whom the poet William Wordsworth, rightly and aptly, declared to be "our tainted nature's solitary boast," namely, the Blessed Virgin Mary. Jesus Christ was born of that same woman. By a special dispensation, she was free from all sin and has now been assumed, body and soul, into heaven, where she makes intercession for us "now and at the hour of our deaths." As the Responsorial Psalm for the Feast of Our Lady of Guadalupe expresses it, she is "the greatest honor of our race."

This has always been the belief of the Catholic Church. At least in part because of it, women are more appreciated and honored in the Catholic Church than in any other world religion. And practically alone among all our institutions today, the Catholic Church retains an accurate and sane view of the difference between men and women as created by God. And the Church also dares to say *vive la différence*! Women do not *need* ordination, nor do they need to serve at the altar, in order to be Christians in the full sense of the word; or in order to be redeemed by Christ, the son of Mary, or to be graced by the Holy Spirit in order to know, love, and serve God in this world, and to be happy with him forever in the next. This, necessarily, should be the goal of us all. The overwhelming majority of men, after all, are not ordained either. Continued agitation for a full, imagined "equality" in this matter within the Church has only distracted some from working towards what should be the true goals of the faith.

Chapter Nineteen
The Vernacular Liturgy

No aspect of the post-Vatican-II liturgical reforms has been of greater moment in the Roman rite than the change from a Latin to a vernacular liturgy. We have already noted how Vatican Council II's Constitution on the Sacred Liturgy, *Sacrosanctum Concilium,* very plainly, it would seem, decreed that Latin was to be retained: "The use of the Latin language, with due respect to particular law, is to be preserved in the Latin rites" (SC 36 §1).

The Constitution further decreed that "care must be taken to ensure that the faithful may also be able to say or sing together in Latin the parts of the Ordinary of the Mass which pertain to them" (SC 54). With regard to the Liturgy of the Hours, or Divine Office, prayed in particular by religious in community, or by the priest with what used to be called his Breviary – but today prayed by many of the laity as well – it was specified that "in accordance with the age-old tradition of the Latin rite, the Latin language is to be retained in the divine office"(SC 101 §1).

All this seems to be quite clear and straightforward, yet these bare statements in the Constitution, as it was finally approved by the Council Fathers, give no hint that, from the opening days of the Council, as reported by all the historians of the Council, there were intense debates and discussions concerning the place of Latin in the Church. Nobody seems to have doubted that Latin provided an exact medium with a fully developed and finely nuanced theological vocabulary for the official documents of the Church; but many of the Council Fathers had come to doubt both the continued suitability of Latin as a liturgical language, as well as its practicality as a working language, especially in view of the fact that the study and use of Latin had fallen off so drastically in education in modern times. Latin was no longer the common language of educated people, as it had once been in centuries past and up until fairly recent times in both Europe and America.

During the time of the Council, many of the Council Fathers even objected to the fact that the proceedings of the Council itself were conducted in Latin. Experience soon proved that many of the bishops were less than adept in the language, were often not able to follow the conciliar interventions with true understanding, and were especially hampered when it came to the give-and-take of conciliar debates.

According to the pseudonymous author, "Xavier Rynne," in his book *Vatican Council II* – the collection of the "Letters from Vatican City" which he periodically published in the *New Yorker* magazine throughout all the four sessions of the Council – Cardinal Richard J. Cushing of Boston candidly shared with Pope John XXIII his unhappiness with the Council's efforts to function efficiently using Latin. The Boston cardinal offered to pay for installing a complete simultaneous translation system for the entire Council. However, this offer was not taken up by Blessed John XXIII (although informal translation services in the various language groups quickly grew up and were eagerly made use of by the bishops; then, in due course, according to Peter Hebblethwaite, in his biography of Pope Paul VI, the Dutch Phillips company finally did install simultaneous translation equipment in October, 1964, towards the end of the Council).

The Melchite Catholic Patriarch of Antioch, Maximos IV Saigh, a venerable, bearded Eastern-rite prelate already in his eighties when the Council began, deliberately defied and violated the Council's rules by insisting upon speaking in French, although he too had been trained in Latin and was probably as competent in it as almost anybody in those days. But he declined on principle to use Latin. It was an indication of where things were going.

This Eastern-rite prelate, who would prove to be one of the more forceful and colorful Vatican II figures, intervened often on a variety of subjects, mostly in a liberalizing vein. In his first address to the Council, he strongly advocated a vernacular liturgy, pointing out that Christ himself had spoken the language of his contemporaries – and Christ, according to him, "offered the first Eucharistic Sacrifice in a language which could be understood by all who heard him, namely, in Aramaic."

This Melchite patriarch then employed a number of the arguments for a vernacular liturgy that would continue to be used by others, during and after the Council. "We Orientals cannot understand," he said, "how the faithful can be gathered together and made to pray in a language which they do not understand. The Latin language is dead, but the Church is alive...The language used must be a living language, since it is meant for men and not for angels."

In response to this kind of initiative, it turned out that there was considerable sentiment in favor of a vernacular liturgy, particularly among missionary bishops; and there were more than 800 such missionary bishops at the Council, most of them still of Western origin. The practice of ordaining "native" bishops was still in its infancy in those days; and the missionary bishops in place largely believed that a vernacular liturgy was called for, especially in their mission fields. This sentiment proved to be enormously influential at the Council.

There was also a fairly wide recognition that the typical products of modern educational systems were untrained in Latin to a degree that the Church in her own educational and training programs – in seminaries, for example – could only with great difficulty compensate for, if at all. Latin was simply not being seriously taught any longer in many places.

What after the Council convened proved to be a very strong groundswell among the bishops in favor of a vernacular liturgy, at first encountered an equally strong determination on the part of the Roman Curia, shared by no small number of the Council Fathers as well, to maintain Latin as the official language of the Church, regardless. There was a real conflict here, in other words, and, as we shall see, the decisions the Council ultimately made about Latin and enshrined in *Sacrosanctum Concilium* were not as strongly in favor of the retention of Latin as appeared at first sight from a simple reading of the text; they were actually rather uneasy "compromise" decisions, which were not destined to endure in the post-conciliar period.

Nearly eight months before the opening of the Council, on February 22, 1962, Pope John XXIII had issued an apostolic constitution on the Promotion of the Study of Latin, *Veterum Sapientia*, in which the pontiff strongly justified the Church's continued use of the ancient language. While recognizing the cultural importance of Latin, the pope also quoted the words of his predecessor, Pope Pius XI, to the effect that the primary reason for the Church's reliance upon the language was not cultural at all but *religious:* "For the Church," Pius XI had written in 1922, "precisely because it embraces all nations and is destined to endure to the end of time...of its very nature requires a language which is universal, immutable, and non-vernacular."

John XXIII made these words his own, and stated that he had decided to issue his own directives following up on it "so as to insure that the ancient and uninterrupted use of Latin be maintained and, where necessary, restored." The pope's "directives" as set forth in *Veterum Sapientia* were quite strict: they forbade churchmen from even writing or speaking against Latin, and they included requirements that seminarians be given "a sufficiently lengthy course in Latin" before beginning their study of philosophy and theology; they stipulated that Latin should be restored to the curriculum in Catholic institutions, and that the major sacred sciences should be taught in Latin using Latin textbooks. More than that, they required that a syllabus for the teaching of Latin be prepared for use throughout the Church, and that a Latin Academy be established in Rome to carry out and promote all these requirements.

This 1962 apostolic constitution of John XXIII represented the firm majority viewpoint in Rome regarding Latin on the eve of the Council. If anything could have preserved Latin in the Roman rite, *Veterum Sapientia*, coming from the pope himself, should have been able to preserve it. Pope John XXIII personally loved Latin, and was well versed in it, like so many of his generation. Any reader of his letters or other writings will find that he was constantly quoting Latin phrases; as was true of so many prelates of his generation. He had been formed in a solid Latinity, and he very much wanted to perpetuate it. But the times had changed, and *Veterum Sapientia* was very soon destined to fall by the wayside. It represented a valiant stand by the pope that was not, however, able to succeed in the end. Nobody overtly "dissented" from it or spoke out against it; it just very soon ceased to apply to what was happening in the world.

Even after the Council convened, and the initial debates and discussions revealed the widespread sentiment among the bishops for a vernacular liturgy, Roman Curia cardinals, among others, were not slow to rush to the defense of Latin, affirming the importance of its use both in the liturgy and generally. The Roman Curia cardinals were not alone in this. Two of the American cardinals of the day, for example, Archbishops Francis J. Spellman of New York and Archbishop James Francis McIntyre of Los Angeles, were among those who strongly favored retaining Latin, as did many of the other prelates – soon to be labeled, for this among other reasons, as diehard "conservatives" by journalists such as Xavier Rynne, breathlessly reporting on the Council in the secular media from a liberal perspective assumed to represent the simple truth at the time.

Prominent among the "conservatives" was the 72-year-old Italian Cardinal Alfredo Ottaviani, prefect of the Sacred Congregation of the Holy Office (later the Congregation for the Doctrine of the Faith). In what was destined to become one of the most famous and emblematic incidents of the whole First Session of the Council, Cardinal Ottaviani rose to protest against the drastic changes that were being proposed for the Latin Mass. "Are we seeking to stir up wonder, or perhaps scandal, among the Christian people, by introducing changes in so venerable a rite, that has been approved for so many centuries and is now so familiar?" Cardinal Ottaviani wondered. "The rite of Holy Mass should not be treated as if it were a piece of cloth to be refashioned according to the whim of each generation."

This was a powerful argument, and one that would continue to echo both inside and outside the *aula* of St. Peter's and down through the postconciliar years, including in the writings on the liturgy of the future Pope Benedict XVI. Cardinal Ottaviani was one of the most influential of the Curia cardinals of his day, then and later. However, he was regularly characterized by reporters as attempting to impede, as the story usually went, good Pope John's desired reforms. In point of fact, he was an able, knowledgeable, and sophisticated theologian, who as often as not presciently saw where at least some of the changes being proposed would be taking the Church.

In an intervention delivered to all the Council fathers protesting against what he saw as undue changes being proposed in the liturgy, Cardinal Ottaviani spoke in fluent Latin without any written text or notes, since he was partially blind. Wholly caught up with his topic and arguments, he exceeded the ten-minute time limit for spoken interventions, which was the Council's rule. When he reached the fifteen-minute point, the prelate presiding over the Council that day, Cardinal Bernard Alfrink of the Netherlands, first rang the warning bell; and then, when Cardinal Ottaviani went on speaking anyway, either oblivious to the warning bell or deliberately ignoring it, Cardinal Alfrink ordered a technician to switch off the Curia cardinal's microphone.

Verifying the loss of sound by tapping his microphone, Cardinal Ottaviani was then obliged, ignominiously, to return back to his seat, amid actual applause from the floor in apparent approval of witnessing this influential Curia cardinal being thus brutally cut off short in his intervention. This was one of the incidents that signaled the definite "liberal" tendency that the Council in many respects was going to pursue.

Moreover, this incident was seen at the time, and has been recounted since, as a just and necessary come-uppance administered to a powerful Curia prefect, too long accustomed to having things his own way, as so many then thought. The whole affair helped form the mythology which would quickly grow up around the Council, and which began to be apparent virtually as soon as the Council began: namely, that the bishops of the world, "democratically," had to rise up and rein in the members of the Roman Curia and blunt their "power," if the Council was ever to realize the dream of Blessed John XXIII. Although it is true, of course, that the bishops of the world meeting together at the Council did see many things in a significantly different light than the bishops working in the Roman Curia, and did succeed in some cases in setting the Church on a new course that they, rather than the Curia, effectively charted, the idea that the "conservatives" in the Roman Curia always had to be check-mated by the "liberals" among the Fathers of the Council coming from dioceses around the world is a thesis that has been grossly exaggerated and has distorted the real truth about the Council down to the present day.

Following the initial rather intense debates on the liturgy during the conciliar First Session, in 1962, the Council fathers representing various points of view agreed that the schema on the liturgy needed to be returned to the Council's Liturgical Commission for extensive reworking along the lines of the many comments and suggestions made in the course of the debates. This was done; and the Constitution on the Sacred Liturgy, *Sacrosanctum Concilium*, as we now know it, was not brought back and approved until near the very end of the Second Session of the Council the following year, 1963. By then, many other topics had been introduced and debated, and, meanwhile, opinions concerning the reform of the liturgy had pretty much been talked through; and, as we have seen, the completed text of *Sacrosanctum Concilium* was finally approved by a huge majority of the Council Fathers with almost no opposition.

When considering post-conciliar liturgical developments, especially negative ones, we need to remind ourselves that the liturgy Constitution itself was, in fact, approved by an overwhelming majority of the Council Fathers, that is, the Catholic bishops of the world. There was *no* significant opposition to it at the time; the troubles that arose later were not generally either foreseen or even imagined; nor, appearances to the contrary, were foreseen or imagined the subsequent conflicts and even the eventual schism that came about at least in part as the result of the enactment of the Constitution on the Sacred Liturgy. Archbishop Marcel Lefebvre himself approved and signed this particular document, and only later objected to the changes that it brought about.

Almost immediately after the approval of *Sacrosanctum Concilium*, in January, 1964, Pope Paul VI established the "Consilium" for the Implementation of the Constitution on the Sacred Liturgy, and, at the same time, the pope ordered the establishment of liturgical commissions in every diocese for the same purpose. The reform of the liturgy thus got underway in earnest, and well before the end of the Council. It would be almost two more years before the Council itself ended in December, 1965.

With regard to the question of Latin versus the vernacular, *Sacrosanctum Concilium* retained, as we have seen, the requirement favored by the Roman Curia and many of the other Council Fathers to the effect that Latin would continue to be the official language of the Western Church. However, immediately following this seemingly very clear provision, the document itself significantly qualified this requirement by stating that "since the use of the vernacular whether in the Mass, the administration of the sacraments, or in other parts of the liturgy, may frequently be of great advantage to the people, wider use may be made of it [the vernacular], especially in readings, directives, and in some prayers and chants" (SC 36 §2). The decision as to "whether and to what extent the vernacular is to be used" was given to "the competent territorial ecclesiastical authority," that is, to the bishops, subject to confirmation by the Apostolic See (SC 36 §3).

These concessions may have seemed neutral and balanced at the time, but they served to open a door which, in the end, could no longer be kept closed; for they actually represented enormous, indeed, unprecedented, concessions to the territorial bishops who had come out so strongly for the vernacular in the conciliar discussions and debates. In fact, these concessions practically constitute "Exhibit A" in the case argued by some about how the bishops of the world came together at the Council and successfully challenged the predominance of Roman Curia in not a few areas. And, in the event, the conferences of bishops virtually everywhere elected to go with the vernacular liturgy.

The decisions of the various bishops' conferences still had to be "approved, that is, confirmed by the apostolic See," according to *Sacrosanctum Concilium*; but the provision that the liturgy *could* be celebrated in the vernacular, in effect, constituted the handwriting on the wall for the Latin liturgy. It would just be a matter of time before Latin would be replaced by the vernacular nearly everywhere, in accordance with what turned out to be the almost universal wishes of the various bishops' conferences. It should be remembered, though, that there was always a legitimate "chain of authority" in the transition from Latin to the vernacular: the various bishops' conferences petitioned the Holy See, and the Holy See in due course responded approving the petition. The change from Latin to the vernacular was thus at no point "illegal," or "illicit," as some traditionalists have charged. The change was made in accordance with existing Church rules which, then as now, accorded ultimate authority in the matter to the Holy See.

It is significant, in fact, that *each* of the paragraphs of *Sacrosanctum Concilium* providing for the retention of Latin was immediately followed by a qualifier providing that the bishops' conferences could, in effect, decide differently. Thus, the provision that the faithful should be able to say or sing together in Latin those parts of the Mass pertaining to them, went on immediately to specify that adaptations could nevertheless be made by the bishops' conferences "whenever a more extended use of the vernacular in the Mass seems desirable" (SC 54). This, again, was pretty much to give *carte blanche* to the bishops' conferences, practically speaking.

Similarly, the requirement in *Sacrosanctum Concilium* that Latin was to be retained in the Divine Office was immediately qualified by the statement that "in individual cases the ordinary [bishop] has the power to grant the use of a vernacular translation in those clerics for whom the use of Latin constitutes a grave obstacle to their praying the office properly" (SC 101 §1). In all of these instances, the final, apparently "compromise" language concerning Latin contained in the Constitution as voted by the Council both affirmed the continued use of Latin *and* allowed for the vernacular under certain circumstances if the bishops so desired.

Thus, although Vatican II seems on the face of it to have stated unequivocally that Latin was to remain the liturgical language of the Church, the fact is that the Council itself allowed and provided for from the outset exceptions which in the end were almost bound to result in the vernacular liturgy that we in fact have today, given the strong sentiment for the latter among the territorial bishops of the world.

Rome, however, seems to have genuinely wished to retain the Latin. The First Instruction on the Proper Implementation of the Constitution on the Sacred Liturgy, *Inter Oecumenici*, dated September 26, 1964, still required publishers to print the Latin text even when publishing translations of the altar Missal or the Breviary (cf. IO 57 & 89); but the fact remains that the pope also appointed known advocates of the vernacular to the Consilium he established to implement the liturgical reforms, including the president of the Consilium, Cardinal Giacomo Lercaro of Bologna, one of the more "liberal" members of the European Alliance of bishops which dominated the Council. According to Father Ralph M. Wiltgen's excellent history of Vatican II, *The Rhine Flows into the Tiber*, some national hierarchies, including those of France and Germany, were determinedly moving to institute a vernacular liturgy from the moment *Sacrosanctum Concilium* was approved, and quite apart, it seems, from any specific approval of this by the Holy See.

In the end, it appears that pressures from the bishops around the world proved to be too great to allow the Latin Mass to survive. Most of the bishops wanted the vernacular liturgy, as the debates during the Council had indicated; and thus, in response to the petitions and requests of the national hierarchies the world over, restrictions on the use of the vernacular were progressively lifted by the Holy See. By 1971, as Austin Flannery, O.P., has stated in his brief summary of the question in his *Vatican Council II: The Conciliar and Post-conciliar Documents*: "The use of the vernacular in public Masses was left entirely to the judgment of episcopal conferences, to the judgment of individual priests for private Masses, and of the ordinary for the divine office, in private, in common, or in choir."

The changeover from Latin to the vernacular, however inevitable it may seem in retrospect to have been, was a prime example of an obviously drastic liturgical change that proved to be way too abrupt and precipitous in the way that it was decided upon and implemented. It represented yet another one of the many liturgical changes for which the laity were ill prepared, and for which no basic explanation or rationale was ever generally provided to them. It was just carried out, and pretty much from one day to the next. To this day, many of the faithful – especially those who have actually read the provisions in *Sacrosanctum Concilium* to the effect that Latin was supposed to be "preserved" – regard this changeover as a mistake, if not as a betrayal. Some have even questioned its legality.

Although the changeover was, in fact, legal, and although permission to adopt the vernacular was properly requested by the various bishops' conferences, and was duly and legally granted by the Holy See, little or none of this, again, has ever been properly *explained* to the faithful at large. Yet this changeover to a vernacular liturgy was unprecedented; it was an epochal change, and one which by its very nature could not but affect the faithful both deeply and broadly. Much more attention should have been given to *how* the changeover was to be effected, once it was decided that there was going to be such a changeover. The seemingly abrupt abandonment by the Church of a Latin liturgy that had been in place for many centuries could not but be experienced as anything but a great and traumatic shock and loss – whatever the expected benefits of the vernacular liturgy that was to replace it.

In recounting, however briefly here, how the changeover from the Latin to the vernacular liturgy occurred, the present writer has tried hard, not without difficulty, to be as neutral and objective about the whole thing as possible. Generally speaking, however, emotions have run very high on this issue, and there has rarely been much neutrality or objectivity in any quarter on the subject of the Latin, and, especially, on the subject of the "Tridentine" Mass, as we have already seen.

What I may appropriately say here, perhaps, is that while I personally loved (and love) the Latin, and in the course of my own life have joyfully participated singing bass in a couple of fine Latin Gregorian choirs, my mind and judgment nevertheless tell me that the changeover to the vernacular liturgy was almost inevitable. If it had not come following Vatican II, it would almost certainly have come not long after, given the state of mind in so many places that was revealed at the Council. Vatican II was merely the crucible in which it became evident that Latin no longer "worked" very well for the Church, broadly and practically speaking. Nor, barring a return to Latin as the basis of liberal education in the West (which seems unlikely), do I see much of a chance for any significant broad revival of the Latin liturgy – although Benedict XVI's *Summorum Pontificum* obviously signals a continuing interest in the Latin liturgy that exists in certain quarters within the Church. But it also remains to be seen how broad this current partial revival of Latin will prove to be. For myself, of course, I greatly regret the general passing of the Latin liturgy, but I fear it is a "done" thing.

It also seems clear in the light of the experience of the post-conciliar years, however, that all along Latin should have been more prominently retained at least as an "option" – not only for its intrinsic value, but also to help preserve the immense treasure of the sacred music of Western Christendom, much of which is based on the use of Latin. Even now, Latin has not been formally "abolished" or "prohibited," as some have too often imagined (and, as some bishops have unfortunately allowed them to go on thinking that such was the case).

However, the use of Latin in regular Masses for the faithful is now rendered quite difficult for the people, if only by the fact that few suitable missals or missalettes exist in Latin for the New Order of the Mass (the Mass of Paul VI), the currently authorized "ordinary" liturgy for the Roman rite contained in the current Roman Missal. Then there is the further fact of how limited any knowledge of Latin is today even among Catholics.

Nevertheless, there remains a strong case for the retention of Latin in the liturgy as an *option*. This, among other things, is one of the things that Pope Benedict XVI finally and wisely allowed for by means of his 2007 *motu proprio* reviving the Tridentine Mass as an "extraordinary" form of the Roman rite.

However, the retention of Latin in the liturgy should not be confined only to the revived Tridentine Mass. The celebration of the New Order of the Mass in Latin should also be more easily available as another option. It is permitted – it has been permitted all along – and it should therefore be available on a more regular basis, if we wish to retain the rich tradition of the Latin liturgy in the Roman rite. Appropriate Missals and other necessary liturgical books should be published in order to allow the *Novus Ordo* to be more easily and widely celebrated in Latin.

Chapter Twenty
Liturgical Translation

Once the basic decision to go with the vernacular liturgy was confirmed by the Holy See's general approval of requests to this effect coming from the bishops' conferences around the world, a whole new set of questions then inevitably arose. These questions were principally concerned with the question of *liturgical translation*. The task of translating all of the Church's liturgical and sacramental books became strictly necessary once the vernacular liturgy was approved. This task would prove to be immense. It was not clear to anyone at the time how it was even going to be done.

In order to examine the problem of producing suitable English versions of the Roman liturgy, a meeting of bishops at the Council from a number of English-speaking countries had already been held as early as October 1963 – even before the final approval of *Sacrosanctum Concilium*. This meeting was called mostly at the initiative, it seems, of an American prelate, Archbishop Paul J. Hallinan of Atlanta, who figured prominently in liturgical circles at that time, and who also became an original member of Pope Paul VI's Consilium charged with implementing the sacred liturgy when the latter eventually got set up.

Meetings among bishops from English-speaking countries soon resulted in the formation of an International Commission on English in the Liturgy (ICEL). ICEL was organized as an independent corporation governed by an episcopal board consisting of a bishop-representative from eleven English-speaking countries. A number of other countries where English was spoken became associate members. ICEL was set up to be responsible for producing the texts of the Church's liturgy in English.

Because of the nature and quality of the translations it produced, however, ICEL itself soon became a rather controversial body. From the outset, many of the faithful found the new English liturgy to be less than inspired. The ICEL translators may have been aiming at the "noble simplicity" desired by *Sacrosanctum Concilium*, but the result they produced all too often turned out to be flat, pedestrian, and prosaic.

More than that, ICEL often seemed oddly given over to a certain kind of what can only be called *mistranslation*. Even Catholics with no claim to be Latinists had to wonder why an expression such as *et cum spiritu tuo* ("and with thy spirit") came to be rendered: "and also with you"); or why the *Credo* ("I believe") at the beginning of the Latin version of the Nicene Creed that we profess on Sundays and holy days was translated as "*we* believe"; or why the once very familiar *mea culpa, mea culpa, mea maxima culpa* ("through my fault, through my fault, through my most grievous fault") mostly got dropped from the new English version of what used to be known as the *Confiteor* ("I confess...").

As regards the "we believe," it certainly seemed to partake of the ubiquitous new theology that tended to see the gathering of the people together at Mass as somehow more important than the presence of Christ in the eucharistic sacrifice. It is true, however, that this particular translation can be justified. *The Catechism of the Catholic Church*, for example, states that the "'I believe' (*Apostles' Creed*) is the faith of the Church professed personally by each believer, principally during Baptism. 'We believe' (*Niceno-Constantinopolitan Creed*) is the faith of the Church confessed by the bishops in Council, or more generally by the liturgical assembly of believers" (CCC 167).

For some of the other mistranslations, however, there seemed to be no apparent explanation at the time; nor has anyone provided any very suitable explanations since. Why, for example, did the ICEL translators so carefully always seem to avoid using the word "soul"? Was this a consequence of the "new theology"? Did the translators no longer believe in the existence of the human soul as the "form" of the body, or as the immaterial principle animating it – or, as the *Catechism of the Catholic Church* puts it, "the innermost aspect of man...that by which he is most especially [made] in God's image"(CCC 363)?

However that may be, the same tendency was to be found among modern biblical translators as readily as among liturgical translators. For example, the old and familiar Douai-Confraternity Bible rendered the well-known passage of Matthew 16:26 as: "What does it profit a man, if he gain the whole world, but suffer the loss of his own soul?" Among the more recent translations, however, the New American Bible substitutes "self" for "soul" here, while the Jerusalem Bible gives "life" instead of "soul" (the Greek is *psyche,* the Latin *anima*). Even the generally excellent Revised Standard Version of the Bible prefers "life" here for some reason, even though it elsewhere retains "soul" in such passages as Matthew 10:28 and I

Peter 1:9. Whatever the explanation for these variations, it certainly seemed to be the case that some modern religious translators apparently did not see themselves as bound to produce translations that were entirely accurate.

As another example of a not untypical translation produced by the ICEL translators along the same lines, let us look at how ICEL handled the *Gloria* ("Glory to God") in the Mass:

LATIN TEXT

Gloria in excelsis Deo, et in terra pax hominibus bonae voluntatis.

Laudamus te, benedicimus te, adoramus te, glorificamus te, gratias agimus tibi propter magnam gloriam tuam, Domine Deus, Rex caelestis, Deus Pater omnipotens.

Domine Fili unigenite, Iesu Christe, Domine Deus, Agnus Dei, Filius Patris, qui tollis peccata mundi, miserere nobis; qui tollis peccata mundi, suscipe deprecationem nostram.

Qui sedes ad dexteram Patris, miserere nobis.

Quoniam tu solus Sanctus, tu solus Dominus, tu solus Altissimus, Iesu Christe, cum Sancto Spiritu: in Gloria Dei Patris.

Amen.

ICEL TRANSLATION

Glory to God in the highest, and peace to his people on earth.

Lord God, heavenly King, almighty God and Father, we worship you, we give you thanks, we praise you for your glory.

Lord Jesus Christ, only Son of the Father, Lord God, Lamb of God, you take away the sin of the world: have mercy on us; you are seated at the right hand of the Father: receive our prayer.

For you alone are the Holy One, you alone are the Lord, you alone are the most High, Jesus Christ, with the Holy Spirit, in the Glory of God the Father.

Amen.

This is surely an unusual translation, first of all, because the Latin version is longer than the English. Yet Latin is known to be the more terse, elliptical language. Normally Latin texts are *shorter* than their English equivalents. What has happened here? Actually, the English simply omits certain words, beginning with *hominibus bonae voluntatis* ("to men of good will"), which the English version leaves out entirely, translating it instead simply as "his people"; this omission is particularly surprising considering that the phrase is scriptural (cf. Lk 2:14).

Then there are the five verbs in the Latin meaning to praise, bless, adore, glorify, and thank. For no obvious reason, these are reduced to three in English: to worship, thank, and praise only. The adjective *magnam* ("great") referring to God's glory is similarly left out entirely. The phrase *Filius Patris* ("Son of the Father") is melded with *unigenitus* ("only begotten"), which is then translated simply as "only." Again, there is no obvious reason why this should have been done. The *sins* of the world (*peccata:* this is definitely a plural in the Latin) are reduced in the English to "sin of the world" (singular).

The phrase *qui tollis peccata mundi* ("who takes away the sins of the world"), repeated twice in the Latin, is given only once in the English. The same thing is true for *miserere nobis* ("have mercy on us"): the *suscipe deprecationem nostram* ("receive our prayer") which follows the second *qui tollis peccata mundi* in the Latin is transposed in the English to follow the *qui sedes ad dexteram Patris* ("who is seated at the right hand of the Father"), in place of the second *miserere nobis*.

Why these changes and omissions and transpositions? It is not at all clear from the text why the ICEL translators felt free to omit and change the plain and simple words in the Latin text in the way that they did here. What does seem clear is that they did feel free to do this. They did not, apparently, feel at all bound by the Latin text. Examples of the same kind could be multiplied many times over by comparing with the original Latin texts the now familiar liturgical texts that have constituted our liturgy in English over the past nearly forty years now.

When we begin to inquire more seriously into why this should be the case, and to delve more deeply into the matter, we discover that, virtually from the time the Roman liturgy first began to be translated into English, the ICEL translators were following a free translation method based upon a little-known document which Pope Paul VI's Consilium produced in 1969.

Known as *Comme le Prévoit* ("As Foreseen") from its French original, this document advocates what it calls a method of "dynamic equivalence" in translations. By definition this means that the translations do not need to be literal. Once it is established that the translations do not need to be literal, we are inevitably at once thrown back upon the subjective idea of the translator as to what the translation should be. According to this method, words and concepts in the original Latin can thus be replaced with terms deemed more relevant today. "Sacral language," for example, is no longer considered necessary or appropriate in the modern world;

adaptations suited to the spirit of the times can be freely adopted. In one place, the document asserts that:

> Many of the phrases of approach to the Almighty were originally adapted from forms of address to the sovereign in the courts of Byzantium and Rome. It is necessary to study how far an attempt should be made to offer equivalents in modern English for such words as *quaesumus* ["we beseech"], *dignare* ["to be considered worthy"], *clementissime* ["most merciful"], *maiestas* [majesty], and the like (13).

This kind of thinking can only remind us of the argument that kneeling is unsuitable today because it supposedly only arose when vassals were required to kneel before their feudal lords. In point of fact, these honorific words tend to be sedulously avoided in the ICEL English liturgy, although they remain very much part of the original Latin text of the revised Roman liturgy. Presumably such words do not accord with the modern democratic spirit (although why they are apparently no longer thought to apply to Almighty God is not at all clear!).

Nevertheless, much that seems odd or strange in the liturgy in English becomes explicable once we realize that ICEL has quite consistently followed a particular method of translation which *allows* for departures, even major departures, it seems, from the original Latin. Not a few of the odd and even strange things sometimes encountered in the English liturgy finally become at least intelligible, if still not always excusable. Once we know about *Comme le Prévoit* and its method of so-called dynamic equivalence in translation, we are able to view the vernacular liturgy in English in a new and different light.

All along, then, it turns out, the typical ICEL translations have been produced in accordance with a conscious theory that, quite apart from literal accuracy, was almost bound to rob them of some of the grandeur, mystery, and dignity that ought to be required in any genuine liturgical text directed towards "the worship of the divine majesty" (SC 33). This was certainly true of the ICEL translations for the Mass and the sacraments that were hurriedly done in the late 1960s and early 1970s and pressed into service on and around our altars throughout the English-speaking world. We had to learn to live with these translations, of course, but that did not mean they could not have been better.

Yet doing translations in accordance with *Comme le Prévoit's* theory of dynamic equivalence was not the only reason the typical ICEL translations turned out to be so unsatisfactory. Yet another defective theory was also being relied on by the ICEL translators, and we must now examine this other theory in the chapter which follows.

Chapter Twenty-One
"Inclusive Language"

It was bad enough that the "first generation" of liturgical translations into English done by ICEL were not only done hastily; they were done in accordance with a defective theory of translation. We might have thought that the Church would do better with a "second generation" of translations. When the time came for a new set of liturgical translations, or retranslations, however, instead of improving with experience, the liturgical translation situation actually began to *get worse*!

Yes. This occurred, at least in part, because the ICEL translators, influenced like practically everybody else in our society by the rise of the organized radical feminist movement, became convinced that liturgical translations henceforth had to be not only free and non-literal; they also had to employ feminist so-called *inclusive language*. Not only would liturgical texts henceforth be translated in accordance with the free method of so-called dynamic equivalence; they would also be translated in accordance with modern radical feminist ideas of acceptable language.

According to the radical feminists, "man" and related words, including the masculine gender pronouns, "he, him, his," refer primarily or exclusively to males only; women are held by them to be "excluded" when these words are used in the generic sense that has been standard in English for over a thousand years, that is, when "man" and the masculine pronouns are used to refer to human beings in general. Since women undeniably are human beings and do need to be included, it follows that specific language which does include them supposedly needed to be devised and used, according to the feminists. This can be accomplished, for example, by saying "person" instead of "man," or "humankind" instead of "mankind" – or, similarly, by saying, instead of "to each his own," "to each his *or her* own," or "to each *their* own"! And so on.

Or again: instead of the saying, "every man for himself," the accepted new locution would presumably have to be, "every man and woman for himself or herself." Or again, instead of saying "man does not live by bread alone," one should say, "people do not live by bread alone." And so on. This is "inclusive language."

We would have to live on another planet not to know how successful the feminists have been in trying to impose this kind of inclusive language on our whole society today. Although the results of trying to use inclusive language are frequently clumsy, unnatural, and sometimes even absurd, many people today still nevertheless go on – "manfully," we might say! – trying to use it. People are even prone to apologize when, as almost inevitably happens, they sometimes cannot help lapsing back into what was once standard English. Dictionaries now expressly sanction inclusive language; teachers teach it; style books for the press and media require it; schools and universities demand it of their students writing term papers.

Familiar religious hymns such as "O God, Our Help in Ages Past" now have to be changed so that the traditional lines that used to say – "Time like an ever rolling stream bears all its sons away" – now must read: "Time like an ever growing stream bears *us* all away"! (which does not even fit the melody!). Similarly, where the beloved Christmas Carol, "Joy to the World," used to read "Let men their songs employ," we must today obligatorily sing: "Let *us* our songs employ." The same thing is true of the carol "Good Christian Men Rejoice," which becomes "Good Christian *Friends* Rejoice." And so on.

We need to notice that today's attempts to turn feminist inclusive language into standard contemporary English speech represent a highly artificial and ideological manipulation of language which has been relentlessly promoted – quite successfully, as it happens, at least for the moment – by an organized radical feminist movement. The radical feminists dictate politically correct feminist language in the same way that the French and Russian Revolutions once imposed the use of such words as "citizen" and "comrade" and other kinds of politically correct speech. How long people will go on trying to speak and write in such an artificial and unnatural way once today's feminist ideology is no longer so dominant is anybody's guess. For the moment it is impossible to escape from the pressures which dictate writing and speaking in such a highly artificial and unnatural way.

As far as the Catholic faith is concerned, however, when we reflect carefully upon God's revelation of himself as, precisely, a *Father*, and, especially, by his Incarnation in a man (male), his Son, Jesus, we soon realize that the masculine gender nouns and pronouns have to be retained in religious discourse, if we are to be true to God's revelation of himself. Attempting to translate Scripture using inclusive language very often distorts the religious meaning of the original scriptural passage. For example, the Church in her authentic tradition has often interpreted passages from the Old Testament as containing a Christological dimension – as looking towards Christ and his coming. This Christological dimension can be weakened or lost entirely when translators insist on using inclusive language. An obvious example of this can be seen in Psalm 1, as translated in the Revised Standard Version (RSV), on the one hand; and in an inclusive-language translation called Today's English Version (TEV), on the other, as follows:

RSV TRANSLATION

Blessed is the man
who walks not in the counsel of the wicked,
nor stands in the way of sinners;
but his delight is in the law of the Lord.

TEV RENDERING

Happy are those
who reject the advice of evil men,
who do not follow the example of sinners,
or join those who have no use for God.
Instead they find joy in obeying the laws of the Lord.

Quite clearly, the Christological dimension (*Jesus* as the prototype of those who "walk not in the counsel of the wicked"!) has vanished from the second of these two translations; it has become just anybody at all who is "happy" (*not* "blessed"!) in rejecting evil advice. There is no longer any suggestion that it is Christ who "delivers us from evil." To lose this *religious* meaning in such scriptural passages is surely a heavy price to pay merely in order to appease the feminists and those who mindlessly follow the lead of the feminists in their view of what constitutes acceptable language today.

Yet this distorted view of what constitutes acceptable language today has too often unfortunately been accepted and shared by, e.g., the Catholic bishops, who have sanctioned it in both scriptural and liturgical translations – when they should have rejected much of it immediately and out of hand, and on first hearing, if they had been proceeding on the basis of a sense of the faith. And as is so often the case, the majority of bishops who have favored and sanctioned such ideologically motivated language are trying to appease a group whose radical feminist members not only care nothing for the Catholic faith; most of them would probably rejoice if the Catholic faith were to disappear from the face of the earth.

Still, a distortion of the religious meaning of a passage is not the only reason why inclusive language is unsuitable for the Church, or, especially, for the Church's liturgy. Experience with attempting to use inclusive language shows that it distorts meaning all along the line. How, for example, can we say that "all men are brothers" using inclusive language? It is always possible, of course, to say that "all men and women are brothers and sisters"; but then by making the phrase sex specific in this way, we end up altering the original *generic* meaning, referring now only to adult male and female human beings, and we thereby exclude *children!*

Similarly, we could always try "all human beings are siblings," but in addition to the loss of the elegance and grace of the original phrase, we have, again, changed the *meaning*. The same thing would be true of saying, "all human beings are brothers and sisters." In hastening to accord supposed "justice" to women, as "justice" has been defined for us by the radical feminists, then, we as a society have given far too little thought to the larger consequences of attempting to change reality by changing language. In the long run, reality is not likely to remain forever artificially changed in this way. As the ancient Roman poet Horace wrote: *Naturam expelles furca, tamen usque recurret;* "You may throw nature out with a pitchfork, but she will keep coming back."

Meanwhile, though, as long as radical feminism still reigns, as it does today, we also generally find the leaders of our society – politicians, judges, TV anchors, newspaper editors, talking heads, academics, university presidents, army generals, navy admirals, CEOs, ministers of religion, and, sadly, not a few Catholic bishops as well – hastening to pay their obeisance to the feminists by approving inclusive language. Perhaps we should not be surprised that the free-wheeling International Commission on English in the Liturgy (ICEL) also decided – entirely on its own authority, by the way – "to avoid words which ignore the place of women in the Christian community altogether or which seem to relegate women to a secondary role." Nothing would do, in the minds of the ICEL translators, but that the liturgy of the Catholic Church should henceforth be celebrated using inclusive language.

According to a 1990 volume prepared by ICEL itself, *Shaping English Liturgy*, the organization began using inclusive language in its translations of Roman liturgical texts from Latin into English as early as 1975. Initially,

ICEL received full Church approval – including Roman approval – for such texts as the 1985 Order of Funerals, which it translated using inclusive language. The same thing was true of the initial segments of a revision of the Roman Missal which ICEL began retranslating as part of the "second generation" of liturgical texts to be used in English. The first ICEL offerings for the revision of this revised Roman Missal were fairly routinely – almost automatically – approved by fairly large majorities of the American bishops, and were then sent on to Rome for final approval. This was pretty much the established pattern through most of the post-conciliar years: just as the bishops were generally accepting of what the professionals and experts came up with in other areas, so was this particularly true in the case of liturgical translations.

This raises the general question of why the bishops, as the official guardians of the liturgy – as Vatican Council II had specifically confirmed – were so relatively passive and permissive in going along with whatever ICEL came up with. We have seen how, from the very beginning of the institution of the vernacular liturgy, the typical ICEL translations were not only inferior; they were sometimes inaccurate; indeed, sometimes they were actual mistranslations, as we have shown (and we could cite many, many more examples). But then, added to all of this, there came the adoption of inclusive language by ICEL. The bishops were never consulted about this; they were never specifically asked whether inclusive language was permissible or necessary; but then they never objected to it either. Where *were* the bishops all this time then? Why *were* what seem in retrospect to have been so many missteps, mistakes, and errors so readily and easily, and, it would seem, almost automatically, tolerated?

There is no easy or single answer to these questions. Both at the Council and in the immediate post-conciliar period, too much was happening too fast in too many areas of the Church's life for the average bishop even to keep up with it all, much less control it. In one sense the bishops *had* to depend upon what the experts were doing, since the bishops could scarcely do it all themselves. And as we have already noted, nobody really knew how to implement a complete reform of the Church's liturgy, including the translation of all liturgical texts from Latin into the vernacular. Much had to be improvised as various questions and problems arose.

The Instructions that began issuing from the Roman congregations even before the Council was over, and later, as far as the liturgy was concerned, those based on the work of Pope Paul VI's Consilium, certainly read then, and mostly still read today, as if everything was being done in proper order; and as if careful thought was being given to at least most of the important questions as they arose. Yet, looking back, we can now see how deficient a liturgical reform was that allowed an area as large and as important as proper liturgical translation to be governed by a document as defective as *Comme le Prévoit*. And this was only one of the problems. Yet the bishops of the English-speaking world seem to have simply accepted without serious examination or question the translations provided by ICEL. More than that, when questions did arise which the bishops had to take a closer look at, the tendency was still to approve and endorse pretty much what the experts had decided upon.

In the matter of inclusive language, the American bishops, in 1990, approved a set of Criteria for the Evaluation of Inclusive Language Translations of Scriptural Texts Proposed for Liturgical Use which largely accepted the feminist viewpoint that the generic use of masculine nouns and pronouns excluded women, and hence should no longer be used in scriptural and liturgical translations.

With these Criteria, the bishops attempted a "compromise" solution, supposedly respectful of divine revelation, by retaining the masculine nouns and pronouns for God and for the Persons of the Holy Trinity ("vertical language"). At the same time, they endorsed the feminist notion that the masculine nouns and pronouns should not be used in a generic sense when referring to human beings ("horizontal language"). As far as references to human beings were concerned, they thus virtually adopted the feminist line, in fact. This is what the bishops' Criteria specified in the matter:

> Words such as *'adam, anthropos,* and *homo* have often been translated in many English biblical and liturgical texts by the collective terms "man" and "family of man." Since in the original languages these words actually denote human beings rather than only males, English terms which are not gender-specific, such as "person," "people," "human family," and "humans," should be used in translating these words (Criterion 19).

The reader may have noticed that these 1990 American bishops' Criteria for translations applied to scriptural texts used in the liturgy, and not just to the liturgical texts translated by ICEL. In point of fact, the Church's problem of so-called inclusive language extended beyond what ICEL had decided on its own to do. The community of biblical scholars too, like the ICEL translators, had by this time largely gone over to the feminist point of view on inclusive language. A veritable profusion of new biblical translations was now coming out prepared with an eye on a desired feminist *"imprimatur."* This phenomenon was not confined to Catholic Scripture scholars only, but, if anything, was even more pronounced among our "separated brothers and sisters"(!).

Entire translations of the Bible were now coming out using inclusive language. For example, the Protestants produced a New Revised Standard Version (NRSV) in place of their generally excellent, indeed outstanding, Revised Standard Version (RSV). (The RSV, in fact, in the midst of a welter of new biblical translations, still remains the best and most suitable of all the modern translations of the Bible in English; and, as the *Ignatius Bible*, for example, it is readily available in an approved Catholic edition as well.)

The New Revised Standard Version, however, proved immediately popular with a number of denominations seeking inclusive language readings from the Scriptures. The Catholic bishops too were urged by their scholars and experts to approve the NRSV; and, in 1992, along with a revision that was in progress of the Catholic New American Bible (NAB) that was entitled the Revised New American Bible (RNAB), the Congregation for Divine Worship actually approved these two inclusive-language Bible translations for Catholic worship. This Roman approval was not destined to endure, however, as we shall see; but the fact that it was granted at all shows how far down the road the inclusive-language band-wagon was able to travel before finally being recognized as the alien intrusion into the liturgy that it actually is.

What kind of a translation was contained in the New Revised Standard Version? A few comparisons will quickly bring this out. Let us take, for example, the Revised Standard Version's rendering of the familiar phrase from the Psalm, "What is man that thou art mindful of him, and the son of man that thou dost care for him?"(Ps 8:4). The NRSV renders this same passage: "What are human beings that you are mindful of them, mortals that you care for them?" Quite apart from the stilted and inelegant diction that we see here, there is the further inconvenient fact that second NRSV rendering *does not mean the same thing* as the first RSV one. "Mortal" is *not* the equivalent even of "human being," much less of the generic "man"; it certainly does *not* adequately convey the meaning that *"son* of man" has in the Bible, particularly as this term came to be used by Jesus Christ to describe himself.

Again, man may be mortal, but a mortal is not necessarily a man. The change in meaning here can readily be seen in yet another passage from the NRSV: "See, the home of God is among *mortals* [instead of "with men," as in the RSV]. He will dwell with them...and death will be no more..." (Rev 21:3–4).

But the question naturally arises here: how can death be "no more" if those among whom God is dwelling are "mortals"? Such changes of meaning – which not infrequently result in outright absurdities – are inevitable when we try to force language and meaning into a radical feminist mold. The NRSV abounds in such instances. Where Exodus 3:15 in the RSV speaks of "the God of your fathers," the NRSV gives "the God of your *ancestors*." According to the RSV, Acts 5:29 records Peter and the other apostles as saying: "We must obey God rather than man"; but the NRSV changes "man" to read *"human authority."*

When we find Jesus saying in the RSV's Matthew 5:22, "But I say to you, anyone who is angry with his brother...," we are no longer surprised to see the NRSV, entirely on its own authority, adding to the words of Jesus himself: "and sister"! Such are the results when it comes to be believed that scriptural translations must employ inclusive language. *Meanings are changed!*

One of the most often quoted boners of the NRSV New Testament, though, is found in Mark 1:17, which the RSV, of course, familiarly renders as: "Follow me and I will make you become fishers of men." The NRSV, however, translates this as: "Follow me and I will make you fish for *people*"! This is almost a parody. And what is remarkable in all of this is that serious scholars and pastors have not only been able to accept this kind of language; they have been prepared to promote it and impose it upon the faithful. The fact that a Roman congregation could actually have approved a translation such as the NRSV, even temporarily, as the Congregation for Divine Worship did in 1992, along with an equally deficient Revised New American Bible, is very hard to understand.

However, the same year, 1992, saw another development which was destined to bring the whole question of deficient scriptural and liturgical translations in English to the attention of the Holy See in a way that would eventually result in Rome's finally beginning to raise serious questions about these faulty translations, as well as about the role and work of ICEL in general. It was not long afterwards that Rome decided that the whole English translation process had to be rethought and redone, finally putting the Church, after more than thirty years, back on the road towards a sane and accurate liturgy in English.

Chapter Twenty-Two
The New Vatican Translation Norms

What occurred in December 1992, to change the Church's course quite decisively with regard to English translations, grew out of the issuance by Pope John Paul II of the *Catechism of the Catholic Church*. The Holy Father promulgated this *Catechism*, the first "universal" Catholic catechism in over 400 years, on December 10, 1992. Seven years in preparation by a drafting committee consisting almost entirely of working Catholic bishops, the document was declared by the pope to be "a sure and certain standard for the teaching of the faith."

At the time the *Catechism* was promulgated, work was already in progress to have the document translated into both Latin and the major modern languages. Originally it had been written in French, which had been the common language of the document's international bishop-drafters. It was fully expected that English-speaking Catholics, among others, would very soon have their own version of the *Catechism*. Inexplicably, however, the appearance of the English-language version kept being delayed. The *Catechism* did not finally appear in English until May 27, 1994, in fact, nearly a year and a half after the appearance of the original French version promulgated by the pope.

It turned out that the reason for the delay was that the original English translation made had been done by a translator who had *used inclusive language*! When the Roman congregations, particularly the Congregation for the Doctrine of the Faith, saw the distortions in meaning and Catholic doctrine that resulted from this attempt to translate the *Catechism* using inclusive language, the Holy See demurred and insisted that the entire translation had to be rejected and a new one prepared. An Australian archbishop, Joseph Eric D'Arcy of Hobart, Tasmania, was commissioned to prepare a wholly new translation of the *Catechism* using standard English. (For an extended account of this whole question of the translation of the *Catechism of the Catholic Church* into English, see the chapter, "The Translation of the *Catechism* into English," in Wrenn, Monsignor Michael J., and

Whitehead, Kenneth D., *Flawed Expectations: The Reception of the Catechism of the Catholic Church* (San Francisco: Ignatius Press, 1996); the full text of this book is available at www.christendom-awake.org.)

Confronted with an extensive text in English using inclusive language, the Holy See could not avoid seeing and judging its glaring inadequacies as a document of faith. Inclusive language in English does not really work, as we have shown. Once this was realized in Rome, the stage was set for a thorough re-examination of the other scriptural and liturgical translations into English that had been employing inclusive language, in particular those prepared by ICEL.

Nor was this re-examination long in coming. In the fall of 1994, the Congregation for the Doctrine of the Faith requested that the approval of the NRSV and RNAB Bibles, which the Congregation for Divine Worship had inexplicably granted two years earlier, be rescinded. This rescission directly affected, among other texts, the revised new Lectionary with Scripture readings for the Mass based on the RNAB which ICEL was engaged in translating. Up to this point the American bishops (although in diminishing numbers) were still generally and rather routinely approving ICEL's work almost automatically.

Soon afterwards, the Congregation for Divine Worship and the Discipline of the Sacraments began holding up the ICEL liturgical translations submitted by the American bishops for the Roman *recognitio*, or approval. The Congregation even began sending some of them back. Throughout the 1990s, in fact, there was a complex and even confused series of liturgical texts going back and forth between Rome and the United States. It would be tedious, if it were even possible, to attempt to trace all this movement in detail. But it is no exaggeration to say that, through the mid–1990s, as it became more and more clear that Rome was no longer going to approve pretty much routinely the liturgical texts being submitted, the concerned American bishops became progressively more anxious and expended enormous efforts trying to get approved in Rome ICEL-translated texts that were more than dubious.

In one dramatic instance, on December 13, 1996, all seven of the U.S. cardinals active at the time went to Rome together in a body to lobby for the approval of the proposed new Lectionary based on the RNAB – the Bible translation from which Rome had withdrawn its approval. That *this* was the subject that could bring all seven of the active American cardinals to Rome together unfortunately speaks volumes about their apparent priorities. Advancing the feminist agenda was evidently the principal thing all these American cardinals could agree upon! What they *should* have learned by then was that trying to appease the feminists was impossible.

Early in the next year, 1997, another delegation of American bishops went to Rome and sat down with Curia officials to work out a compromise on modified inclusive language for the new Lectionary being prepared for the United States. The American bishops agreed to modify some of the RNAB inclusive language in the Lectionary. The compromise they achieved may have solved the immediate problem of an impasse between the American bishops and Rome, but their product proved to be far from entirely satisfactory, though Rome apparently decided that it was minimally acceptable. (In August 2007, the Congregation for Divine Worship and the Discipline of the Sacraments similarly finally gave the *recognitio* of the Holy See to a Canadian Lectionary originally published in 1992 based on the New Revised Standard Version of the Bible; a press release from the Canadian Conference of Catholic Bishops spoke of a "revision of the Lectionary . . . [based] on an agreed set of principles"; one surmises that the Canadian bishops agreed to modify some of the more excessive NRSV inclusive language, just as the American bishops had.)

Yet the melancholy fact remained that the bishops *had been accepting* of the manifest distortions of feminist inclusive language. No greater example of misplaced episcopal priorities can be imagined than that this kind of feminist-inspired inclusive language, of all things, should have been the cause that for once united the efforts of all seven of the then active U.S. cardinals and of the later delegation of U.S. bishops that followed them to Rome (the same thing was surely true of the Canadian bishops later on). All these prelates were evidently concerned and worried precisely *because* it was becoming more and more clear that the Congregation was now seriously scrutinizing the ICEL translations being sent in; and approval was no longer going to be easy, if it was going to be granted at all to some of these defective translations.

At the same time, by the late 1990s, an increasing number of American bishops were themselves now actually beginning to question the adequacy of the translations which, formerly, had been almost automatically approved – first, by the Bishops' Committee on the Liturgy (BCL), which over the years had more or less worked hand in glove with ICEL; and then by large majorities of the bishops in the conference itself. But a new wind was now blowing; it was increasingly coming to be understood that not only could ICEL-type translations no longer be given virtual rubber-stamp approval; some of them could no longer be approved at all; and more and more American bishops were not only coming to see this, but some of them were even beginning to agree with Rome in the matter.

There had been intimations of Roman dissatisfaction with English liturgical translations even before the affair of the *Catechism* translation. On the 25th anniversary of *Sacrosanctum Concilium,* in December 1988, Pope John Paul II, in his apostolic letter *Vicesimus Quintus Annus,* spoke of the work of the "commissions," such as ICEL, which had been established "for the work of translation, as well as for the wider implications of liturgical renewal." The pontiff stated on that occasion that "the time has come to evaluate [these] commission[s]." Again in December 1993, in an address to a group of American bishops from the Western United States who were making their five-year *ad limina* visit to the pope – at the very time when the *Catechism* was undergoing re-translation, and at the same time that many of the American bishops were complaining that no authorized version of the *Catechism* was yet available in English – the pontiff pointedly said to these territorial bishops, on the subject of liturgical translations, the following:

> One of your responsibilities in this regard...is to make available exact and appropriate translations of the official liturgical books so that, following the required review and confirmation by the Holy See, they may be an instrument and guarantee of a genuine sharing in the mystery of Christ and the Church: *lex orandi, lex credendi.* The arduous task of translation must guard *the full doctrinal integrity* and, according to the genius of each language, *the beauty* of the original texts. When so many people are thirsting for the living God (Ps 42:2)...the Church must respond with a language of praise and worship which fosters respect and gratitude for God's greatness, compassion, and power. When the faithful gather to celebrate the work of our redemption, the language of their prayer – *free from doctrinal ambiguity and ideological influence* – should foster the dignity and beauty of the celebration itself, while faithfully expressing the Church's faith and unity (*L'Osservatore Romano* (English Edition), December 15, 1993; emphasis added throughout).

These remarks of Pope John Paul II, especially his reference to "doctrinal ambiguity and ideological influence" in liturgical texts, quite clearly reflected what the Congregation for Divine Worship and the Discipline of the Sacraments was now noticing in some of the translated English liturgical texts that had been submitted for approval. It was while the first volume of the proposed new English Lectionary based on the RNAB was under consideration that the Congregation evidently concluded that entirely new liturgical translation Norms had become necessary. The Congregation therefore proceeded forthwith to develop such Norms.

These Norms for the Translation of Biblical Texts for Use in the Liturgy, as they were called, were developed and completed around 1995, and were probably already coming into use when the seven U.S. cardinals made their last-ditch visit to Rome in December 1996 to plead for inclusive language. It was already too late. Rome was already seriously on the case. Nevertheless, the new Norms did not come into the public domain until somewhat later, after they had been distributed to all the U.S. bishops, along with a packet of other liturgical materials from the Congregation for Divine Worship and the Discipline of the Sacraments, sent out just prior to the American bishops' semi-annual meeting in June 1997.

The new translation Norms were not actually made public officially. They seem to have been leaked to the leftist *National Catholic Reporter*, which then published them, much as the same radical journal in 1967 had published the leaked confidential reports made to Pope Paul VI by the Papal Birth Control Commission – which had then led so many people to expect, mistakenly, that the Church's teaching prohibiting artificial birth control would be changed.

The new Vatican Norms for the Translation of Biblical Texts for Use in the Liturgy, however, hardly commanded public attention on the same level as the continuation of the Church's ban on birth control! Nevertheless they provoked no small tempest in some liturgical circles. They contained practically a point-by-point annulling of the 1990 U.S. bishops' Criteria for the Evaluation of Inclusive Language Translations of Scriptural Texts Proposed for Liturgical Use that we described above. While the bishops had followed their experts and scholars in deciding that inclusive language had become necessary in "justice" to "women," Rome looked rather at the resulting English translations, and at the way in which the doctrines of the faith were being distorted in them. The new Vatican Norms do not even mention inclusive language by name, as a matter of fact, anymore than they *say* that they are superseding the bishops' Norms that accepted inclusive language; they nevertheless effectively do eliminate inclusive language by what they prescribe.

Specifically, the new Vatican Translation Norms require: (1) accurate translations made with (2) "maximum possible fidelity to the words of the text" and "faithful to the sense of sacred Scripture understood as a unity and totality." Translations must (3) "faithfully reflect the Word of God in the original languages...without 'correction' or 'improvement' in the service of modern sensitivities." In cases of obscurity, translations should be made (3a) with "due regard" to the Church's Latin Neo-Vulgate Bible; and, if explanations are necessary, they should be given (3b) in appended notes, not incorporated into the translated text.

Vatican Translation Norm 4 is subdivided into six subparts, each of which prohibits a specific translation practice: (4 §1) "the natural gender of *personae* in the Bible...must not be changed"; (4 §2) "the grammatical gender of God, pagan deities, angels, and demons...must not be changed"; (4 §3) "in fidelity to the inspired Word of God, the traditional biblical usage for naming the persons of the Trinity as Father, Son, and Holy Spirit is to be retained"; (4 §4) "...in keeping with the Church's tradition, the feminine and the neuter pronouns are not to be used to refer to the person of the Holy Spirit"; (4 §5) "there shall be no systematic substitution of the masculine pronoun or possessive adjective to refer to God in correspondence to the original text"; and (4 §6) "kinship terms that are clearly gender specific...should be respected in translation."

Each of these subparts of Vatican Translation Norm 4 prohibits a specific and favored ICEL translation practice identified from various inclusive-language translations submitted to the Holy See. Observance of this six-part Norm alone would by itself eliminate most of the errors in such translations as the NRSV and the RNAB. Taken together, these prohibitions would eliminate such errors as substituting "Creator, Redeemer, and Sanctifier" for "Father, Son, and Holy Spirit"; avoiding the use of masculine pronouns referring to God by repeating the word God; referring to the Holy Spirit as "she" or "it"; or changing either the natural or the grammatical genders found in original texts.

Vatican Translation Norm 5 follows up on this last point and specifies that "grammatical number and person in the original texts should ordinarily be maintained." What this means is that the practice of switching to the plural, "they," in order to avoid having to use the generic "he," is eliminated. This is one of the most common practices in inclusive language translations, of course, and it often results in serious mistranslations; for it cannot be seriously maintained that the plural always means the same thing as the singular. With regard to the religious meaning, as we have noted, the Christological dimension may be lost in many Old Testament texts which prefigure Christ or refer to his coming (as Norm 6 §2 below also points out) when singulars are changed to plurals.

Translation Norm 6 is divided into three subparts, the first of which (6 §1) specifies that "translations should strive to preserve the connotations as well as the denotations of words or expressions in the original, and not preclude possible layers of meaning." This subpart is evidently intended to eliminate errors such as those which inevitably arise when translators focus upon one preoccupation such as "male dominance," and thereby ignore other important nuances and layers of meaning. Norm (6 §2) deals with a point that we have already covered when it notes that "...where the New Testament of the Church's tradition has interpreted certain texts of the Old Testament in a Christological fashion, special care should be observed in the translation of these texts so that a Christological meaning is not precluded." Finally, Norm (6 §3) says that "the word 'man' in English should translate [Hebrew] *'adam* and [Greek] *anthropos,* since there is no one synonym which effectively conveys the play between the individual, the collectivity, and the unity of the human family..."

"Man," in English, does have multiple meanings related to the individual, as well as to the collectivity, and to the human race generally. We can still consult any dictionary to verify the multiple meanings that the word "man" has always had in English and still has. It may be true that, under current feminist influence, the definition of "man" as "an adult male human being" may now have been moved up to be definition number one in many dictionaries; but this does not mean that the other meanings are obsolete or have been eliminated; and, indeed, all dictionaries still continue to include these other meanings among the definitions they give. Nor does it mean that speakers of English today would ever fail to understand what is meant when "man" is used in the generic sense, whatever the feminists and their fellow travelers may think or say.

All in all, then, these new Vatican Translation Norms reflect a sane and realistic view of what is required in liturgical translations, even in the present heightened and ideological atmosphere. We must be grateful for the clear-sightedness of the Roman congregations; they were able to see how acceptance of inclusive language (along with the other features of "dynamic equivalence" in translation) was deforming and debasing the Church's liturgy – and this at a time when most of the English-speaking bishops, along with their *periti* and the majority of today's biblical scholars, were generally not seeing this at all, but were just going along with the supposed demands of today's secular culture that remains under such radical feminist influence.

That the new Norms would remain in place and govern future scriptural and liturgical translations became a reality on March 28, 2001, when the Congregation for Divine Worship and the Discipline of the Sacraments issued its Fifth Instruction on the Right Implementation of the Constitution on the Sacred Liturgy, *Liturgiam Authenticam* ("Authentic Liturgy"). The subtitle of this document was: "On the Use of the Vernacular in the Publication of the Books of the Roman Liturgy."

This Fifth Instruction, *Liturgiam Authenticam,* truly inaugurated a new era in the use of the vernacular liturgy. The Instruction brought together and laid out systematically in one authoritative document all the points and corrections which Rome had been engaged in making piece-meal in the course of the 1990s. The document expressly aimed to correct what it called "the omissions and errors which affect certain vernacular translations" (LA 6); and it declared its intention of establishing "anew the true notion of liturgical translation in order that the translations of the sacred liturgy into the vernacular languages may stand secure as the authentic voice of the Church of God" (LA 7). Liturgical translation, according to this definitive new instruction:

> ...is not so much a work of creative innovation as it is of rendering the original texts faithfully and accurately into the vernacular language. While it is permissible to arrange the wording, the syntax, and the style in such a way as to prepare a flowing vernacular text suitable to the rhythm of popular prayer, the original text, insofar as possible, must be translated integrally and in the most exact manner, without omissions or additions in terms of their content, and without paraphrases or glosses (LA 20).

Divided into five chapters following a short Introduction, *Liturgiam Authenticam* speaks about and lays down the rules concerning: 1) the choice of vernacular languages to be introduced into liturgical use; 2) the translation of liturgical texts into vernacular languages; 3) the preparation of translations and the establishment of commissions to carry out the work; 4) the publication of liturgical books; and 5) the translation of proper liturgical texts. The meat of the document which bears most directly upon past ICEL translations – and upon the hopefully much improved translations that will be produced in the future now that this particular document has been issued as guidance – is to be found in Chapter Two of the Instruction, which covers the actual translation of liturgical texts into vernacular languages.

There we find a veritable treasure trove, both of solid general principles applicable to all translations, and of specific norms which go into enough salutary detail to exclude the kinds of defects found in past ICEL liturgical texts. In particular, the new Vatican Translation Norms which we have already examined above have all been fully incorporated into this document, almost word for word. *Liturgiam Authenticam* even goes farther, though, and specifies that "the term 'fathers,' found in many biblical passages and liturgical texts of ecclesiastical composition, is to be rendered by the corresponding masculine word into vernacular languages insofar as it may be seen to refer to the patriarchs or the kings of the chosen people in the Old Testament" (LA 31). This will entail another change, since for some time now we have been hearing about our "ancestors" instead of our "fathers" in these particular passages!

With the promulgation of *Liturgiam Authenticam*, it would seem that so-called "inclusive language" as such, although it is scarcely even specifically mentioned in the document – nor does the document concede that there is any such thing in a real sense – nevertheless has hopefully once and for all and finally been laid to rest by this Fifth Instruction. That this was going to happen seemed already evident from the nature of the Vatican Translation Norms developed earlier; but this document as written has now definitely completed the task. It is even worth quoting in full the following paragraph in this connection:

> In many languages there exist nouns and pronouns denoting both genders, masculine and feminine, together in a single term. The insistence that such a usage should be changed is not necessarily to be regarded as the effect or the manifestation of an authentic development of the language as such. Even if it may be necessary by means of catechesis to ensure that such words continue to be understood in the "inclusive" sense..., it may not be possible to employ different words in the translations themselves without detriment to the precise intended meaning of the text, the correlation of its various words or expressions, or its aesthetic qualities. When the original text, for example, employs a single term [e.g., "man"] in expressing the interplay between the individual and the universality and unity of the human family or community (such as the Hebrew word *'adam,* the Greek word *anthropos*, or the Latin *homo*), the property of the language of the original text should be maintained in the translation. Just as has occurred at other times in

history, the Church herself must freely decide upon the system of language that will serve her doctrinal mission most effectively, and should not be subject to externally imposed linguistic norms that are detrimental to the mission (LA 30).

In other words, inclusive language which attempts to get around plainly saying "man" in a generic sense distorts both the meaning and the beauty of the original scriptural texts. The Church cannot therefore abandon this usage in response to some alleged "development" in the English language which now supposedly understands the term "man" only as denoting an adult male human being. This is not, in any case, correct; it is merely a claim of the radical feminists; but to the extent that such language in the liturgy might ever be misinterpreted as somehow discriminatory or demeaning to women, the paragraph preceding the one just quoted makes clear that "it is the task of catechists or of the homilist to transmit that right interpretation of the texts that excludes any prejudice or unjust discrimination on the basis of persons, gender, social condition, race, or other criteria."

By means of the new Vatican Translation Norms and *Liturgiam Authenticam*, then, the Church in the English-speaking world got rescued from feminist-inspired translations that would surely have come to seem stale and clumsy, and sometimes even absurd, once the current fashionable feminist tide recedes (which it eventually will, because what the old Roman poet said is true, namely, that nature will indeed "keep coming back").

Chapter Twenty-Three
New Liturgical Leadership in the Church

The new Vatican Translation Norms and the eventual issuance of *Liturgiam Authenticam* represented only one indication of Rome's thinking on the subject of liturgical texts. There were other indications that Rome was now determined, at long last, to see English liturgical texts more suitable to Catholic worship put in place. Among these indications had to be counted the appointment of the former bishop of Valparaiso, Chile, Jorge Arturo Medina Estevez, to head the Congregation for Divine Worship and the Discipline of the Sacraments. Archbishop Medina was named pro-prefect of the Congregation in 1996 and prefect in 1998, and he was also made a cardinal in the latter year. This Chilean prelate had already by then distinguished himself, among other ways, as one of the eight bishop-authors of the *Catechism of the Catholic Church*. Later on after his retirement, as cardinal protodeacon, he was the one who announced to the world from the balcony of St. Peter's the election of Cardinal Joseph Ratzinger to the papacy in 2005.

The choice of Cardinal Medina in 1996 to head the Vatican congregation in charge of the liturgy proved to be a very fortunate one, even though he was destined to remain there for only six years. Nevertheless, from the outset of his term, he showed that he knew what he was doing and where the Church needed to be going, especially, it turned out, in the matter of the English translations of the Roman liturgy. It is, of course, ironic that a Chilean should have proved to be so instrumental in setting in place provisions for remedying the defects of the liturgy in English (just as it is ironic that the Congregation for the Doctrine of the Faith headed by a German, then Cardinal Joseph Ratzinger, should have been the first to realize the defects of the translated *Catechism* that had originally been "Englished" using inclusive language).

Yet another very important ecclesiastical appointment that was made around the same time as Cardinal Medina's appointment was the replacement as the American ICEL representative, in June 1997, of Cincinnati's

Archbishop Daniel E. Pilarczyk by the new archbishop of Chicago, Cardinal Francis E. George. The Cincinnati prelate had been a protegé and successor of the late Cardinal Joseph Bernardin while the latter was still archbishop of Cincinnati. When the latter himself became the archbishop of Chicago and was raised to the cardinalate, Archbishop Pilarczyk became archbishop of Cincinnati in his turn.

This same Archbishop Pilarczyk served for nearly a dozen years as the ICEL chairman as well as the American representative on ICEL. During that same period, he also served both as president of the conference of Catholic bishops (1989–1992), and, for a number of years, as chairman of the Bishops' Committee on the Liturgy (BCL). He thus counted as a very influential bishop and had unparalleled influence on the liturgy in those years. Indeed, he could correctly be said to be one of the more important members of the post-conciliar "liturgical establishment," such as it was. However, there is no public evidence at all, it is important to state, that he ever expressed or had the slightest doubt about the kind and quality of the typical ICEL translations into English. On the contrary, Archbishop Pilarczyk, throughout his career as archbishop, could on more than one occasion be found to be bowing to the culture while allowing to Rome only the minimum he was obliged to grant.

His replacement by the new Chicago archbishop, Cardinal George, in June 1997, then, at the very time that the new Vatican Translation Norms also surfaced, was one more indication that a new wind was finally blowing. Cardinal George was a native Chicagoan and a religious order priest (the Oblates of Mary Immaculate). In a meteoric career, he had previously been bishop of Yakima, Washington, then archbishop of Portland in Oregon. A scholar and intellectual as well as a shepherd, Cardinal George had the reputation of being both sound and tough-minded on liturgical questions. He had been openly critical of certain ICEL translations at some of the earlier American bishops' meetings. According to the *National Catholic Reporter*, at the ICEL meeting in 1998, he was the bearer of the bad news to the organization that Rome would be demanding serious and extensive changes in ICEL's translation procedures. Later, in 2002, he became chairman of the U.S. Bishops' Committee on the Liturgy as well, until he had to relinquish that post upon his election as USCCB vice president in 2004. He was elected president of the USCCB itself in November 2007.

With the advent of Cardinal Medina at the Congregation for Divine Worship and the Discipline of the Sacraments, and with that of Cardinal

George as the American ICEL representative representing views closer to Roman thinking, the Holy See's tardy but increasingly effective series of interventions in English-language liturgical questions became even more insistent. On September 20, 1997, Cardinal Medina wrote to the then president of the U.S. bishops' conference, Bishop Anthony Pilla of Cleveland, flatly turning down an ICEL-translated revised book of Rites of Ordination of the Bishop, of Priests, and of Deacons, which had been submitted to the Holy See for the required Roman *recognitio* the year before. These revised ordination Rites, Cardinal Medina wrote bluntly, "cannot be approved or confirmed by the Holy See for liturgical use." He added that the document's "shortcomings are so diffused that minor, isolated corrections will not suffice"; the translation, according to this curial cardinal, "fails to transmit faithfully important doctrinal aspects of the Latin original."

This 1997 letter of Cardinal Medina's – made public by Bishop Pilla – went on to say what should have been said about some of the ICEL's liturgical translations years, if not decades, earlier. Cardinal Medina continued:

> . . . It is also cause for concern that the translators have felt free to introduce changes at will, to "improve" the order of the text, the rubrics, and the numbering. To the above-mentioned translation have been added new compositions. These have been found to be in disharmony with the conventions of the Roman liturgy, confused, largely unsuited to the circumstances in which they would be used, and at best theologically impoverished.

This blunt Medina letter concluded with the recommendation that an entirely new translation from the Latin texts of the ordination Rites was called for. This letter, strong as it was, was still only a harbinger of more things to come. In 1998, the Congregation again required more than 400 changes in a revised Introduction to the Lectionary in English that had been submitted for approval. The Lectionary is the book of scriptural texts used at Mass during the year. The Congregation also insisted on the withdrawal of a bishops' *imprimatur* ("let it be printed") from the so-called "ICEL Psalter" – an inclusive-language version of the Psalms which had been prepared by ICEL, and which was already in fairly wide use in some religious orders without any formal ecclesiastical approval.

By this time almost anybody at all knowledgeable or involved with the liturgy in English was waiting for the other shoe to drop in Rome. On October 26, 1999, it dropped with a rather loud bang, though a somewhat delayed one; this came in the form of a letter from Cardinal Medina to

Bishop Maurice Taylor of Galloway, Scotland, then chairman of ICEL. The public effect of this Medina letter was delayed because it did not become public knowledge until two months later. The reverberations from it are still echoing, however.

Once again, this letter was never officially released to the public, either by the Congregation or by the ICEL; instead it was leaked to the *National Catholic Reporter*, which published it in its issue of December 24, 1999, under the headline, "Vatican Moves to Take Control of Translation Agency."

This headline was actually not a bad description of both the tone and import of this 1999 Medina letter, for in it the prefect of the Divine Worship Congregation laid out, in effect, an entirely new procedure for producing English translations of the Roman liturgy, a procedure in which the Congregation itself would henceforth be directly involved; the letter thus marked the end of an era for what had been up to then a free-wheeling, essentially autonomous ICEL organization. Since the English-speaking bishops had not proved either willing or able to keep or bring the organization under effective Church control, the Congregation for Divine Worship and the Discipline of the Sacraments announced with this 1999 Medina letter its own firm intention of doing so.

The Medina letter seems to have been prompted by a letter from Bishop Taylor requesting a meeting between ICEL officials and the Congregation, presumably in order to clear up what ICEL regarded as some mere misunderstandings. The Congregation thought the problem went much deeper and was more serious than any mere misunderstandings, however. Cardinal Medina responded to Bishop Taylor first by saying that "such a meeting, in order to be truly productive, ought to follow upon certain steps which should no longer be deferred."

The Divine Worship prefect then referred to his earlier letter of September 20, 1997, quoted above, in which the ICEL translation of the Rites of Ordination of the Bishop, of Priests, and of Deacons had been turned down, and a whole series of defects in the ICEL translation of it had been identified. Cardinal Medina noted that the defects listed had not been "exhaustive" but only "illustrative." He then went on to identify other defects in ICEL translations generally, notably the "undue autonomy" that characterized them, as well as the fact that ICEL translations generally "paraphrase or redraft the Latin *editiones typicae*, while revising the rubrics so extensively as to impede effective recourse to the Latin text for the sake of clarification." In other words, the variations were so extensive that the English text could no longer even properly be compared with the Latin original. Cardinal Medina added that "the rubrics have sometimes been altered in substance without prior authorization of the Holy See, and indeed without even a request for such authorization."

That was not all. Cardinal Medina had still other complaints. He faulted the ICEL translators for composing their own texts; for producing the so called "ICEL Psalter," which had been "employed in ways which directly contravene liturgical law"; for allowing the publication and use, in some cases by non-Catholic denominations, of yet other ICEL texts and documents not approved by the Holy See; and, finally, for *not* producing in a timely fashion other material essential to the completion of the new *Missale Romanum.*

"All of these factors," the Medina letter concluded, "appear to converge towards the conclusion that the Mixed Commission" – the Congregation's name for the ICEL organization – "is not in a position to render to the bishops, to the Holy See, and to the English-speaking faithful, nor to produce with appropriate promptness, the texts that will be needed in the foreseeable future..."

Basing its actions on a provision in the 1988 apostolic constitution of Pope John Paul II reorganizing the Roman Curia, *Pastor Bonus* (62), relating to the superintendence of "those matters which pertain to the Holy See in relation to the moderation and promotion of the sacred liturgy," the Medina letter then mandated a series of reforms, including: a thorough and immediate revision of the ICEL statutes, to be carried out in consultation with the Congregation; a new definition of the mission of the organization limiting its work to "the translation into English of the Latin *editiones typicae* of the Roman liturgical texts and books in their integrity"; provision for the replacement and rotation of ICEL staff and advisors – the appointment of all of them to receive a *nihil obstat* ("nothing against") from the Congregation itself; the prohibition of copyrights or permissions for use of materials not approved by Rome; and yet other provisions.

All of these provisions reflected a considered and markedly adverse judgment by the Congregation on the work of the ICEL over many years. This judgment effectively meant that the entire corpus of liturgical books and texts in English was going to have to be redone in accordance with the stricter new Vatican Translation Norms which had been developed by the Congregation. Although the ICEL translators had already embarked on their own retranslation project with some of their own "second generation" translations, it was the installments of the latter submitted to the

Congregation for *recognitio* that had finally served, at long last, to bring upon the ICEL the adverse Roman judgment it had so long deserved – and which finally got delivered in Cardinal Medina's letter.

This judgment was confirmed in March 2002, when Cardinal Medina officially rejected the ICEL re-translation of the Roman Missal which had been in use since 1975. The bishops had been debating and even trying to modify the ICEL re-translation of this document since around 1993; and their latest version of it had finally been sent to Rome for the required *recognitio* in January 1999. In turning it down – not until three years later! – Cardinal Medina included yet another set of "Observations" animadverting again upon the unacceptable quality of the ICEL translations. The staff of the Congregation was evidently spending a great deal of time going over English liturgy texts, and was now clearly doing so quite exhaustively.

At the same time, Cardinal Medina expressed his acute dissatisfaction with the progress of the reorganization of ICEL itself, which he had ordered in his 1999 letter. Although ICEL had "taken a number of steps in response to the Congregation's request for such a restructuring of the Commission," Cardinal Medina noted, there was still lacking, in his opinion "a fresh group of experts and administrators appropriately positioned to collaborate with the Holy See."

The desired reorganization of ICEL was never likely to be completed, it seemed, as long as the same old people remained in place. Finally, though, in September 2002, the chairman of the ICEL episcopal board, Bishop Maurice Taylor of Galloway, Scotland, who had been in office since 1997, was replaced by Bishop Arthur Roche of Leeds, England. At the same time, the long-time executive secretary of ICEL, Dr. John R. Page, an American who had worked for ICEL for some thirty years and had been executive secretary since 1980, was replaced by yet another Englishman, Father Bruce Harbert, of Birmingham, England. A specialist in Latin and Greek, Father Harbert had previously written articles critical of ICEL translations. In the journal *Antiphon*, for example, he once wrote that ICEL's work was "redolent as much of the 1960s as of the fourth century. Yet the liturgical reform that gave us the vernacular liturgy was intended to be, not so much a fresh start with a clean sheet, as a recovery of primitive tradition."

With such new leadership, the prospect of a real reform of ICEL and its work thus seemed at long last possible and perhaps even now likely. This remained true even though, only a month later, in October 2002, Cardinal Medina himself, having reached the mandatory retirement age of

75, stepped down as prefect of the Divine Worship Congregation. He was replaced by Cardinal Francis Arinze, then aged 69, an African bishop who since 1984 had been president of the Pontifical Council for Interreligious Dialogue. From all indications, Cardinal Arinze – who as a Nigerian was already completely acclimated to a liturgy celebrated in English – seemed likely to continue, and, in fact, did continue, the authentic reforms so vigorously put in place and promoted by Cardinal Medina in the latter's six short years as pro-prefect or prefect. These years proved, however, to be the decisive years in laying the groundwork for what can now finally – some forty years after the Council – result in suitable and authentic texts for liturgical celebration in English.

Nor were the steps that we have briefly described here the only steps taken during Cardinal Medina's tenure. In June 2001, for example, the Holy See had created yet another entity, *Vox Clara* ("Clear Voice"), an international committee of English-speaking bishops who were charged with overseeing the translation work of the – soon to be reformed! – ICEL operation. Headed by the archbishop of Sydney, Australia, George Pell – named to the College of Cardinals in 2003 – the *Vox Clara* Committee included several American prelates as members, namely: Archbishop Oscar Lipscomb of Mobile, Alabama; Archbishop Justin Rigali of St. Louis (later transferred to Philadelphia, and also named cardinal in 2003); Archbishop Alfred Hughes of New Orleans; and Cardinal Francis George of Chicago. Most of these prelates had the reputation of being "papal loyalists," and thus seemed likely to be more sympathetic to Rome's efforts to insure at long last exact and accurate English translations of the liturgy of the Roman rite.

As things turned out, the *Vox Clara* Committee turned out to be a very active group. It met frequently and its members reviewed and provided substantive comments on new, on-going liturgical translations that were being produced. It was a case where bishops (rather than just "experts") were taking an active role in carrying out the Church's liturgical reforms. A similar body of bishops should have been named at the outset of the liturgical reforms, perhaps even before the end of the Council; if that had been done, some of the mistakes that were made might have been avoided.

The *Vox Clara* Committee was still going strong at the beginning of 2008, reviewing translations of the new Roman Missal, and offering suggestions for possible alternate words and phrases more faithful to the Latin original and easier to proclaim and comprehend. During its fourteenth meeting in September 2007, the committee was engaged in discussing initiatives to insure the effective reception and implementation of the new Missal which at that point it was hoped would be completed by the end of 2010.

Clearly, English translations were now being produced in the way that Cardinal Medina had prescribed. Another earlier indication that the strict Roman oversight of liturgical texts in English instituted by Cardinal Medina was being continued under Cardinal Arinze came in October 2002, when the Nigerian cardinal wrote a letter to the president of the U.S. Conference of Catholic Bishops, Bishop Wilton D. Gregory of Belleville, Illinois – and apparently also to the presidents of other English-speaking bishops' conferences. The major burden of this Arinze letter, dated October 23, 2002, was that the long-awaited reorganization of ICEL originally demanded by Cardinal Medina's 1999 letter to ICEL president Bishop Taylor was still not being completed satisfactorily or within the time limits called for by Rome. Cardinal Medina had originally asked that this reorganization be completed by Easter, 2000. Yet more than two years later this had still not been done. But what seemed especially significant, though, was that Rome was now continuing to follow up and insisting that it be done.

It seems that new draft statutes for ICEL were in the process of being examined by the various English-speaking bishops' conferences before being finally approved. Cardinal Arinze's letter to Bishop Gregory was quite critical of the draft statutes in question, however, in part because they had evidently been prepared without the consultation with the Congregation, a consultation which had plainly been requested by Cardinal Medina. Cardinal Arinze also faulted the statutes for failing to acknowledge that it is the Congregation for Divine Worship itself, not the various bishops' conferences, that properly "erects" a commission to carry out liturgical translations into vernacular languages.

Another deficiency of the draft statutes was their failure to provide for any term limits for ICEL staff, something which had definitely also been called for; nor did they provide for a *nihil obstat,* or veto power, by the Congregation over the hiring of ICEL staff, as had similarly been called for. It thus became clear that, in spite of ICEL foot-dragging, Rome was not backing away from the original requirements that had been laid down for a reorganized ICEL in the 1999 Medina letter.

Once again, though, the 2002 letter from Cardinal Arinze was not made public by the Congregation. As before, it was leaked to the *National Catholic Reporter*, which then produced yet another alarmist headline (which once again was essentially true!): "Vatican Insists on Greater Control over Language Agency" (NCR 12/13/02). Given the long drawn-out history of the whole affair, it should certainly not have been any surprise to anyone by that time. Or, rather, the surprise was perhaps that Rome was simply not backing off; nor was foot dragging going to gain any kind of a reprieve for ICEL.

Cardinal Arinze's persistence seems to have paid off. After so much reluctance and even resistance, an acceptable set of ICEL statutes finally was produced and was approved by the U.S. bishops in June 2003; these revised new statutes then received the Roman *recognitio* in time to be published in conjunction with a high level meeting called by Cardinal Arinze in Rome in October 2003. It was this meeting that reportedly re-launched a whole new effort to produce acceptable liturgical texts in English. Thus at long last was ICEL finally "reorganized."

The time was long overdue for developments such as those we have just been describing – developments which now gave definite promise of a new era for the vernacular liturgy in English. All this seemed especially appropriate since, in the Jubilee Year 2000, the Holy Father had announced the preparation of a new edition of the Roman Missal. This new Roman Missal would now come out under the new arrangements in place, and would obviously have to be translated anew from scratch. Thus, it could fittingly serve as the foundation stone for the whole corpus of liturgical texts in English hopefully to be re-translated according to the new Norms.

New introductory rules for the proper celebration of Mass contained in the new *General Instruction on the Roman Missal* (GIRM) were actually published ahead of the Roman Missal itself and quickly became the subject of intense study. As we have already seen in connection with our discussion of kneeling earlier in these pages, the American bishops produced a set of "American Adaptations" of the new GIRM rules for the Mass, but these represented only minor variations in the text. These American Adaptations were finally approved by the Congregation for Divine Worship and the Discipline of the Sacraments in April 2002. The Latin *editio typica* of the new Roman Missal itself had been presented to Pope John Paul II just one month before, on March 18, 2002.

Unfortunately, Rome has a long-standing – and unhappily merited – reputation for taking its own sweet time about things. Officials of the Roman Curia even pride themselves on this; the old saying in Italian often attributed to the Roman Curia being, *qui pensiamo in secoli* ("here we think in centuries"). This saying, however, only too often accurately reflects the outlook of Vatican officials. Still, no one could any longer say that Rome had not finally acted concerning ICEL, beginning especially with Cardinal Medina's 1999 letter to Galloway Bishop Maurice Taylor.

Bishop Taylor, for his part, was evidently not happy with the Roman judgment. When his term as chairman of the ICEL episcopal board expired in August 2002, after several years of evidently quite reluctant activity on his part related to carrying out the Congregation-mandated ICEL reorganization, the Scottish bishop issued as what he called "a duty of conscience" a statement strongly defending the work of ICEL prior to the Roman interventions we have been describing. "Many good people connected with ICEL have suffered during this time of transition," Bishop Taylor wrote; he went on as follows:

> The members of ICEL's episcopal board have in effect been judged to be irresponsible in the liturgical texts that they have approved over the years. The bishops of the English-speaking conferences, voting by large majorities to approve the vernacular liturgical texts approved by ICEL, have been similarly judged. And the labors of all those faithful and dedicated priests, religious and lay people who over the years devoted many hours of their lives to the work of ICEL have been called into question.

Well, yes! The ICEL mode of operating did reflect negatively both on the organization's staff and on its episcopal board, as well as on the bishops of the English-speaking conferences generally, who went on approving deficient ICEL translations year after year. Bishop Taylor nevertheless denied that ICEL was "a recalcitrant group of people, uncooperative, even disobedient." This was "mistaken and untrue," he said. He went on to single out for praise some of the past key figures in ICEL, such as former ICEL executive secretary, John R. Page, Cincinnati Archbishop Daniel Pilarczyk, and the retired South African prelate, Archbishop Denis Hurley, O.M.I., who, prior to Archbishop Pilarczyk, had long served as the ICEL episcopal board chairman. (Archbishop Hurley died in February, 2004, at age 88, and liberal commentators deplored how he had been neglected in his last years. He had been the youngest bishop in the world when he was appointed in 1947 at the age of 31, and he had been very active at and after Vatican II. The fact remained, though, that he was also one of the few Catholic bishops anywhere in the world to dissent publicly from Pope Paul VI's encyclical *Humanae Vitae*, and this may have had something to do with his relative eclipse in later years.)

We can surely grant that Bishop Taylor's task following his receipt of the 1999 letter from Cardinal Medina can scarcely have been a pleasant one for him; it is equally to be regretted that the ICEL staff "suffered," as he contended, as a result of the Roman judgment. The record nevertheless shows a long-standing and consistent pattern of ICEL's by-passing of Church authority while operating according to its own lights in an area, the liturgy, which *Sacrosanctum Concilium* plainly says "depends solely on the authority of the Church" (SC 22).

This tendentious pattern persisted in the face of repeated Roman requests and admonitions. Since the English-speaking bishop-representatives on the ICEL board did not, or could not, set the organization on a better operational path, the Congregation for Divine Worship and the Discipline of the Sacraments ultimately had no choice but to intervene in the way that Cardinal Medina finally did intervene, and Cardinal Arinze very commendably continued to carry on. Bishop Taylor himself retired as bishop of Galloway, Scotland, in the spring of 2004.

In an interview in Rome in March 2005, Chicago Cardinal Francis George, still the American ICEL representative, when asked if all this did not represent "Rome's desire to take control of liturgical translation away from local Churches," replied that it was "more accurate to say that control has been taken away from the experts and given back to the bishops." Cardinal George did not minimize the fact that, as Bishop Taylor had indicated, there were "deep wounds among people, very faithful people, who worked on liturgical issues over the years." Still, the whole process could only be judged in the light of what was hoped would be the success of the new translations when completed.

Chapter Twenty-Four
Resistance to Liturgiam Authenticam

With the adoption of the new Vatican Translation Norms and the issuance of *Liturgiam Authenticam,* what became necessary in the light of the new specifications for liturgical translations was the prospect of a complete new set of translations of all the Church's liturgical books – this time done in accordance with the sound principles and norms laid out in *Liturgiam Authenticam.* Since the reorganization of ICEL, such new translations were now underway with regard to the Roman Missal and other liturgical books. It was likely to take awhile longer to get suitable scriptural texts, of course, given the broad sentiments of the current generation of Scripture scholars in favor of inclusive language. In the long run, however, the principles of *Liturgiam Authenticiam* should ultimately prevail.

In order to help this process along, the document provided for the preparation of a *Ratio Translationis*, a guide or style manual of basic principles for the translation of liturgical texts. The *Vox Clara* Committee consisting as it did mostly of bishops regularly took a particular interest in overseeing the preparation of this guide. The English-speaking conferences of bishops received a preliminary version of this *Ratio Translationis* in 2005 and by the end of 2007 the guide was said to be ready for release "soon."

In addition to the translation principles and norms contained in Chapter Two of *Liturgiam Authenticam*, which come close to reversing those which have been in use up to then, the document clearly bolstered the authority of the Holy See in the regulation of the Church's liturgy generally. Vatican II's *Sacrosanctum Concilium* had already made clear that "regulation of the liturgy depends solely on the authority of the Church, that is, on the Apostolic See" (SC 22 §1). Only subsequently does the very same paragraph of the liturgy Constitution add: "And, as the laws may determine, on the bishop." But *Liturgiam Authenticam* was now one of those "laws" which the bishop too had to abide by.

And *Liturgiam Authenticam* specifies as well that (what was in some ways true all along) a *recognitio* from the Holy See for all translated liturgical texts is necessary before they can be used or published. This rule was made firm and specific because in the United States, for example, some questionable translations, including some featuring inclusive language, had been published for "experimental" or "private" use, without any ecclesiastical permission. That kind of thing had to cease, Rome specified in *Liturgiam Authenticam*. The "practice of seeking the *recognitio* from the Apostolic See for all translations of liturgical books," the Roman document specified, "accords the necessary assurance of the authenticity of the translation and its correspondence with the original texts. This practice both expressed and effected a bond of communion between the successor of Blessed Peter and his brothers in the episcopate" (LA 80).

Furthermore, it was clearly necessary to uphold the principle according to which each particular Church:

> . . . must be in accord with the universal Church not only as regards the doctrine of the faith and the sacramental signs, but also as regards those practices universally received through apostolic and continuous tradition. For these reasons, the required *recognitio* of the Apostolic See is intended to ensure that the translations themselves, as well as any variations introduced into them, will not harm the unity of God's people, but will serve it instead (LA 80).

However, this was probably not the unanimous view of so-called "public opinion" within the Church today. Many of the "usual suspects" among Catholics, long accustomed to benignly tolerated dissidence within the Church, were dismayed and even not a little disoriented by the evidence that the Holy See evidently finally meant business with *Liturgiam Authenticam*. We could quote a number of such critics, but not untypical among them would have to be, again, the self-styled "independent" *National Catholic Reporter*: predictably dissident in the face of almost anything authentically Catholic. The newspaper printed a story by its Rome correspondent about *Liturgiam Authenticam* opining that "critics say that the document strikes at the heart of Vatican II ecclesiology by centralizing power in the Curia and by insisting that local cultures adopt an essentially Roman style of worship."

This same point of view proved to be that of the then chairman of the U.S. Bishops' Committee on the Liturgy (BCL), Bishop Donald Trautman of Erie, Pennsylvania, who declared that the document "points away from the liturgical and biblical renewal of Vatican II. In many aspects, the document is a disappointment."

The ultra-liberal Call to Action organization said even more pointedly that "*Liturgiam Authenticam* is a slap in the face to Catholics worldwide . . . a way the Roman Curia is continuing to clamp down and control the English-speaking world of Catholicism, including the National Conference of Catholic Bishops, which has made strides forward in liturgical, church, and social justice issues."

It was only too predictably typical, of course, that such critics would see fit to go after the Holy See in the name of Vatican II. It was equally typical for them to see the whole thing in terms of "power" (as if "power" were the essence of the authority that was granted to Peter and the other apostles by Christ). In the same issue of NCR in which this negative news report about *Liturgiam Authenticam* appeared, there was also an editorial complaining that "under the guise of fostering a 'sacred style,' Vatican bureaucrats have up-ended the understanding of Vatican II as put into practice by bishops from English-speaking countries...[C]ertain functionaries, in league with the most reactionary elements in local churches, could not tolerate movement toward inclusive language...[This] latest assault on the work of bishops and professional liturgists...illustrates why significant Church leaders have risked their reputations in recent years to call for the decentralization of power" (NCR 5/25/01).

The alleged harm of *Liturgiam Authenticam* was here ascribed to "Vatican bureaucrats," and not specifically to the vigorous and outstanding Chilean Cardinal Medina, who had shepherded the preparation and issuance of the document. When the document was also described as "up-ending" Vatican II, it was as if a clear re-assertion of what Vatican II actually called for liturgically was somehow antithetical to the Council itself! And, of course, it had to be nobody but the "most reactionary elements," surely, and not perhaps those actually responsible within the Holy See itself, that could "not tolerate" inclusive language.

Meanwhile, the whole laudable effort to bring the liturgy back into conformity with the principles of Vatican II could only be seen by the *National Catholic Reporter* as an "assault" on the work of "bishops and professional liturgists." And as for those who had "risked their reputations" in calling for "decentralization," surely they were the very ones who should now have been considered to have *lost* their reputations: they were the ones, after all, who were always calling for the Holy See to back off and "decentralize," as they characterized the whole business, and this at the very moment when the Holy See was almost alone in defending the authentic Catholic tradition.

Dissident publications such as the *National Catholic Reporter,* however, were not the only critics of *Liturgiam Authenticam.* The document got an equally chilly reception, not only from many professional liturgists with a stake in the current liturgical status quo which they had helped develop, but also from some of the bishops who have been prominent members of the current liturgical establishment. BCL Chairman Bishop Donald W. Trautman, again, whom we have already just quoted, was a long-time member of the Bishops' Committee on the Liturgy, and was its chairman between 1993 and 1996. He was also an active, determined partisan for the status quo of the "renewed liturgy" as he understood it – and especially with regard to the use of inclusive language. In an address to the National Association of Pastoral Musicians in July, 2002, Bishop Trautman took it for granted that typical liturgical ministers today, with the advent of *Liturgiam Authenticam*, would be "disillusioned, dejected, and disheartened because of liturgical backsliding." For him, Roman efforts to return the vernacular liturgy to the authentic principles that *Sacrosanctum Concilium* had, in fact, called for represented instead "a new rigidity" and a "reversal" of the "liturgical renewal begun at Vatican II." According to him, *Liturgiam Authenticam* signaled "an orchestrated applying of the brakes to liturgical renewal."

In yet another address to the Federation of Diocesan Liturgical Commissions (FDLC) in October 2003, Bishop Trautman adopted the same "aggrieved victim" stance assumed earlier by ICEL's Bishop Taylor in Scotland. Urging the FDLC members to continue to resist "Vatican interference," as he styled it, he also objected to those who advocated "a reform of the reform" (a formula often employed by the then Cardinal Joseph Ratzinger, for example). Bishop Trautman went on to claim a Vatican II sanction for the earlier liturgical reforms now being corrected. He declared:

> The Holy Spirit was present at Vatican II and gave us new direction. When we encounter people who hearken back to rigidity in rubrics, we must say, "Do not quench the Spirit." When inculturation is denied and one liturgical form is forced on all, we must say, "Do not quench the spirit." When the Scripture translations in our Lectionary are flawed, and not proclaimable, we must say, "Give us the richness of God's Word. Do not quench the Spirit." The

Holy Spirit prompted the renewal and reform of the liturgy. Now,
more than ever, we must say, "Do not quench the Spirit . . . "

Bishop Trautman no doubt honestly and sincerely believed that the
current vernacular liturgy represented a true renewal of the liturgy and an
authentic implementation of what Vatican Council II called for. Again like
Bishop Taylor, he was able to ask, rather querulously: "Are we to tell our
people now that the bishops' approval of these texts some 35 years ago and
Rome's confirmation of that approval was flawed? Has the English-speaking world been praying with inaccurate texts confirmed by the Holy See?"

The answer to both of these questions would seem to be, once again:
"Well, yes"! As we have repeatedly had to observe in these pages, nobody
in the beginning actually knew how to go about reforming the entire liturgy of the Catholic Church, including the changeover to vernacular languages. Nor should it be all that surprising now that not a few mistakes
were made in the course of carrying out such a vast and complicated effort.
But the time was now long past to admit the mistakes that had been made
and to correct them. That even after nearly forty years, Rome should only
in the last several years have finally gotten around to noticing in a serious
way that all had *not* necessarily always been for the best in the carrying out
of the Vatican-II-mandated liturgical reforms, was really a rather amazing
commentary on how organizations sometimes operate in a "time warp"
that bears little relation to what is happening in reality – even, it seems,
holy Church!

One test of a viable organization, though, lies in its ability to recover
from even its worst mistakes and reform itself anew. The Catholic Church
has had to undergo and pass that test many times in the course of her long
history. The history of the last forty years surely provides yet one more
example of the Church once again coming up against but ultimately passing that same kind of test.

A comparison of what *Sacrosanctum Concilium* says with at least
some of what we actually have had out there with the current liturgy clearly suggests that the Congregation for Divine Worship and the Discipline of
the Sacraments *needed* to intervene. This was the case because the bishops' conferences, by themselves, sometimes proved to be very far from
being entirely successful in achieving the Council's aims. A comparison of
what *Liturgiam Authenticam* says with at least some of what has for so long
served as our vernacular liturgy similarly suggests that a Roman intervention was indeed needed in order to get translations more suitable for "the

worship of the divine majesty" (SC 33) than some of those we unfortunately had to live with for so long.

What now seemed very clear and hopeful about all of these more recent developments was that the Holy See, with its *Liturgiam Authenticam*, along with some of the other measures it had increasingly been taking over the previous decade and a half, had finally decisively moved to insure that henceforth the sacred liturgy celebrated in English would finally, at long last, begin to conform to some of the original plans and hopes of the Fathers of Vatican II when they decided upon their comprehensive reform of the Church's entire liturgy.

Furthermore, it is worth noting that the American bishops ultimately more or less began to go along with Rome. They may not always have liked it – quite clearly at least some of them did not always like it – but they were beginning to go along anyway, once Rome made clear that they *had* to go along. Too often in the past Rome did *not* always insist on making this clear. From their own point of view, the American bishops may sometimes have thought that they had cause to resent some of the actions handed down and insisted upon by the various Roman curial dicasteries and offices. This is certainly the attitude conveyed by Bishop Donald Trautman in the remarks of his quoted above. And thus one negative and perhaps even ominous sign amid the generally favorable liturgical developments of the previous several years was the fact that the American bishops, at their annual meeting in November 2004, actually *re-elected* Bishop Trautman to be the chairman of the Bishops' Liturgy Committee! They not only re-elected him to head the BCL; they did so as a result of a nomination from the floor.

This came about because Cardinal Francis George was obliged to relinquish the position of BCL head after having been elected vice president of the USCCB. A number of bishops thereupon decided to place the name of Bishop Trautman in nomination up against the names of the two other candidates being considered, Cardinal Justin Rigali of Philadelphia and Bishop Allen Vigneron of Oakland, California. Bishop Trautman was the winner with 53 percent of the vote of his brother bishops.

It was earnestly to be hoped that the bishops who voted for him, though, did so because of his perceived "expertise" in liturgical matters. It would certainly be a very disturbing development if the American bishops had elected a new head of the BCL *because* he was known to have steadily opposed what he himself characterized as "Roman interference" in the liturgy!

In any event, though, during his tenure as head of the BCL, Bishop Trautman seems to have pretty routinely done his job; and the job in question seems to have consisted largely during the same period in presenting at successive meetings of the bishops' conference further installments of the new liturgical translations being carried out by the reorganized ICEL, after they had been examined and commented on by the BCL. He does not seem to have changed his mind on any of his positions in opposition to *Liturgiam Authenticam* and the other post-Medina changes; but at the same time, the process set in motion by Cardinal Medina seems to have continued more or less intact, and Bishop Trautman appears to have for the most part gone along with it up until the meeting of the bishops in November, 2006, when Bishop Arthur Serratelli of Paterson, New Jersey, who had been creditably serving on the Bishops' Committee on Doctrine, was elected to succeed Bishop Trautman as head of the BCL beginning in November, 2007. Subsequently, too, the bishops' committee in question was renamed the Committee on Divine Worship.

Nevertheless, the fact that a certain amount of Trautman-style sentiment persisted among the American bishops was indicated by the vote of the bishops' conference at their meeting in June, 2008, in Orlando, Florida. On that occasion, the bishops *rejected* a translation by the new, reorganized ICEL of a segment of the new Roman Missal containing propers for Sundays and holy days. This rejection came about when the vote in favor of approving the translation in question failed to receive the two-thirds majority required by USCCB rules. Apparently there was some dissatisfaction with the new style of translation. According to press reports, some of the bishops during the debate in Orlando expressed problems with words such as "gibbet," "wrought," and "ineffable," complaining that these words were no longer common in standard English. "These orations need reworking if we are going to proclaim them without leaving people scratching their heads," Bishop Victor Galeone of St. Augustine, Florida, was quoted as declaring.

In his diocesan newspaper, however, Bishop Arthur Serratelli contended that while the liturgical translations were not "dumbed down to the most common denominator," they remained "readily accessible to anyone." He added that "there is something more at stake than pleasing individual tastes and preferences in the new liturgical translations." Certainly one hoped that the new ICEL would as a matter of principle take into account the legitimate comments and suggestions of the American bishops (unlike the old ICEL which so often simply proceeded on its own); at the same time, however, it was of the greatest importance that the process of going forward in accordance with the standards of *Liturgiam Authenticam* should be continued.

And, in fact, it seemed likely that the translation which failed to garner the required two-thirds majority on this occasion would later be approved with whatever modifications came to be agreed upon. The American bishops have tended to "come around" eventually on liturgical matters where Rome has insisted, even if not always immediately – and even if not always enthusiastically. In this sense, the Church's typical "system" can generally be said to have "worked." In the case of the liturgy, it was the particular curial office ultimately responsible for the conciliar liturgical reforms, namely, the Congregation for Divine Worship and the Discipline of the Sacraments, which eventually did get around to doing its job (even if more than a little tardily!). The end result was that, even if it did not come until some forty years after the Council, the Church seemed finally on the way to getting something like the reformed liturgy that the Council had originally called for.

Meanwhile, the Church also more or less held together in spite of all the confusion and turmoil that followed the Council, particularly in the area of the so-called "liturgical renewal." The great majority of the faithful, meanwhile, had long since accepted the revised liturgy, as Pope John Paul II reminded us; and, at this point, it was likely that most Catholics would probably be disturbed at any further attempts to change the liturgy yet again. It would simply not be wise or right, as the former Cardinal Joseph Ratzinger and future Pope Benedict XVI, among others, pertinently noted in his *Feast of Faith*, "after the upheavals of past years, to press for further external changes."

Chapter Twenty-Five
The End of the Process

With the revitalized leadership provided by Cardinals Medina and Arinze in Rome and by Cardinals George and Pell among the English-speaking bishops, and with the reorganization of ICEL, along with the issuance of such instructions as those contained in *Liturgiam Authenticam* in 2001, as well as of the third edition in Latin of the Roman Missal itself in 2002, it could finally be said that something like what the Fathers of Vatican II had originally envisaged as the reform of the liturgy seemed finally to be possible. On the occasion of the fortieth anniversary of *Sacrosanctum Concilium* in December, 2003, Pope John Paul II issued an Apostolic Letter on the Liturgy, *Spiritus et Sponsa*, as well as a chirograph on sacred music commemorating the one-hundredth anniversary of Pope St. Pius X's *Tra le Sollecitudini*. The election of Pope Benedict XVI in 2005, of course, could only have had the effect of reinforcing these trends, and this proved to be the case.

More than that, as we have already noted, the reorganized ICEL by then had already been hard at work on a new English translation of the *Ordo Missae*, or Order of the Mass. A complete English translation of it was approved by the ICEL episcopal board in January 2004, and, in February of the same year, copies of this revised version of the Mass prayers were sent out for comment to all English-speaking bishops by ICEL chairman, Bishop Arthur Roche (who became ordinary of the Diocese of Leeds, England, in April 2004, having been coadjutor bishop until then). Comments were to be returned for re-consideration by ICEL, after which revised drafts were supposed to be sent back to the various bishops' conferences for their approval. Following approval by the bishops' conferences, the usual *recognitio* by the Congregation for Divine Worship and the Discipline of the Sacraments would eventually be required for such texts.

This was the process that continued to be followed in subsequent years concerning the translations for various segments of the Roman Missal and other texts. From 2004 on, the American bishops pretty extensively discussed and debated Missal translations at nearly every one of their biannual meetings held in June and November of each year. Besides the 2008 session which has just been mentioned above, a particularly extensive discussion of the same type, for example, took place at the bishops' meeting in November 2005, when it became clear that bishops were becoming increasingly active in liturgical matters and were no longer content just to "sign off" on what the "experts" had decided and done. At their meeting in Baltimore in November 2007, again, the bishops reviewed the revised readings from the Lectionary for the Sundays in Lent (they had approved those for Advent the year before).

But the way forward was not always entirely smooth. Considering how intense the opposition has been all along to the liturgical and translation norms Rome was now insisting on, it was probably inevitable that this opposition would resurface from time to time and require firm action. On May 2, 2006, for example, the prefect of the Congregation for Divine Worship and the Discipline of the Sacraments, Cardinal Francis Arinze, found it necessary to send yet another letter to the American bishops. This letter came just prior to the meeting of the bishops in June 2006. Cardinal Arinze wrote, *inter alia*:

> It is not acceptable to maintain that people have become accustomed to a certain translation for the past thirty or forty years, and therefore that it is pastorally advisable to make no changes. Where there are good and strong reasons for a change, as has been determined by this Dicastery in regard to the entire translation of the *Missale Romanum* as well as other important texts, then the revised text should make the needed changes. The attitude of bishops and priests will certainly influence the acceptance of the texts by the lay faithful as well.

So the process continued on, and, on November 1, 2007, the chairman of the International Commission on English in the Liturgy (ICEL), Bishop Arthur Roche of Leeds, England, announced that the draft phase of the process of translating the 2002 Roman Missal from Latin into English had finally been completed. At the same time, he noted that the actual introduction of the new text in each country would be a matter for the bishops' conferences and hence the completed text was not immediately available. Other voices, including the Vox Clara Committee, had meanwhile spoken of the end of 2009 as the probable time of the introduction of the new texts.

At the time of this writing the actual date was not yet known, but the end of 2010 did not seem unlikely.

Nor is it yet possible to say what the final version as a whole will look like, since only parts of it have been generally circulated. The indications are, though, that the new version will be a great improvement over the Mass in English that English-speaking Catholics have been accustomed to throughout the post-conciliar era up to now. Some of the current translation anomalies that have been noted in these pages will hopefully – and most probably – be eliminated: "I believe" ("*Credo*") will replace the "we believe" that has introduced the recitation of the Creed up to now. "And with your spirit" ("*et cum spiritu tuo*") will replace that truly strange expression, "and also with you." And "through my fault" ("*mea culpa*") will again be repeated three times, as in the old Latin *Confiteor.* Generally speaking, greater formality and solemnity will characterize the new translation. It is worth comparing, for example, the 1973 and 2004 versions of the introductory paragraph of Eucharistic Prayer I (the "Roman Canon"):

LATIN

Te igitur, clementissime Pater,
Per Iesum Christum, Filium tuum
Dominum nostrum,
Supplices rogamus ac petimus,
Uti accepta habeas et benedicas +
haec dona, haec munera,
hanc sancta sacrificial illibata . . .

OLD ICEL VERSION

We come to you, Father,
with praise and thanksgiving,
through Jesus Christ your Son.
Though him we ask you to accept and bless +
These gifts we offer you in sacrifice . . .

NEW ICEL VERSION (?)

Most merciful Father,
We therefore humbly pray and implore you
through Jesus Christ, your Son, our Lord,
to accept and bless +

these gifts, these offerings,
these holy and undefiled sacrifices . . .

And so on. This comparison represents only one small sample, but it
seems safe to say that the new version does not avoid formal and sacral language ("merciful," "implore," "holy," "undefiled," etc.), in the way that the
old version did. Where the version long in place has "Deliver us, Lord,
from every evil," the new version has "Deliver us, *we pray*, from every
evil" – thus including a translation of the Latin *quaesumus* which the original ICEL translators assiduously avoided. Many more examples of the
same kind could no doubt be cited. The secretary of the U.S. bishops'
Committee on the Liturgy at the time, Monsignor James P. Moroney, was
quoted in the press as saying that "we will need to grow into these texts,"
but what is likely is that Monsignor Moroney has exaggerated the degree
to which American Catholics have ever been wedded to the current ICEL
version now slated to be replaced. It would be more accurate to say that we
have had to take what we were given all along and get used to it. On the
whole, though, I think that American Catholics are going to prefer the new
version once the initial shock reaction to *any* change in an accustomed
liturgy has been gotten over.

Accuracy in translation is also a notable factor in the new version, as
required by *Liturgiam Authenticam*. For example, the familiar response,
"Dying you destroyed our death, rising you restored our life, Lord Jesus,
come in glory," is really a rather plain *mis*-translation of the Latin,
"*Mortem tuam annuntiamus, Domine, et tuam resurrectionem confitemur,
donec venias.*" The new version renders this more accurately as: "We proclaim your death, O Lord, and profess your resurrection until you come."

Accuracy does not appear to govern in absolutely every case, however. One rather troubling instance is the change of the phrase in the Creed
"for us men and for our salvation" into simply "for *us* and for our salvation," dropping the word "men" ("*homines*"). Does the new team of ICEL
bishops and translators continue to be bewitched by the radical feminists
and their demand for so-called inclusive language, as the old team was?
Perhaps not, even though the usage is employed in this case. This particular point arose during one of the bishops' meetings, in fact, and the motion
to include "men" was *voted down* by a clear majority of the American bishops. *They* are evidently not yet disenthralled from feminist influence! Thus,
the clear requirements of *Liturgiam Authenticam* may not in every single
instance be followed.

On the whole, though, the new translation of the Order of the Mass seems likely to be a huge improvement over the one we have had up to now. After all these years we may finally have a Mass text in English that does justice to the sacred dimensions of our Catholic tradition. One major question that continues to be troubling, though, is why it took the Church so long, traveling by such devious routes, to arrive at a simple, sensible, and straightforward implementation of liturgical reforms that were themselves not unreasonable, at least as they were set forth in *Sacrosanctum Concilium* and in the principal post-conciliar liturgical documents. We have, of course, already in this book discussed or pointed to some of the reasons for what occurred after the reform of the liturgy was undertaken. To describe what happened does not, however, excuse everything that happened, even though it does perhaps help to explain it.

And what happened did undeniably include some unhappy results. Not to labor unduly the expression, but the post-conciliar Mass misunderstandings were in fact massive. It was simply not clear to many of the faithful what was happening to the Church, and, whatever it was, it did not always seem auspicious to many of them. For example, one of the effects of the post-conciliar confusion on the faithful was to prompt some of them to *leave* the Church, sometimes to join Evangelical sects. These latter sects may sometimes have at least had the merit of continuing wholeheartedly to believe in Jesus and in the salvation he announced, unlike the case with some of the liberals, apparently, including a few of those responsible for implementing the Vatican II reforms. Still, the sects to which some confused Catholics repaired remained deplorably far from the fullness of Christ's true faith and authentic Christian practice, as these are found in the Catholic Church.

Then there were those members of the faithful who turned to traditionalist groups adhering to the unreformed pre-Vatican-II Latin Tridentine Mass as the supposed single hallmark of authentic Catholicism. We have already reviewed in some detail how Pope Benedict XVI's *Summorum Pontificum* in 2007 represented a late attempt – perhaps too late? – to deal with *them*. That Benedict believed he had to allow for such a significant departure from what the Council had decreed surely itself pointed to this result as yet another one of the Mass misunderstandings that followed upon the liturgical reforms. Benedict was surely correct in believing that the Church had a strict obligation to try to reconcile those who had not been reconciled to the reforms called for by the Council. Even though the Tridentine Mass is unlikely ever to be anything but the "extraordinary" form the pope has now designated it to be, it was nevertheless important and indeed necessary that those who prefer this form not be neglected or left out simply in order to achieve liturgical uniformity. Benedict was quite correct in his belief that liturgical pluralism should be one of the marks of the true Church of Christ. While the Council Fathers certainly never imagined any such outcome as the one that came about, still the forty plus years since the Council have certainly made us only too well aware of what it was and what it entailed.

In addition to such unintended and unhappy consequences as the traditionalist disaffection and the Lefebvrist schism, though, there have also been, undeniably, not a few positive benefits as well for the Church that have stemmed from the liturgical reform. We cannot forget these benefits just because *some* of the other results of the reform have not been happy. Now, however, in the final part of this book, we need to take a brief look at the unfortunate traditionalist schism that, tragically, did develop out of the conciliar reforms. We also need to look (even more briefly) at a recent misguided high-level effort to revive and perhaps carry on with the kind of "creative" liturgy that caused so much trouble in the first place in the post-conciliar era and should by now long since have been discredited in view of all that has happened.

In August, 2008, the U.S. Bishops' Committee on Divine Worship announced the opening of a Missal Information website where interested people can find and read the new English translations of liturgical texts as they are completed and approved. The link to this Missal Information website is: http://www.usccb.org/liturgy/missalformation/index.shtml.

On December 9, 2008, Cardinal Antonio Cañizares Llovera of Toledo, Spain, was appointed prefect of the Congregation for Divine Worship and the Discipline of the Sacraments, replacing Cardinal Francis Arinze. Cardinal Cañizares had been archbishop of Toledo since 2002, and was named a cardinal in 2006. For many years he taught at the University of Salamanca.

PART THREE

THE REFORM STANDS IN SPITE OF
THE UNINTENDED CONSEQUENCES

Chapter Twenty-Six
The Traditionalist Schism

The only real schism that resulted from Vatican Council II has been the movement identified with the late French Archbishop Marcel Lefebvre and his followers. Among other things, the Lefebvrites wished to retain the Latin Tridentine Mass, and their movement, like that of some other traditionalists holding out for the retention or return of the Tridentine Mass, has often been characterized as having been caused mostly or solely by objections to the Vatican II liturgical reforms. Actually, though, this kind of traditionalism, as it has manifested itself in the post-conciliar years – and not only in the case of the Lefebvre Schism alone – really had somewhat different and deeper causes, most of them doubts about the validity of the Second Vatican Council itself and about some of its acts and decisions, in particular, Vatican II's Declaration on Religious Liberty, *Dignitatis Humanae*, and its Pastoral Constitution on the Church in the Modern World, *Gaudium et Spes*.

But since the Lefebvre Schism has been so prominently identified in the public mind with the rejection of the New Order of the Mass, we must look at it here, even though the true roots of the Lefebvre Schism, like the rejection of the new Mass by some other traditionalists, really do extend far beyond the questions of the Latin Tridentine Mass and Vatican II's reform of the liturgy. They sometimes extend, in fact, to doubting whether the Second Vatican Council was even a valid general council of the Catholic Church – and, in the minds of some traditionalists, they even extend to the further question of whether the "conciliar popes" elected just before, during, or following the Council, John XXIII, Paul VI, John Paul I, and John Paul II, were even "true popes." Since he was elected on the same basis as these immediate predecessors of his, these doubts can apply equally to Pope Benedict XVI in the minds of some traditionalists.

On these questions, however, there can perforce not be two points of view: either these men are true, validly elected successors of the apostle Peter, and the Second Vatican Council too is valid in the same way as the twenty ecumenical councils of the Church which preceded it, *or* the claims of the Catholic Church herself cannot be allowed to stand. The Church herself has validated these popes and this Council with the authority she has from Christ; and so if she is wrong about these things, then she can be wrong about anything that she holds and teaches, and hence cannot really be the Church that she has always claimed to be.

Meanwhile, though, there still remains the burning question for some of the "validity" – or at the very least, the desirability – of the New Order of the Mass, the post-Vatican-II rite promulgated by Pope Paul VI with his *Missale Romanum* on March 26, 1970, and in general use in the Church since then. The rejection of this new Mass has figured prominently and insistently, not only in the revolt of Archbishop Lefebvre and his followers, but also in the actions of some other "traditionalists" who, although they are not necessarily formally connected with the Lefebvrites, have also rejected the New Order of the Mass.

Thus, in this and in the next chapter, we must briefly describe both the Lefebvre schism and the phenomenon of rigid traditionalism in the postconciliar era generally. Both *seem,* at any rate, to have been fueled by the decision of Vatican II to reform the traditional liturgy of the Church, although the ultimate causes of both are more complex, as we have noted, and as Pope Benedict XVI himself also indicated in *Summorum Pontificum.*

Historically speaking, many general councils of the Church were followed by schisms – breaks or ruptures in the Body of Christ sometimes brought about by decisions of the councils which some within the Church disagreed with at the time. In the case of the ancient Church councils, for example, after the Council of Ephesus in 431 A.D., the communion today known as the Assyrian Church of the East (formerly, "the Nestorian Church"), did not accept the decisions of the Council, which prominently included the question of whether the Blessed Virgin Mary was "the mother of God," or merely "the mother of Christ." As a result of this disagreement, communion with the Catholic Church was broken.

Following the Council of Chalcedon in 451 A.D. – which among its acts prominently defined that Jesus Christ was both true God and true man – there was yet another splitting away from universal Church unity on the part of those communions identified thereafter in history with "Monophysitism," or the view that Christ had only one nature, not two (a divine as well as a human nature), as the Council of Chalcedon had taught and insisted. These schismatic communions included the Armenian

Apostolic Church, as well as the Coptic, Ethiopian, and Malankara Jacobite and Orthodox Syrian Churches, all of which are still to be found today among the Ancient Churches of the East. Post-Vatican-II ecumenical discussions and dialogues have now established, however, that these historical "Monophysite" communions, like the "Nestorian" Assyrian Church of the East mentioned immediately above, are perhaps not as far from strict Catholic orthodoxy as was once believed. Some agreed statements on belief have now been concluded between them and the Catholic Church, and there is even some hope today that eventual reunion with the Catholic Church could prove to be easier, and perhaps could come about sooner, than once was commonly thought.

The split between the Catholic Church, with more than a billion adherents, and the fifteen autonomous Eastern Orthodox Churches consisting of a membership of more than 300 million adherents in all – a split which is conventionally dated from the mutual excommunications of the year 1054 – involved a number of complex issues, including especially the claims of the papacy, which were eventually rejected in the East. Today both the Eastern and Western Churches continue to agree on most doctrinal questions as well as on the seven sacraments instituted by Christ, but the schism between them nevertheless persists in spite of the mutual expressions of great good will and the various efforts that have been manifested between East and West since Vatican Council II.

In more recent times, and in addition to the major disagreements that arose out of the Protestant Reformation and continue to persist today, the solemn definitions of the First Vatican Council in 1870 especially continue to be strongly questioned by many non-Catholic Christians. These definitions concerned the pope's universal primacy over the whole Church, as well as his doctrinal infallibility when formally defining a teaching on faith and morals while speaking as pastor and teacher of all Christians. These definitions have not only constituted a huge obstacle to any possible reunion with either the Protestants or the Eastern Orthodox Churches; they also produced a schism among some Catholics in Germany who believed that Vatican I had gone too far in defining the nature and scope of the pope's authority in such precise and concrete, and, they thought, highly questionable, terms. In particular, the notable German historian J. Ignace von Döllinger led a number of his followers into the schismatic Old Catholic Church as a result of their opposition to Vatican I's definitions concerning the pope's primacy and infallibility. This was the major schism that arose out of Vatican I.

As for Vatican II, however, the single, formal schism that has come about to date is, as we have noted, the one that became effective on June 30, 1988, when French Archbishop Marcel Lefebvre illicitly ordained four bishops in Écône, Switzerland, in open defiance of an express prohibition and warning from the Holy See. As a result, both the archbishop and the four bishops he ordained were immediately and automatically excommunicated. As the Vatican press office declared at the time:

> According to Canon 1013, the consecration of bishops on June 30 by Monsignor Lefebvre, in spite of the admonition on June 17, has been carried out explicitly against the pope's will; this is a formally schismatic act according to Canon 751, inasmuch as he openly refused submission to the Holy Father and communion with the members of the Church under his jurisdiction.

Occurring as it did nearly a quarter of a century after the end of the Council in 1965, this formalization of the Lefebvre Schism had actually been a long time in coming, and the Holy See had diligently tried to head it off. That it was inevitably going to come, however, had been pretty evident for quite awhile to most knowledgeable observers, in spite of extraordinary efforts exerted by the Holy See to try to avert it. The root causes of the schism went back to Archbishop Lefebvre's participation at the Council, which he attended as superior general of the Holy Ghost Fathers, a position to which he had been elected in 1962. Prior to that, he had for many years been a missionary priest and bishop in Africa, where he had eventually become the archbishop of Dakar.

At the Council, Archbishop Lefebvre became part of a conservative bloc called the *Coetus Internationalis Patrum*, or International Group of Fathers, which generally tried to modify and even counter some of the initiatives of the generally dominant liberal bloc of bishops from northern Europe known as the European Alliance. Among the trends opposed by this International Group of Fathers were the pronounced conciliar thrusts in favor of religious liberty and ecumenism and towards greater "collegiality" (or cooperation) among the bishops and with the pope. Vatican II ended up strongly emphasizing all three of these subjects in the various documents it issued.

In the eyes of Archbishop Lefebvre, however, religious liberty, ecumenism, and collegiality all represented distinct *errors* as far as the Church was concerned; he equated them with the "liberty, equality, and fraternity" of the French Revolution, which, of course, had so strongly rejected

Christianity and persecuted the Church. That the French Revolution could in any way ever have been an inspiration for the acts of a general council of the Catholic Church was unthinkable for a traditionally-minded French Catholic such as Archbishop Lefebvre. In actual fact, of course, the Council's understanding of ecumenism, religious liberty, and collegiality were *not* equivalent to the French revolutionary ideals of liberty, equality, and fraternity; but if Archbishop Lefebvre nevertheless somehow thought they were, it was easy to see how he could have concluded that the Council had gone astray

Later, Archbishop Lefebvre even declared explicitly that "Vatican II is the 1789 in the Church." He belonged to a strong anti-revolutionary tradition among Catholics in France, whose ancestors had been royalist as well as Catholic, and had suffered exile, loss of property, and even death at the hands of the French Revolution. To equate Vatican II with 1789 was to condemn the Council unreservedly and out of hand. The French Revolution was quite generally understood to have been militantly anti-religious and anti-Catholic.

Another effort identified with the International Group of Fathers at Vatican II to which Archbishop Lefebvre belonged was to try to secure a strong statement by the Council against Communism. In this the International Group did not succeed, at least to the satisfaction of its members, who had to be satisfied with the strong sections on atheism in the Council's Pastoral Constitution on the Church in the Modern World, *Gaudium et Spes* (GS 19–21). Blessed Pope John XXIII had made clear when he convoked the Council that it would not be issuing condemnations or anathemas, and this papal stricture was apparently supposed to apply even to Communism, or at least a fair number of the Council Fathers seemed to believe that this was the case. However that may be, the Council did *not* condemn Communism directly and by name.

The failure to get more conservative and traditional ideas and *schemas* approved by the Council no doubt contributed to Archbishop Lefebvre's growing disillusionment with the whole conciliar process. Later on, he would typically denounce what he soon came to call "conciliar Rome."

Although he took part in the conciliar process throughout the entire Council, and even ended up signing fourteen of the sixteen Vatican II documents – including the Constitution on the Sacred Liturgy! – Archbishop Lefebvre's growing disenchantment with the Council was reflected in his eventual refusal to sign either Vatican II's Pastoral Constitution on the Church, *Gaudium et Spes,* or, especially, the Council's Declaration on

Religious Liberty, *Dignitatis Humanae*. At some point in the conciliar or immediate post-conciliar years, he evidently decided with finality to set his face firmly against the Council and all its works. Henceforth he acted as if it were Marcel Lefebvre's mission in life to save the Catholic Church from the damage being self-inflicted upon her, as he saw it, as a result of Vatican II.

In 1968, Archbishp Lefebvre had a falling out with the religious order to which he belonged, the Holy Ghost Fathers, which he had continued to head up to that point. His falling out with the order came at a meeting concerned with the implementation of the Council. After walking out of that meeting, the archbishop then effectively left the order. A little later, he went to Écône, Switzerland, where, in 1969, he founded the Society of St. Pius X (SSPX) and opened a seminary to train priests in what he and his followers would come to claim was the true "Catholic tradition," sans Vatican II. This true Catholic tradition, according to him, had been betrayed by the Council. "This is an operation of survival for tradition," Archbishop Lefebvre would later say about his own efforts, at the time of his illicit ordination of the four bishops. "They are in the process of destroying the Church...It is to show our attachment to the Rome of forever that we perform this ceremony . . . We will be thanked one day by the bishops of Rome for having maintained the traditions of the Church."

The "Catholic tradition," in the view of Archbishop Lefebvre and the SSPX, quite naturally included the Mass and other rites as they had been celebrated in the Church prior to the Vatican II liturgical reforms. Archbishop Lefebvre and the SSPX thus came to be primarily identified in the public mind with their adherence to the Latin Tridentine Mass, although their revolt against the Church quite obviously extended far beyond liturgical matters, as we have noted.

The Lefebvrites were not the only ones who insisted upon retaining the Latin Tridentine Mass. Other groups of Catholics reacting adversely to the post-conciliar changes here and there broke away from obedience to the hierarchical Church and continued to celebrate "motel Masses" or other independent Masses in separate churches or chapels, for which they often hired, Protestant-Congregation-style, their own "loyalist" priests. In one notorious case, a so-called St. Athanasius Chapel in Virginia long employed the services of a "traditionalist priest" who turned out never to have been ordained at all; he was only masquerading as a priest.

The Catholic Traditionalist Movement (CTM) in New York was another organization which very early in the game began offering Tridentine

Masses, including a popular broadcast Mass presented on radio and TV. The CTM has actually continued down to the present day offering this broadcast Mass. Yet other groups, in various places, some of them ephemeral, also defiantly held out against the "tyranny" of Vatican II and its changes. Still at the present day there are even groups of so-called *"sedevacantists,"* – those who hold that there has been no valid pope since the death of Pope Pius XII. For these people the See of Peter has been "vacant" since then, the popes subsequently elected having "betrayed the Catholic tradition" by their acceptance of the Second Vatican Council as valid.

From time to time, other traditionalist organizations even now still emerge here and there to announce that they, and not the hierarchical Church, represent the true "Catholic tradition." In particular, a number of mostly polemical traditionalist publications such as *The Remnant* or the *Catholic Family News* have continued to appear, and, it seems, even to flourish to some extent, at least in some quarters. And occasionally yet another often ephemeral new traditionalist publication is launched and offered to the Catholic people. Accurate numbers of how many Catholics belong to these splinter groups and are thus formally separated from the Church and attending illicit Tridentine Masses, however, are hard to come by. Probably a larger number reads some of their publications, hoping against hope for a roll-back of the Vatican II reforms, while remaining in communion with the Catholic Church and attending the only Masses that are approved by the local bishop.

One notable case of a traditionalist group that rivaled the Lefebvrite schism was that of Bishop Antonio de Castro Mayer of Campos, Brazil. An ally of Archbishop Lefebvre's during the Council, Bishop de Castro Mayer spoke out there against the evils being brought about by the modern media, against religious liberty, and against the vernacular Mass. He was among those in favor of condemning Communism by name; and, in one intervention, he deplored the absence of any reference, in the *schema* that became *Gaudium et Spes*, to the Devil – "who nevertheless exists," the Brazilian bishop declared. (In the event, a reference to "the powers of evil" was added to the final version of *Gaudium et Spes* (GS 37), along with a footnote referring to one of the Gospel passages where Christ himself affirms the existence of the Devil – so the Devil was not entirely ignored by the Council in the end! Similarly, both *Lumen Gentium* 16 and *Ad Gentes* 9 make reference to, and hence assume the existence of, the Devil).

Following the Council, in 1969, Bishop de Castro Mayer refused to implement the liturgical reforms called for by *Sacrosanctum Concilium*. In his diocese, the Tridentine Mass continued to be celebrated – actually, it only generally began to be called "Tridentine" when it turned out that it was continuing to be celebrated in some places, even though the Roman Missal had meanwhile been revised and was henceforth the standard Mass of the Roman rite. Although not formally affiliated with Archbishop Lefebvre's movement, Bishop de Castro Mayer regularly supported the latter; and, meanwhile, he himself managed to maintain his own "traditionalist" diocese in the face of steady pressures from Rome. This situation obtained for well over a decade. His resistance endured until he was finally forced into retirement in 1981. In that year, his successor at long last instituted the New Order of the Mass in Campos.

Nevertheless, considerable numbers of Catholics still remained loyal to the outgoing bishop, and Tridentine Masses were then organized quite widely outside the actual churches of the diocese themselves. When Bishop de Castro Mayer died in 1991, the four SSPX bishops ordained by Archbishop Lefebvre at Ecône in 1988 duly, though illicitly, ordained a "successor" to him. Later still, and somewhat surprisingly, as we shall presently see, a reconciliation was actually effected by the Holy See with the numerous traditionalists in Campos, and a bishop was appointed by Rome to lead them.

Thus, Archbishop Lefebvre and his Society of St. Pius X were never the only schismatic traditionalists in the field. Nevertheless, the SSPX continued to be both the most representative of the traditionalist (Tridentinist) movement, as well as very probably commanding the greatest numbers. Since he was steadily training priests at his seminary at Ecône, Switzerland, Archbishop Lefebvre was also able to send his graduates out to staff "parishes" in a number of countries. This remains the case today, even after the archbishop's own death. By the time the schism became formalized in 1988, the archbishop had ordained more than 200 priests, and he claimed to have organized followers in over 25 countries. Accurate numbers were, again, hard to come by, with Lefebvrite sympathizers sometimes claiming as many as a million followers worldwide. Meanwhile, the Vatican estimated the numbers involved in the schism to be somewhere less. Such is the broad brush background of the single formal schism that issued from Vatican Council II.

Chapter Twenty-Seven
The Holy See Fails to Reconcile the Schismatics but the Door Remains Open

It was an initial illicit ordination of priests by Archbishop Marcel Lefebvre that first got him into formal and serious trouble with the Holy See and eventually brought about his suspension *a divinis* in 1976. In the beginning, the seminary he founded at Écône was actually approved ecclesiastically. Only after the archbishop began his harsh public denunciations of what he saw as the errors of the Council did Church authorities begin to have second thoughts about what was going on at Écône. As a result of Archbishop Lefebvre's illicitly ordaining thirteen priests in July 1976, Pope Paul VI was finally obliged to suspend him officially from exercising his priestly and episcopal ministries. In the case of these priestly ordinations, the archbishop had acted in defiance of a formal warning from the pope – indeed, an anguished personal plea from Paul VI – not to carry out the illicit ordinations.

Later, in September 1976, a meeting to try to heal the breech was arranged between the archbishop and Paul VI himself (who, earlier, had declined to meet with the disobedient prelate in person). Nothing came of this meeting, however; everything broke down over the archbishop's refusal to accept the Second Vatican Council. In the archbishop's view, it was the "conciliar Church" that was "disobedient" and "in schism." For him, the principles of the French Revolution had successfully entered into, and had undermined, the historic Catholic Church. According to him, "the new Mass expresses a new faith which is not Catholic." He employed even stronger language on occasion, characterizing the new Mass as a "bastard rite" and the Church's new sacramental rites as "bastard sacraments...[and] the priests coming from the seminaries are bastard priests..."

Archbishop Lefebvre, in other words, was no moderate either in his sentiments or in his language, and he frequently resorted to rhetoric that was quite recognizably extremist in tone. To verify this, we need only sample a few lines of his from a document that he called his "profession of faith," as follows:

> We adhere with all our heart and all our soul to Catholic Rome, guardian of the Catholic faith and of the traditions necessary to the maintenance of that faith – to eternal Rome, mistress of wisdom and truth.
>
> By contrast we refuse . . . to follow the Rome of neo-Modernist and neo-Protestant tendencies that manifested itself so clearly in Vatican Council II and after the Council in all of the reforms which issued from it. All these reforms, in effect, have contributed and continue to contribute to the demolition of the Church, the ruin of the priesthood, the annihilation of the sacrifice and of the sacraments, the disappearance of the religious life, and a naturalistic and Teilhardian teaching in the universities and seminaries and in catechesis – a teaching issuing from liberalism and Protestantism many times condemned by the solemn magisterium of the Church.

Not much could be added to that! This was no simple misunderstanding. It was hard to see how Archbishop Lefebvre could be reconciled to the Church short of renunciation by the latter of the decisions of Vatican Council II. This situation remained unchanged up to the end of the pontificate of Pope Paul VI.

After the election of Pope John Paul II in 1979, negotiations were resumed between the archbishop and the Holy See. From the beginning of his pontificate, the new pope was most anxious to find a way to reconcile the Lefebvrites to the Church. At first sight, one might have thought that he would be more successful in this than Paul VI had been, since the latter was himself generally perceived in traditionalist circles as a Vatican II "liberal pope," while John Paul II was considered to be much more "conservative," at least at the beginning of his pontificate. Certainly John Paul was a somewhat stricter disciplinarian than his predecessor (e.g., in no longer allowing virtually automatic laicization of priests). Moreover, it was not very long after his election that the Polish pope began to be attacked by *liberal* Catholic writers – on the grounds that he was much too "traditional" and "restorationist," and wished to "roll back" the Council and "restore" the pre-Vatican-II scheme of things.

This was not true; of course, nor did the traditionalists really tend to credit it or see him in that light. The fact of the matter was that John Paul II came under attack from the liberal side mostly because he wanted the Council's decisions as contained in the conciliar documents applied more faithfully, whereas the liberals saw everything more in terms of what they considered "the spirit of Vatican II."

The traditionalists, however, never considered John Paul II to be anything but a Vatican II "liberal bishop" himself. In this they were basically correct. At the Council, along with the Polish bishops, Archbishop Karol Wojtyla, among other things, took a prominent part in promoting the very *schemas* on religious liberty and the Church in the modern world to which the traditionalists objected so strongly, and still continue to object. And quite apart from that, moreover, the traditionalists strenuously opposed many of the Polish pope's initiatives over the years. Archbishop Lefebvre himself, for example, severely condemned John Paul II's initial interreligious World Day of Prayer for Peace, held at Assisi on October 27, 1986, to which dozens of leaders of various religions were invited to come to the birthplace of St. Francis to pray for peace together. Pope John Paul II may well have been sincerely focused merely on praying for peace, but the traditionalists tended to see his initiative in this regard as a scandalous and even disgraceful departure from the Catholic tradition. Subsequently, this interreligious Prayer for Peace event at Assisi was nevertheless to become a recurring affair under John Paul II (though it was significantly modified by Benedict XVI.)

Archbishop Lefebvre, for his part, branded the whole very widely publicized affair as a "public blasphemy" – although prayers for peace in common with other "men of good will" surely in no way compromise the integrity of Catholic worship as such; nor do they change any Catholic teaching or doctrine in the slightest; nor do they alter the Church's continuing claim, reiterated and reinforced by the Council and by the popes, to possess the fullness of the revelation of Jesus Christ, and also to possess all of the means of sanctification and salvation that were especially present in the seven sacraments that Christ instituted in the Church which he himself founded, according to the Catholic Church's own account of herself. Be that as it may, however, the traditionalists nevertheless believed and believe that such irenical and ecumenical interreligious gestures as the prayers in common at Assisi *do* water down the faith, and *do* compromise and betray the Church's teaching and mission, as they understand it.

The traditionalists were no less severe concerning some other actions of the same kind in the Church. They opposed, for example, among yet other things, John Paul II's emphasis on ecumenism generally in his pontificate. The pontiff himself, of course, saw himself as simply carrying out the mandate of Vatican II – and, indeed, of the Gospels! Nevertheless, the traditionalists quite regularly derided in particular such things as the pope's visits to synagogues and mosques and to Muslim countries and to Jerusalem, his prayers at the Wailing Wall, his many common declarations and joint statements with leaders of separated Christian bodies, and his various "apologies" for the past sins and shortcomings of Catholics.

Nevertheless, even though the traditionalists never did think much of John Paul II, nor of his approach to various contemporary issues, the Polish pope regularly sought reconciliation with *them*. He sought this at least as vigorously as he ever cultivated relations with any other "separated brethren." No doubt the pope thought of the traditionalists *as* tragically "separated brethren" themselves, even though they were obviously of more recent vintage than the Protestants or the Eastern Orthodox. It was four years before the final break with the Lefebvrites, in 1984, that John Paul II had directed the Congregation for Divine Worship to issue his *Quattuor Abhinc Annos*. This document authorized bishops to allow the celebration of Masses using the old Roman Missal, which the faithful preferring the Tridentine Mass could then attend as special "indult" Masses. We have already had occasion to look at *Quattor Abhinc Annos* and the "indult" Masses it authorized earlier in this book, and therefore we need not detain ourselves further on these topics here.

Archbishop Lefebvre and the SSPX, however, would have nothing to do with the proffered indult Masses. To have accepted them would have been a good deal less than a half loaf for them; it would have meant abandoning the whole SSPX position, in fact, which holds the Vatican II liturgical reforms to be invalid because the Council itself was questionably invalid. The Society was thus unwilling to consider changing its stance. And many other traditionalists continued to follow the lead of the SSPX in the matter.

The Holy See nevertheless continued its efforts to effect a reconciliation, in spite of the repeated rebuffs of the SSPX. Various discussions took place from time to time between the SSPX and Roman emissaries or go-betweens, but they came to nothing. Faced with the threat that the archbishop would probably soon be ordaining a bishop to succeed him, however – he was 82 years old in 1988, not getting any younger, and his movement could hardly continue without a bishop to ordain its priests – John Paul II urged the Congregation for the Doctrine of the Faith to try harder. In October 1987, the Congregation announced the appointment of an apostolic visitor, the late "conservative" Canadian Cardinal Edouard Gagnon, to examine the status of the SSPX. Cardinal Gagnon was probably as trusted by the SSPXers as any official from the current Roman Curia could possibly be, and while his efforts did not ultimately result in any reconciliation, he probably helped make the continuing conversations easier.

Eventually the Congregation for the Doctrine of the Faith thought that a tentative agreement had been reached. It was set forth in a protocol dated May 5, 1988, signed by both Archbishop Lefebvre and Cardinal Joseph Ratzinger, in accordance with which the Holy See would recognize the Society of St. Pius X and allow the archbishop to nominate one of his followers to be ordained a bishop as his successor, subject to Roman approval. In return, the validity of Vatican II and its teachings would have to be accepted by the SSPX. Archbishop Lefebvre himself actually stated publicly at one point that he had reached agreement with the Vatican on this.

But this tentative agreement nevertheless broke down. The SSPX people claimed that it broke down because "liberal bishops" continued to complain that too many concessions were being made by the pope. It was more likely, however, as some Roman officials told the press, that Archbishop Lefebvre's followers had persuaded him that it would be wrong after all that had happened for him to come to terms with Vatican II. Although nearing death, he no doubt wished to see the whole question settled with Rome. Still, probably little persuasion was required as far as him ever accepting Vatican II was concerned. Rejection of the Council, after all, had been the principal motive for nearly all of his activities from the time he left the Holy Ghost Fathers and founded his seminary at Écône.

However that may be, Archbishop Lefebvre did finally end up rejecting the tentative agreement that was thought to have been reached in May 1988. Instead, a month later, at the end of June 1988, he proceeded to ordain four new bishops, thereby incurring excommunication both for himself and for them, as we have recorded earlier. How seriously Rome regarded the whole matter can be gauged by the fact that excommunication finally did have to be resorted to. Excommunications had become extremely rare in the post-conciliar Church, and were almost never employed except in the case of sacramental (not doctrinal) cases. In the Lefebvre case, the Holy See had at one time or another tried to stretch or bend or delay almost every one of its own rules. Unlike those American bishops who decided that kneeling or genuflecting before receiving Communion was "disobedient" once the norm of standing to receive had been officially established, John Paul II proved perhaps even too ready to allow worship according to the Tridentine mode even though what Benedict XVI would eventually style the "ordinary" mode had long since been put in place following the Council.

For John Paul II it was apparently enough if the traditionalists would simply state that they "accepted" Vatican II. He had showed himself quite willing to accommodate those who wished to worship according to the Tridentine mode, provided only that they would publicly agree that the Council and its revised mode of worship were also valid. Illicit ordinations of new bishops, however, proved to be something else again; such ordinations were too much even for this pope. Anxious as he was for a reconciliation with the traditionalists, he was nevertheless acutely conscious that Archbishop Lefebvre's act was clearly illegal and represented a conscious, defiant setting aside and rejection of his, the pope's, authority.

Authority is the power to command; it requires obedience on the part of those subject to it; and defiance or rejection of it amounts to a practical denial of it. There was no other way an act such as Archbishop Lefebvre's illicit ordinations of four schismatic bishops could be handled except to let the Church's automatic provision of excommunication in such a case proceed against all those involved.

Following the excommunications, Pope John Paul II proceeded almost immediately – only two days later, as a matter of fact – to issue his apostolic letter *Ecclesia Dei*, dated July 2, 1988, in which he established the special Commission, to be headed by a cardinal, in order to try to salvage what could be salvaged out of the now accomplished Lefebvre schism. The German Cardinal Paul Augustin Mayer, known to have strongly "traditionalist" sympathies, was named the first head of this *Ecclesia Dei* Commission. We have already, of course, discussed this Commission in some detail earlier in these pages; it was later to become an integral part of the arrangements put in place by Pope Benedict XVI's *Summorum Pontificum* in July 2007.

At the time, though, two specific tasks were assigned to the *Ecclesia Dei* Commission: the first one was that the Commission was to make every effort to reconcile to the Church those among Archbishop Lefebvre's followers (and any other willing traditionalists) who might not wish to follow the archbishop into formal schism, but rather, who desired "to remain united with the successor of Peter in the Catholic Church, while preserving their spiritual and liturgical traditions." By this was meant that Rome was still willing to recognize traditionalist groups and allow them to continue to celebrate the Tridentine Mass, provided only that they would also accept the validity of the Second Vatican Council and of the new Mass.

This provision of *Ecclesia Dei* soon bore immediate fruit. It turned out that no small number of priests was willing to defect from the ranks of the SSPX. It was one thing to be a strict traditionalist while Archbishop Lefebvre himself still remained un-excommunicated, and, indeed, was still actively engaged in negotiating with the Holy See as more or less an "equal." It was something else again once the archbishop had been formally excommunicated and thereby officially declared to be in schism. A fair number of Tridentinist priests very soon decided they did not want to follow the Lefebvrites into actual schism, and they therefore indicated their willingness to become reconciled with the Church.

Within two months after the excommunication of Archbishop Lefebvre, for example, the monks at the Benedictine Abbey in Barrous, France, agreed to a return to doctrinal and disciplinary loyalty to the Church (while being allowed to continue celebrating the Tridentine Mass). More importantly, a new order of priests, the Priestly Fraternity of St. Peter (FSSP) was formed with its own religious superior and a membership of ex-Lefebvrite priests unwilling to follow their former leader into formal schism. The FSSP's ranks would shortly be augmented by the ordination of new priests attached to the Latin Tridentine Mass, but desirous of remaining in communion with the Church.

The Holy See's policy of fairly wide latitude in all of this under *Ecclesia Dei* was thus made very clear: the "traditional" Mass and sacraments would be allowed, provided those wishing to have them otherwise recognized the validity of Vatican II, and of the new Order of the Mass, as well as the legitimate authority of the pope and of the bishops.

The second specific task of the *Ecclesia Dei* Commission established by Pope John Paul II in the wake of the Lefebvre Schism was to promote more vigorously the "indult" Tridentine Masses already allowed by the 1984 *Quattuor Abhinc Annos*. We have seen that this effort proved to be only partially successful. Nevertheless, the existence and functioning of the *Eccleia Dei* Commission proved to be a boon when Pope Benedict XVI issued his *motu propio* in 2007 allowing the celebration of the Tridentine Mass on a wider basis.

Pope John Paul II continued to be anxious to accommodate those who wanted the Latin Tridentine Mass as long as they otherwise accepted the authority of the Church and Vatican II. In April 2000, the prefect of the Congregation for the Clergy, the Columbian Cardinal Dario Castrillón Hoyos, was named president of the *Ecclesia Dei* Commission (while continuing to head the clergy Congregation as well) and was given a mandate to try again to heal the Lefebvre Schism. Almost immediately he began negotiations with the SSPX and, in June 2000, he even met personally with Bishop Bernard Fellay, the new superior general of the SSPX, along with the other three bishops who had been ordained by Archbishop Lefebvre. This meeting took place while these four SSPX bishops just happened to be on a "pilgrimage" to Rome (they still profess allegiance to "eternal Rome," although this allegiance does not apparently extend to the pope currently in office!).

Other negotiations between Rome and the SSPX followed over the next year, including additional meetings between Bishop Fellay and Cardinal Castrillón in person. The Roman plan appears to have been to offer the Society the status of an *apostolic administration* without territorial limits, whereby the SSPX – and its bishops, priests, and communicants – would operate pretty much apart from the Church's regular diocesan structure as a kind of separate "Latin Tridentine rite," and be answerable directly to the Congregation of Bishops in Rome rather than to the local bishop.

In the history of the Church, the Holy See has frequently authorized religious orders to exist and function separately and apart from regular diocesan structures. This idea of operating under such a separate apostolic administration would seem to be an eminently sensible way to reconcile those dissatisfied with the conciliar reforms, in fact. It nevertheless turned out to be unsatisfactory for the SSPX, since the Society necessarily saw itself in that situation as being "under" Rome and subject to the authority of the "conciliar" Church, while in the Society's view, *it* rather than the Holy See represented the authentic Catholic tradition.

For, as we have seen earlier, the SSPX believes Rome to be simply in the wrong on the principal matters at issue; it sees itself as simply in the right; it believes Vatican II was a bad dream which will one day simply have to be reversed when, say, another "true Catholic" is finally again elected to occupy Peter's chair, and will then presumably proceed to quash the acts of the illicit Council. This view of the matter is apparently shared by not a few traditionalists, since it is hard to see on what basis they are acting otherwise. But there is no way that any of this is ever really going to happen, of course; there is no way that the Catholic Church could ever go back on one of her general or ecumenical councils. General councils since ancient times have always been considered to constitute a significant part of the true "Catholic tradition" to which the Catholic traditionalists erroneously lay claim. Meanwhile, the post-conciliar Church, including especially the Holy See, in the SSPX view, is believed to be adrift on the seas of modernist error.

One of the SSPX demands, made in the course of negotiations with Rome, was that every priest in the world should be given permission to say the Tridentine Mass, what the traditionalists like to call "the traditional Mass of all time" (although, in fact, it only dates back to 1570). However, the idea that Catholic priests should somehow have a *right* to go against what a general council of the Church has decreed can surely in no way be considered a *traditional* Catholic doctrine. Yet it was precisely this "right" which Pope Benedict XVI was essentially willing to grant in his *Summorum Pontificum*. This was surely an indication that Benedict XVI, like John Paul II before him, was prepared to go very far indeed in order to achieve reconciliation with the traditionalists. Far from being "intransigent," the Holy See has been consistently accommodating in trying to reconcile the traditionalists – provided only that elements essential to the authentic Catholic tradition be maintained, such as, e.g., that a general council of the Church speaks authentically for the Church as it does for Jesus Christ.

Speaking about the Vatican officials with whom he negotiated, the SSPX superior general who succeeded Archbishop Lefebvre, Bishop Bernard Fellay, said: "They do not want to touch Vatican II. Until we can break the taboo on discussing the new Mass and Vatican II, any talk of a rapprochement is premature." The Council simply *has* to be abrogated, in the SSPX view, and there can apparently be no reconciliation of the Society with the Church until it is.

However, the Catholic Church does not, never has, and never will, go back on the solemn decisions of one of her general councils. These conciliar decisions have traditionally been believed to have been arrived at "with the assistance of the Holy Spirit." The Church can no more go back on them than she could repudiate the solemn declarations and decisions of a supreme pontiff. This is what the true "tradition" of the Catholic Church actually is. Anyone who has even seriously studied the history of the Church must realize how unreal the traditionalist position, and the expectations that stem from it, actually are.

Even though, therefore, the SSPX could no longer see how far outside the true tradition of the Church it had ventured, the efforts of Cardinal Dario Castrillón Hoyos to come to an agreement and achieve reconciliation with traditionalists nevertheless turned out to be successful in another quarter. On January 18, 2002, a new "apostolic administration" of the kind that had been offered to the SSPX *was* established in Campos, Brazil. Named after St. John Mary Vianney, the new apostolic administration was created for the benefit of the 15 to 30 thousand traditionalist Catholics there who have continued to attend the Tridentine Masses maintained in that diocese following the refusal of the late Bishop Antonio de Castro Mayer to implement the Vatican II liturgical reforms. On August 18, 2002, a new coadjutor bishop, Dom Fernando Arêas Rifan, was consecrated by Cardinal Castrillon himself as the head of the new apostolic administration. The new bishop described himself in a letter to his supporters as:

> ...the first "traditionalist" bishop appointed for Catholics who attend Mass in the old Latin rite which was the norm before the Second Vatican Council...I have been appointed bishop by the pope with the goal of serving Catholics who are attached to the traditional Mass, in perfect communion with the Church. The Holy See has granted to us as a proper rite the traditional Mass, the sacraments, sacramentals, and Divine Office...Our booming group of traditionalist faithful is served by priests who observe the traditional ways of life, wear cassocks every day, and faithfully pray the traditional Breviary. We have almost 30 priests, all staunchly attached to tradition and most quite young...

Thus, there evidently *is* a way to reconcile traditionalists who at least recognize the legitimate authority of the pope and the validity of the Council, even if they dislike what the Council decided as well as how the popes and the bishops have carried out some of the conciliar mandates following the Council. The Church is *ready* to be reconciled to the traditionalists, in other words, provided certain essentials are maintained. This was evident in the words and actions of Pope John Paul II, as it has subsequently also been evident in the case of Pope Benedict XVI's *Summorum Pontificum*. But reconciliation cannot be merely a one-way street. The traditionalists too have to agree to certain things if reconciliation is ever to come about.

John Paul II, in *Ecclesia Dei*, quoting the Council, aptly put his finger on the fundamental *error* of the kind of thinking that, tragically, led to the Lefebvre ordinations and to the formal schism that followed. Extensively quoting from Vatican II, the pope pointed out in this regard that:

> The *root* of this schismatic act can be discerned in an incomplete and contradictory notion of the tradition. Incomplete, because it

does not take sufficiently into account the *living* character of tradition, which, as the Second Vatican Council clearly taught, "comes from the apostles and progresses in the Church with the help of the Holy Spirit. There is a growth in insight into the realities and words that are being passed on. This comes about in various ways. It comes through the contemplation and study of believers who ponder these things in their hearts. It comes from the intimate sense of spiritual realities which they experience. And it comes from the preaching of those who have received, along with their right of succession in the episcopate, the sure charism of truth" (Dogmatic Constitution on Divine Revelation, *Dei Verbum* 8).

But especially contradictory is a notion of tradition which opposes the universal magisterium of the Church possessed by the bishop of Rome and the body of bishops. It is impossible to remain faithful to the tradition while breaking the ecclesial bond with him to whom, in the person of the Apostle Peter, Christ himself entrusted the ministry of unity in his Church (Cf. Mt 16:18; Lk 10:16).

The Church, in other words, is a living entity: she is not summed up and circumscribed by, say, a particular rite, such as the Tridentine Mass of 1570, any more than she is circumscribed and summed up only by what is explicitly found in sacred Scripture – as many Protestants believe. Rather, as Vatican II taught, the Church was founded upon the living apostles of Jesus under the headship of Peter and she lives and moves today in their successors, the bishops of the Catholic Church, in union with the successor of Peter, the bishop of Rome, the pope.

Two of the successors of Peter, Popes John Paul II and Benedict XVI, have in our day quite amply proved, both by their words and their actions, that the Church is prepared to go to great lengths to be reconciled with the Catholic traditionalists. The Church ardently desires this reconciliation. The Church is *not* prepared, however, to compromise doctrinal essentials, such as that the official acts of a general council become part of the Church's authentic tradition and enjoy the guarantee of the Holy Spirit. *That* the Church is not prepared to compromise such essentials is simply one more indication that the Church is what she says she is, namely, what Jesus Christ said she would be when he declared at Caesarea Philippi that he was founding her upon the rock of Peter.

Chapter Twenty-Eight
A Resurgence of "Creative" Liturgies?

One of the most talked about recent books on the liturgy, entitled *A Challenging Reform*, authored by Piero Marini, and published by the Liturgical Press in 2007, was ostensibly just a history of the "Consilium," the temporary body of bishops and experts organized after Vatican Council II to implement the Council's Constitution on the Sacred Liturgy, *Sacrosanctum Concilium*. Once it appeared, however, the book was immediately taken in some quarters to be much more than a simple history. That it was considered to be much more than a simple history was even implied by its subtitle: *Realizing the Vision of the Liturgical Renewal*. But it was especially so considered because of the identity of its author, who for some twenty years had been the master of ceremonies for papal liturgies, and who was widely noted, especially in progressive circles, for the "creative" liturgies he organized.

Thus, those who favored the kind of "creative" liturgies thought by some to have been the essence of what Vatican II's mandated reform of the liturgy really called for – but steadily curtailed in recent years by the actions of the Congregation for Divine Worship and the Discipline of the Sacraments – welcomed this book as possibly signaling a revitalization of the free and easy liturgical style too often found in the post-conciliar era. After all, if the pope's own master of ceremonies could go on organizing "creative" liturgies, regardless of existing liturgical regulations, why would anyone else be obliged to follow those regulations?

On October 1, 2007, John L. Allen, Jr., of the *National Catholic Reporter* already quoted several times in this book, published a story headlined "Vatican's Top Liturgical Liberal Steps Down." In this story Allen reported that, after serving some twenty years as head of the Vatican Office for the Liturgical Celebrations of the Supreme Pontiff, Archbishop Piero Marini was being replaced by a younger man of the same name, Guido Marini (no relation), and was being transferred to become president of the Pontifical Commission for International Eucharistic Congresses.

As head of the Vatican liturgical office in question, Archbishop Marini was from 1987 to 2007 the master of ceremonies for papal liturgical ceremonies, and, as such, he was a perennially familiar face for the watchers of televised papal liturgical celebrations. For journalist Allen and for many other Roman cognoscenti, however, this same Archbishop Marini was a Vatican figure of special interest, particularly because the papal Masses and other liturgical ceremonies he organized were not always carried out in strict conformity with the Church's liturgical rules and regulations. Allen noted that Archbishop Marini's liturgies were "sometimes more innovative than a strict reading of official policy might permit."

For example, as related in a later interview with the same John Allen published in NCR on December 28, 2007, the admiring American journalist noted that it was Archbishop Marini who, among other departures from the Church's normal liturgical practice, "allowed an indigenous Mexican shaman to exorcise John Paul II during the canonization Mass for Juan Diego in Mexico City in 2002, and who permitted scantily clad Pacific Islanders to dance for the pope during the opening liturgy of the Synod for Oceania in St. Peter's Basilica in 1998." This latter event, of course, went directly contrary to the Congregation for Divine Worship's 1975 document entitled "Dance in the Liturgy," in which it is stated unequivocally that dance "cannot be introduced into liturgical celebrations of any kind whatsoever. That would be to inject into the liturgy one of the most desacralized and desacralizing of elements . . . "

No such considerations, however, apparently deterred this papal master of ceremonies, on this and on other occasions. Nor, after twenty years in his position, did it seem that his removal and replacement could be considered either hasty or precipitous or perhaps somehow "for cause." Some voices did suggest that the archbishop's lack of sympathy for Pope Benedict XVI's *Summorum Pontificum* could have been the cause of his removal. John Allen had earlier reported that "although Marini never took a public position on the move, it is widely known that he . . . expressed reservations in private" – reservations which evidently did not remain very "private," if they quickly became so "widely known"! However that may be, Archbishop Marini was, apparently, not being demoted; since he was being named as president of a pontifical commission, and hence he could actually then be in line to be named a cardinal.

And in spite of his frequent and rather obvious departures from the Church's liturgical rules, however, the fact is that he was kept on year after year as the papal master of ceremonies. Pope Benedict XVI kept him on for more than two more years after the long seventeen years he had already served John Paul II. Allen could plausibly describe him in that capacity as "a great champion of the reforming spirit in Catholic liturgy" at the same time that he qualified as the Vatican's "top liturgical liberal."

Nor does it seem that his actions and reputation ever bothered unduly the popes who employed him. Not unlike most of the liturgical innovators in the post-conciliar era, Archbishop Marini typically justified his innovations by characterizing them as truer to the authentic spirit of Vatican Council II than was the case with the Church's own codification of the reforms decreed by the Council. In the examples just cited pertaining to Mexico and Oceania, he claimed to have been acting on requests from local bishops. After all, was not Vatican II supposed to have decentralized authority and responsibility in the Church, giving more power to the local bishops?

Still, it might be wondered why Pope John Paul II, who was strict about so many things, could have tolerated and, indeed, sanctioned, Archbishop Marini's "creative" liturgies for so long – at the same time that he was repeatedly calling for more faithful adherence to the Church's liturgical regulations in not a few papal documents. One possible answer to this question that comes to mind seems to be that the pope somehow did not view the aberrations of his master of ceremonies as really being as serious as in fact they were. Obviously, any pope's own regular experience of the liturgy diverges markedly from the experience of the average person in the pews, and John Paul II, like many other high-ranking churchmen, was often slow to grasp how the reformed liturgy was in fact affecting many of the faithful. Too often, Church authorities even seemed incapable of comprehending what the problems were.

That John Paul II did eventually achieve some grasp of the existence and extent of liturgical abuses is certainly shown by the strictures that from time to time he issued against them in the course of his long pontificate. Nevertheless, just as this same pontiff was able to accept a novel interpretation of canon law which allowed for the approval of female altar servers, "altar girls" – at the very same time that he was attempting to cut off once and for all any further discussion or debate on the question of the ordination of women with his *Ordinatio Sacerdotalis* – so, it seems, that John Paul II, in spite of his manifest greatness, simply had a blind spot in certain areas, not only where altar girls were concerned, but also, it seems, where the example and the effects of the aberrations of his master of ceremonies were concerned.

It is true that "inculturation," or the adaptation of Church practices to local cultures, was one of the "in" things in the pontificate of John Paul II. It is also true that Archbishop Marini, and others of his ilk, regularly invoked "inculturation" in justification of their "creative" innovations. Nevertheless, it was true then, and it remains the case now, that "inculturation" *cannot* be the pretext or excuse for the disregard or violation of established Church regulations.

It is even harder to understand how Benedict XVI could have gone on countenancing such liturgies in the case of the man who became *his* master of ceremonies – he who had so frequently deplored and criticized liturgical abuses, and who had specifically cited the incidence of "deformations" in the liturgy as resulting from excessive "creativity," and as one of the principal reasons why his *Summorum Pontificum* became necessary.

Be that as it may, the former papal master of ceremonies certainly turned out to be a hardy and long-lasting survivor in the papal service. Yet no sooner had Archbishop Marini stepped down from his position than he was again in the news as a result of the publication in an English translation of his book on the liturgy. The appearance of the book was the occasion for the long, admiring December 2007 John Allen interview with him in the NCR quoted above, in which the NCR journalist reported, *inter alia*, on the extensive publicity and promotions being given in liturgical circles to the publication of this book.

A Challenging Reform was formally launched on December 14, 2007, with a presentation in the throne room of the residence of Cardinal Cormac Murphy-O'Connor of Westminster, England. Plans called for similar presentations in Boston, Chicago, Notre Dame, and New York in February 2008. Clearly Archbishop Marini continued to enjoy the patronage if not the friendship of an impressive number of high-ranking churchmen. His book bears numerous laudatory blurbs on its covers by such as Belgian Cardinal Godfried Danneels, retired San Francisco Archbishop John R. Quinn, and former Dominican Master General Timothy Radcliffe – churchmen who had in recent years expressed dissatisfaction with what they saw as "conservative" or "centralizing" trends in the Church; but who seemed to see the publication of this book of Archbishop Marini's as the harbinger of a new trend much more favorable to their way of seeing things. For them the book even seemed to signal some kind of comeback for "creative" liturgies.

Another indication of Archbishop Marini's continuing status as a "champion" of liturgical reform was the appearance on the book's title page of the names of three English-speaking liturgists who "edited" and "reworked" the text for publication here, namely: Mark R. Francis, C.S.V., John R. Page, and Keith F. Pecklers, s.j. John Page, of course, was for many years the executive director of the International Commission on English in the Liturgy (ICEL) – *before* the extensive reforms of that organization begun by Cardinal Jorge Medina in the late 1990s and continued by Cardinal Francis Arinze after that.

Both the manner and the matter of the publication and promotion of *A Challenging Reform*, then, suggested that Archbishop Marini was seen as a new leader and rallying point for the forces that continued to favor what they considered to be the authentic reforming spirit that grew out of Vatican II. Perhaps Marini was even seen as the focus of a new counter-move or resurgence by the same kinds of people who had dominated the liturgical scene throughout most of the post-conciliar era, but who were then thought to have been somewhat eclipsed beginning in the late 1990s by the actions and leadership of such as Cardinals Medina and Arinze at the head of the Congregation for Divine Worship and the Discipline of the Sacraments, by Cardinals George and Pell at ICEL and *Vox Clara,* by Bishop Roche at ICEL – and by the election in 2005 of the very liturgy-conscious Benedict XVI, whose previous writings on the liturgy, as well as his frank reaching out as pope in *Summorum Pontificum* to those dissatisfied with or even alienated by the reformed liturgy, had suggested that the era of constant liturgical innovations and "creative" liturgies was finally at long last over.

Nevertheless, the fact remained that Archbishop Piero Marini too also continued to be prominent on the liturgical scene throughout this same entire period. And he was "the pope's man," after all! If he could continue to "do his thing" regardless of what the Church's liturgical rules specified, why could not others do the same? What the publication of his book, along with the extensive promotion of it by the "usual suspects" among the "liberal" liturgical elements, thus indicated, then, was that, in spite of all the signs indicating that their "creative" way of approaching the liturgy had become less in vogue or was even no longer permitted, they nevertheless had no intention of "going gently into that good night," as the poet had phrased it. On the contrary, they quite firmly indicated that they intended to stay around, with Archbishop Marini as an obvious new leader and his book as a new focal point for "creative" liturgists.

In addition, *A Challenging Reform,* is quite revealing about how the Vatican II liturgical reforms proceeded in the way that they did. As already noted, the book is basically a history of the *Consilium ad esequandam Constutionem de sacra liturgia,* or the "Consilium," the special body or task force of bishops and experts that was set up to carry out the extensive work that was involved in implementing the entire reform of the Roman rite envisaged by the Council. This "Consilium," which operated between 1964 and 1969, at its peak strength consisted of a couple of hundred expert collaborators from many different countries – it was always "international" – who were divided up into more than 30 separate working groups (which this author, oddly, calls "study groups").

These groups were each assigned specific aspects of the overall project of reform. These aspects included such things as concelebration, communion under both kinds, the liturgical calendar, the Psalter, the Lectionary, the Missal, the Divine Office, hymns, sacred music, prefaces, the Rites for the other sacraments, and so on. The revised liturgy of the Church, as we now know it today – which is, of course, much more than simply the *Novus Ordo* Missal alone – was essentially researched and crafted by the members of these Consilium groups, most of whom appear to have been qualified and authentic experts, serious about the Church's liturgy. They did not "invent" a new liturgy, but worked from the established Roman liturgy long in place. The author lists in several places the names of those involved in the work, only a few of whom were widely known. Most of them were recognized at the time as qualified in their respective specialties, however, and thus were called upon to assist in the massive task of liturgical revision that had been assigned to the Consilium.

With respect to the common criticism made in the post-conciliar era that those who devised the new liturgy were ignorant or unappreciative of "the Catholic tradition," however, I have to say that I detected among Archbishop Marini's plethora of names none of the names, for example, of the many disloyal and dissident theologians who otherwise became so deplorably common in the post-conciliar period. Whatever one may think of the work of the Consilium's working groups, those who composed them and crafted the new liturgy seem genuinely to have been mostly able and loyal men of the Church. They appear to be a decidedly different group from that of the dissident theologians who later became so prominent on the scene in the post-conciliar era.

Some among them already were, or later became, well known scholars and liturgical experts. I think, for example, of Aimé-Georges Martimort, later the author of the book *Deaconesses,* translated into English by the present author in the 1980s – and which, in my opinion, constitutes one of the solidest existing historical bulwarks in favor of the proposition that the Church is *unable* to confer sacred ordination on women. The very same Father Martimort was quite active in the work of the Consilium, and played a significant leadership role in it, according to this account.

As for the charge often made in traditionalist circles that "Protestants" had been brought in to help devise a new Mass undermining the true Catholic tradition, although Archbishop Marini did not address this issue directly, he did record in passing that non-Catholic observers were not invited to observe the reform process until 1966, some *three years* after the process had been set in motion.

In short, those who harbor dark suspicions about the process that produced the *Novus Ordo* will not be able to find too much evidence in support of their suspicions in this prosaic, rather repetitious, and even rather fussy and pedantic account of the work of the Consilium. This is not to say that there is nothing amiss or wrong with the liturgical ideas of our formal papal master of ceremonies or with this book. As we shall shortly see, there is plenty wrong with both, but it is just not what some have sometimes imagined it to be.

For the Consilium and its work have been much criticized. This is especially true of the man who was the principal leader and co-ordinator of the work of the Consilium, Father (later Archbishop) Annibale Bugnini, C.M., who was named secretary of the Consilium and later was made secretary of the Congregation for Divine Worship. Archbishop Bugnini certainly was one of the important liturgical figures at and after the Council. He had earlier been secretary of the Pontifical Preparatory Commission on the Liturgy. He was, according to this and other accounts, a hard-driving and indefatigable worker; he became almost legendary among Italian bishops for his devotion to the work ethic. The president of the Consilium, Cardinal Giacomo Lercaro of Bologna, apparently had enormous confidence in Bugnini and very often apparently let him "run the show." It was surely also these qualities in Archbishop Bugnini, however, that helped make possible the completion of the immense amount of work that the Consilium produced during the five years of its existence.

Many of those who question the value of the reformed liturgy, however, find in Archbishop Bugnini much to blame. He himself wrote his own account of his work: *The Reform of the Liturgy, 1948–1975,* also published by the Liturgical Press (in 1990). Critics of the Vatican-II liturgical reforms, in fact, have frequently gone to this source to seek documentation in support of their views. For many of a traditionalist caste of mind,

Archbishop Bugnini is still today considered to have been an evil genius dedicated to the decomposition of the Roman liturgy and a *bête noire* quite beyond any possibility of redemption. There were sighs of considerable relief in many quarters in 1975 when he was finally shorn of any further responsibility for liturgy, and was shunted off to Iran as the apostolic pronuncio to that Muslim country.

But this view of him and his supposed baneful influence seems exaggerated. He may indeed have been the designated "secretary" and "coordinator" of the Consilium and, later, of the Congregation; but the work of liturgical reform was nevertheless the work of many hands, and every aspect of it had to pass through many layers of scrutiny before it could be approved. Whatever his personal aims and intentions, Archbishop Bugnini could not have engineered any really substantial subversion all by himself. While he was undoubtedly a "liberal" in his views on the liturgy – as were many, if not perhaps most, of the experts at the time, especially before anyone had actually *tried* to reform the liturgy – and while he also had great influence by virtue of his position as coordinator of the reform that was carried out, in the end what was produced and decided upon still had to pass muster with the Roman Curia and, finally, with the pope himself.

The bureaucratic review process that was in place at the time, in fact, is one of the principal and repeated complaints of Archbishop Marini in his book. He complains frequently about what he considers to have been the negative and obstructionist attitudes towards the work of the Consilium on the part of the staffs of both the Congregation of Rites and its successor body, the Congregation for Divine Worship. Although Archbishop Marini was throughout most of his career *in* the Roman Curia, by the testimony of this book he was never *of* the Roman Curia. His comments about it resemble the kind of thing generally printed about it in liberal publications such as the *National Catholic Reporter*, namely, that it was always standing in the way of what was regarded as the true promise of the Council. His view of most of his Curia colleagues, in fact, generally is severely critical.

While still a young priest, Archbishop Marini got assigned to the Consilium. Later he was named personal secretary to Archbishop Bugnini himself. He then served for many years in the Congregation for Divine Worship and the Discipline of the Sacraments before finally being assigned to head the Vatican Office for the Liturgical Celebrations of the Supreme Pontiff. According to the three English-speaking liturgist "editors" of the English version of this book, Francis, Page, and Pecklers, "in preparing numerous papal liturgies in Rome under John Paul II and

Benedict XVI, and in his travels around the world, Archbishop Marini had a unique experience of seeing the liturgical reforms carried out in Rome and in the local churches worldwide."

When we look at the actual merits of the book, however, this build up of its author, like that in the admiring article and interview by John Allen in the NCR, must be judged to be more than a little exaggerated. The book is no doubt a competent enough, and probably even mostly accurate, history of the work of the Consilium. But it is also a markedly slanted account. A resounding celebration or vindication of the merits of the Vatican II liturgical reforms in general it is not. If the launching of the book, accompanied by all its laudatory blurbs, is really supposed to represent some kind of new initiative by advocates of a more permissive liturgy whose typical efforts have been rather blunted in recent years, then it must be said that the book would seem to be a wholly inadequate instrument to further their cause very effectively. Instead it is a labored, rather repetitive, and even at times boring piece of work, and it certainly lacks balance. The high praise lavished upon it is misplaced.

Nor does the author really come across as any "great champion of the reforming spirit in Catholic liturgy." Rather, although he generally presents a smooth enough façade – as one would have expected of someone who lasted so long in the papal entourage – he nevertheless mostly comes across as a rather uncritical and even sometimes almost simple-minded proponent of whatever is new in liturgy; and, at the same time, he shows himself to be quite small-minded, and even peevish, towards anyone, especially his putative colleagues in the Roman Curia, considered to be critical or unappreciative of what Archbishop Bugnini and his allies may have decided or favored back in the days of the Consilium.

Archbishop Marini's critical references to the Roman Curia – his employer – are quite frequent and sometimes quite severe. For example, he tosses off phrases such as "the Curia's attempts to *interfere* in the implementation of the reform," "the *resistance* of the Roman Curia," and "the *danger* of the Roman Curia, which historically tended to impede the reforming impetus of councils and bishops." The Congregation of Rites, according to his account, had "a *polemical attitude* toward the Constitution on the Sacred Liturgy [that was] quite evident," and aimed "to *restrain* the Consilium in order to *limit* the reform" (emphasis added throughout).

Moreover, as one might, sadly, expect of a master of ceremonies given to regular contravention of existing liturgical regulations, he shows himself in a number of instances to be quite insouciant, if not actually disrespectful, of the idea that adherence to the existing Church regulations ought to be a requirement of good liturgy. He describes with approval how Archbishop Bugnini "sought to solve problems . . . often *not* taking into account the point of view of the Curia and *the limits set by legislation in force*" (emphasis added again). In another place, he notes that "consultors were not always appointed following the regulations of the Roman Curia." In short, Marini turns out to have been a willing pupil of his mentor Bugnini.

We can only wonder what the reactions of such as Cardinal Danneels and Murphy-O'Connor and Archbishop Quinn could have been in reading passages such as these – and yet these prelates still felt able to praise this book as enthusiastically as they have. The apparent inability of such prelates to understand that the rules of the Church ought to be *upheld* by those in authority can scarcely redound to their credit. How such bishops could presume to deplore or criticize the disobedience of the Lefebvrists is hard to see. While Archbishop Marini's liturgical permissiveness may not be as serious as illicit ordinations, it is still hard to see how his disrespect for legitimate Church authority can be openly countenanced in the way that it is by such prominent ecclesiastics.

A good part of Archbishop Marini's narrative is preoccupied with the question of the status of the Consilium within the Church's official structures. Established as a special body of bishops and experts to accomplish the specific task of getting underway the reforms called for by the Council – what we today would commonly style a "task force" – the Consilium was never accorded any actual juridical status within the Roman Curia, as Marini bitterly complains more than once. His idea clearly seems to be that the Consilium's typical free-wheeling style of operation should have become the Holy See's *normal* way of exercising Church authority generally. Yet on the evidence that he himself provides, it was surely never the intention of Pope Paul VI that the Consilium should ever have been anything but an *ad hoc* body organized to perform the specific task of implementing *Sacrosanctum Consilium*.

And once the specific texts and documents implementing this liturgy Constitution had been prepared and approved, they were then – and necessarily – officially issued by the Congregation of Rites (later the Congregation for Divine Worship), as anyone can verify by looking at the documents contained in Dominican Father Austin Flannery's valuable collection, *Vatican Council II: The Conciliar and Post-Conciliar Documents*. The necessary implementing documents were *not* issued directly by the

Consilium, in other words, but had to undergo an approval process by the permanent established organs of Church authority.

Ironically, as the author's own account consistently attests, while the Consilium was still in being and actively working, Pope Paul VI almost invariably favored the Consilium in the various bureaucratic disputes and squabbles that arose within the Curia. The pontiff no doubt took this position because he wanted to see the implementation process proceed with all deliberate speed. In practice this sometimes even led to what Archbishop Marini describes as the prefect of the Congregation of Rites being "forced to sign documents prepared by the very group that he had consistently opposed." The former papal master of ceremonies erroneously concludes from this fact that "the role that fell to the Congregation of Rites was purely formal."

On the contrary, the Congregation of Rites was ultimately *responsible*, as the pope well knew and wished, and this became perfectly clear once the major implementing task was completed, when the Consilium was simply allowed to go out of existence. Archbishop Marini's depiction of the liturgical liberals as *victims* is unconvincing if not laughable. Had the pope or the Congregations attempted to operate on a regular basis in the way the archbishop consistently recommends throughout this book, the result would have been chaos on an even greater scale than the chaos that in fact too often did accompany the Church's implementation of the liturgical reform. His view of the liturgy *cannot* constitute any kind of model for the Church's practice.

Thus, any kind of attempted resurgence of the "creative" liturgy which so many thought was to be the new *modus operandi* after Vatican II – and which Archbishop Marini and his admirers apparently still think is the proper way to go – is bound to be a non-starter: this approach has been tried, and has failed. Piero Marini is neither a suitable leader or inspiration for any kind of "creative " liturgical revival, nor does his 2007 book, *A Challenging Reform,* point the way to anywhere the Church should be going.

Chapter Twenty-Nine
The Reform Stands

Vatican Council II's decision to reform the entire liturgy of the Catholic Church proved to be a vast and complex enterprise which is not completed yet. In the nature of the case, it was surely possible that many things could go wrong; and, in retrospect, it almost seems as if whatever could go wrong, in accordance with "Murphy's Law," did often go wrong.

We have had to dwell upon so many of the negative aspects of the liturgical reform, and at such length, in fact, that we have said up to this point far too little about the positive aspects of the Vatican II reform of the liturgy. That there were such positive results, Pope John Paul II, among others, was certain. In his apostolic letter *Vicesimus Quintus Annus* on the 25th Anniversary of the Constitution on the Sacred Liturgy, which he issued on December 4, 1988, the pope provided his own summary of the positive results of the reform. We quoted extensively from this summary of John Paul II's earlier in this book (in Chapter Nine). At the same time, the pontiff accurately noted, as we also quoted, that "the vast majority of the pastors and the Christian people have accepted the liturgical reform in a spirit of obedience and indeed joyful fervor" (VQA 12).

This represented pretty much the considered views of Pope John Paul II on the positive aspects of the reform of the liturgy. He said the same thing on the fortieth anniversary of *Sacrosanctum Concilium*, on December 4, 2003, when he issued yet another apostolic letter, *Spiritus et Sponsa,* on the same subject. We have already taken note of this document as well. In this latter document, however, he mostly referred back to the same twenty-fifth anniversary *Vicesimus Quintus Annus* document. Similarly, in a major address on the "Positive Results of Vatican II's Liturgy Constitution" delivered to the Federation of Diocesan Liturgy Commissions in the United States in October 2003, Cardinal Francis Arinze, prefect of the Congregation for Divine Worship and the Discipline of the Sacraments, went back to the same 1988 document of John Paul II's to illustrate what he thought had been the most successful things about the

Church's reform of the liturgy. While we might expect that both the pope and the Curia cardinal currently responsible for the liturgy worldwide *would* want to accentuate the positive, we should not exclude the idea that there may have actually been, in fact, many such positive aspects. All this was *not* just a matter of Church leaders wishing to focus on the "positive aspects."

And although we have touched upon some of these positive aspects, we have said far too little about some of the really important and characteristic things about the Church's liturgy and of Vatican Council II's reform of it. For example, we have said almost nothing about the other rites besides the Mass or about art, architecture, music, or the reformed liturgical calendar. In various ways, of course, these topics, like some of the other topics we have discussed in these pages, have sometimes exhibited a troublesome side. Church architecture, in particular, has been a frequent bone of contention in the post-conciliar era, exhibiting changes sometimes quite disturbing to the faithful. This has been true both with regard to the tearing down of venerable older church structures, and to the kinds and styles of some of the new church structures being built. These new styles have sometimes exhibited little respect for traditional Catholic ideas of the "sacred."

For years what now passes as "sacred architecture" in America was heavily influenced by a controversial modernistic 1978 document, *Environment and Art in Catholic Worship,* which was never even approved by the full body of the American bishops; but which nevertheless came to be treated by some architects and builders as if it were a kind of Holy Writ. Only in November 2000, did the American bishops finally approve a replacement document, *Built of Living Stones,* which it is hoped will eventually lead to improvement in contemporary Catholic Church architecture.

Again, as regards sacred music, for much of the post-conciliar period, some of the new forms of music employed in the liturgy have hardly been inspiring, in particular some of the pseudo-"folk" music that has been brought forward as supposedly suitable for worship of the Divine Majesty. For much of this same period, the Church in America at least has unfortunately been guided by such documents as those produced by the Bishops' Committee on the Liturgy (BCL) as "Music in Catholic Worship" (1972) and "Liturgical Music Today" (1983). These documents were drawn up and published almost without reference to the Holy See's 1967 Instruction on Sacred Music, *Musicam Sacram.* The experience of most Mass-goers during that same period would tend to confirm the conclusion that liturgical music in the post-conciliar era has at the very least been *inadequate.*

Only at their meeting in November, 2007, did the U.S. bishops finally send to Rome for approval a new document entitled "Sing to the Lord: Music in Divine Worship," following up on a Directory on Music in the Liturgy that was sent to Rome for the *recognitio* the year before. Only time will tell to what extent these new documents will represent improvements over what American Catholics have been obliged to live with over the past generation in the way of liturgical music.

Nevertheless, it remains true that, properly and reverently celebrated, in an appropriate ecclesial setting, and especially when accompanied by truly sacral music, the reformed vernacular Mass of Vatican II can be a thing of great beauty which truly does – as it is supposed to – offer us a foretaste of the heavenly liturgy (cf. SC 8). Moreover, its meaning and import are immediately accessible to the average person without any special introduction or training. Nor is this only true on an exceptional basis and in some places. In my own parish, for example, Sunday Masses have long since become quite stabilized; the great drama of the re-enactment of Christ's sacrifice on the cross for the sake of our sanctification and salvation is regularly presented within our own very average parish Sunday worship.

Nor is this true only in my parish. At our cathedral parish, where the musicians are professionals, and the music outstanding, the celebration of weddings, funerals, ordinations, and the like have often truly been occasions of rare moment and great beauty and reverence. Encountering such beauty in Catholic worship, far from being unusual or a surprise, on the contrary is a common thing, even today. As the Venerable Cardinal John Henry Newman wrote in the eighth of his famous lectures *On the Difficulties of Anglicans*, the Catholic Church *"cannot help being beautiful*; it is her gift; as she moves the many worship and adore: *Et vera incessu patuit Dea"* (Virgil, *Aeneid*, I, 402: "And in her gait was a true Goddess seen...").

"Cannot help being beautiful"! This beauty, which is an integral part of the Catholic Church, has not failed to manifest itself in many ways in our day even in spite of the failures and depredations of some of the failed liturgical experiments.

Among the other successes of the liturgical reforms, apart from the Mass, there have been the revisions of all the various rites for each of the sacraments as well as for ordinations, consecrations, weddings, funerals, and so on. These revised rites generally exhibit a dignity and a high seriousness which point back to the supernatural world of truth and grace that necessarily informs them. I marvel almost daily, for example, at the truth and beauty I encounter when I pray the revised Divine Office, or Liturgy of the Hours, as it is now called, especially its Office of Readings. I had no idea of the existence of such richness before the Council. Like many laymen, I took up praying the Liturgy of the Hours in the 1970s. Prior to Vatican II, it was almost unthinkable for laymen to pray what was then known as the Breviary, which was popularly thought to be reserved to the priests (and was in Latin). This was surely another one of the *good* changes inspired by Vatican II. Other similar spiritual blessings have also flowed from the Council's decision to reform the liturgy, and we should not forget them.

That the Vatican II liturgical reform did not come without its problems, though, was long recognized by the highest authorities of the Church. As early as February 24, 1980, for example, in a Letter addressed to the Catholic bishops of the world on the Mystery and Worship of the Eucharist, *Dominicae Cenae*, Pope John Paul II wrote, *inter alia* – it was another one of his famous "apologies"! – anyway, he wrote:

> I would like to ask forgiveness – in my own name and in the name of all of you, venerable and dear brothers in the episcopate – for everything which, for whatever reason, through whatever human weakness, impatience, or negligence, and also through the at times partial, one-sided, and erroneous application of the directives of the Second Vatican Council, may have caused scandal and disturbance concerning the interpretation of the doctrine and the veneration due to this great sacrament. And I pray the Lord Jesus that in the future we may avoid in our manner of dealing with this sacred mystery anything which could weaken or disorient in any way the sense of reverence and love that exists in our faithful people (DC 12).

This, surely, was a heartfelt admission on the part of the Church's supreme pastor that things certainly could have been better. Furthermore, just a few months after this frank "apology" of the pope's, on April 3, 1980, the Congregation for Divine Worship issued a rather stern Instruction on Certain Norms concerning the Worship of the Eucharistic Mystery, *Inaestimabile Donum*. In the Foreword to this Instruction, the Congregation both recognized the positive results of the liturgical reforms and deplored the abuses that had been so often reported:

This Sacred Congregation notes with great joy the many positive results of the liturgical reform: a more active and conscious participation by the faithful in the liturgical mysteries, doctrinal and catechetical enrichment through the use of the vernacular and the wealth of readings from the Bible, a growth in the community sense of liturgical life, and successful efforts to close the gap between life and worship, between liturgical piety and personal piety, and between liturgy and popular piety.

But these encouraging and positive aspects cannot suppress concern at the varied and frequent abuses being reported from different parts of the Catholic world: the confusion of roles, especially regarding the priestly ministry and the role of the laity (indiscriminate shared recitation of the Eucharistic Prayer, homilies given by lay people, lay people distributing Communion while the priests refrain from doing so); an increasing loss of the sense of the sacred (abandonment of liturgical vestments, the Eucharist celebrated outside the church without real need, lack of reverence and respect for the Blessed Sacrament, etc.); and misunderstanding of the ecclesial character of the liturgy (the use of private texts, the proliferation of unapproved Eucharistic Prayers, the manipulation of the liturgical texts for social and political ends). In these cases we are face to face with a falsification of the Catholic liturgy: "One who offers worship to God on the Church's behalf in a way contrary to that which is laid down by the Church with God-given authority, and which is customary in the Church, is guilty of *falsification*" (St Thomas Aquinas, *Summa Theologiae,* 2–2, q. 93, a. 1; emphasis added).

Thus, well over twenty years ago, the Church had already officially recognized, at the highest levels, that the Vatican II liturgical reforms, as actually carried out, had sometimes resulted in (or were accompanied by) serious problems and sometimes abuses. It is true that the Church was both slow to recognize this, and slower yet to provide effective remedies. In some dioceses there does not seem to be any great concern about the matter even now. More than twenty years later, though, the subject was still very much on the pope's mind. In his encyclical on the Eucharist, *Ecclesia de Eucharistia* ("Church of the Eucharist"), issued on Holy Thursday, April 17, 2003, John Paul II, after an obligatory mention of the benefits of the liturgical reform in contributing to "a more conscious, active, and fruitful participation in the Holy Sacrifice," went on to catalogue some of the problems still besetting the proper celebration of the Eucharist:

> In some places the practice of eucharistic adoration has been almost completely abandoned. In various parts of the Church, abuses have occurred, leading to confusion with regard to sound faith and Catholic doctrine concerning this wonderful sacrament. At times one encounters an extremely reductive understanding of the eucharistic mystery. Stripped of its sacrificial meaning, it is celebrated as if it were merely a formal banquet. Furthermore, the necessity of the ministerial priesthood, grounded in apostolic succession, is at times obscured and the sacramental nature of the Eucharist is reduced to its mere effectiveness as a form of proclamation. This has led here and there to ecumenical initiatives which, albeit well-intentioned, indulge in eucharistic practices contrary to the discipline by which the Church expresses her faith.
>
> How can we not express profound grief at all this? The Eucharist is too great a gift to tolerate ambiguity and depreciation. It is my hope that the present encyclical letter will effectively help to banish the dark clouds of unacceptable doctrine and practice so that the Eucharist will continue to shine forth in all its radiant mystery (EE 10).

In order to underline the importance of the Eucharist as the center of the Church's worship, John Paul II decreed, on Corpus Christi, June 10, 2004, a Eucharistic Year to extend from October of 2004 to October of 2005, following which the 11th ordinary assembly of the Synod of Bishops, to be held on October 2–23, 2005, would be devoted to the theme of "The Eucharist: Source and Summit of the Life and Mission of the Church." In the encyclical *Ecclesia de Eucharistia* itself, John Paul II noted that in order to banish those "dark clouds of unacceptable doctrine and practice," he had "asked the competent offices of the Roman Curia to prepare a more specific document, including prescriptions of a juridical nature, on this very important subject. No one is permitted to undervalue the mystery entrusted to our hands" (EE 52).

Nearly a year later, on March 25, 2004, the Congregation for Divine Worship and the Discipline of the Sacraments issued an Instruction entitled *Redemptionis Sacramentum* ("Sacrament of Redemption"), in which the Church's rules for the celebration and

reception of the great sacrament of the Eucharist were strongly reiterated and reaffirmed.

There was little or nothing that was new in this Instruction; the
Church's rules had long been on the record, as had the various prescriptions
that these rules be followed – as we have seen them laid out in such documents as *Dominicae Cenae* and *Inaestimabile Donum*. However, the fact
that the Church was reiterating them once again in this Instruction, and at
the highest level, indicated that they were still not being universally followed. In such a situation, it was therefore certainly important *that* the
Church should again remind everyone of these existing rules. Each time
the Church does so at least leaves less room for free-wheeling liturgists to
take it upon themselves to engage in some of the common abuses that have
unfortunately too often marred the post-conciliar era.

Redemptionis Sacramentum covered practically every possible abuse,
including such things as the habit of some priests to compose their own
Eucharistic Prayers, a habit that the document declared was "not to be tolerated" (RS 51). Similarly excluded were such things as the use of singing
or music during the Eucharistic Prayer; the breaking of the host at the time
of the consecration; preaching at Mass by anyone other than an ordained
priest or deacon; giving First Communion to children who have not yet
made their First Confession; and excessive commotion associated with the
giving of the sign of peace. One prescription of particular interest was the
following:

> It is altogether laudable to maintain the noble custom by which
> boys or youths, customarily termed *servers*, provide service at the
> altar after the manner of acolytes and receive catechesis regarding
> their function in accordance with their power of comprehension.
> Nor should it be forgotten that a great number of sacred ministers
> over the course of the centuries have come from among boys such
> as these (RS 47).

During the course of the drafting of this Instruction, it was rumored at
one point, and stories to that effect appeared in the press, that the document
was going to go back on an earlier decision of the pope's and, once again,
exclude women and girls from serving at the altar. The press stories about
this caused quite a flurry, in fact, and evidently caused not a few bishops
to weigh in with the Congregation concerning their views on this subject.
It is easy to guess what some of those views probably were. In the event,
as can be gathered from the above numbered paragraph from the

Instruction, if there really were those in the Curia who seriously wished to return to the former discipline of reserving altar service to men and boys alone – especially in the interests of encouraging vocations to the priesthood! – then those advocates clearly failed to win the argument in this instance ("once again," one is tempted to add!).

The Instruction, while encouraging the "noble custom" of boys serving at the altar, did not go beyond such encouragement; but instead, in fact, rather lamely, at the end, conceded that "girls or women may also be admitted to this service at the altar, at the discretion of the diocesan bishop and in observance of the established norms" (by which is probably meant that woman still cannot be *installed* in the ministry as acolytes, but can only be "temporarily" deputed to perform the functions of acolytes). It seems clear that those who are determined to keep women functioning in ministries that they can never officially fulfill, according to the current law of the Church, still enjoy a veto power over an issue, altar service, that ought to have been settled long since in accordance with properly Catholic principles so that the Church can move on to more important things.

Yet another post-conciliar document which fully accepted the Vatican II liturgical reforms, while recognizing that the result of all of them was not always perfect, was the post-synodal apostolic exhortation issued by Pope Benedict XVI following the 2005 Synod of Bishops on the subject of "The Eucharist: Source and Summit of the Life and Mission of the Church." Dated February 22, 2007, and entitled *Sacramentum Caritatis*, this document addressed some of the questions with which we have been concerned in this book. In particular, we may quote the following passage with profit:

> The Second Vatican Council rightly emphasized the active, full, and fruitful participation of the entire people of God in the eucharistic celebration. Certainly the renewal carried out in these past decades has made considerable progress toward fulfilling the wishes of the Council Fathers. Yet we must not overlook the fact that some misunderstanding has occasionally arisen concerning the precise meaning of this participation. It should be made clear that the word *participation* does not refer to mere external activity during the celebration. In fact, the active participation called for by the Council must be understood in more substantial terms, on the basis of a greater awareness of the mystery being celebrated and its relationship to daily life. The conciliar Constitution *Sacrosanctum Concilium* encouraged the faithful to take part in

the eucharistic liturgy not "as strangers or silent spectators," but as participants in the "sacred actions, conscious of what they are doing, actively and devoutly" (SC 48) (*Sacramentum Caritatis*, 52).

Thus was the most recent Synod of Bishops actively concerned with the questions we have been examining in this book. We may certainly hope, therefore, that we are authentically engaged in "thinking with the Church," as St. Ignatius of Loyola so aptly expressed it. However that may be, as we have seen in the course of this chapter, Church authorities truly have for the most part come to recognize the extent to which the Vatican II liturgical reforms have failed to measure up to the expectations of the Council Fathers; and they have for some time now been attempting to put in place a "reform of the reform" in order to restore the Church's liturgy and worship to the condition originally envisaged in Vatican Council II's liturgy Constitution. This is not only true of the Holy See, but it is also now true of many of the bishops as well, namely: the recognition that something has to be done; this recognition has become increasingly general and is growing.

The phrase "reform of the reform" began to be heard with increasing frequency in the late 1990s and early 2000s; and, as we have noted, was often employed by Cardinal Joseph Ratzinger before his election to the chair of Peter as Pope Benedict XVI. The phrase undoubtedly represents the way the Church now must go, liturgically speaking. In this connection, the reader can be referred to the excellent book entitled *The Reform of the Reform* by Fr. Thomas M. Kocik published by Ignatius Press in 2003; and also to the excellent *Adoremus Bulletin*, a publication of the Society for the Renewal of the Sacred Liturgy, edited by Helen Hull Hitchcock (P.O. Box 300561, St. Louis, MO 63130; and at www.adoremus.org). How to build on what the Church's liturgical situation now is – regardless of what perhaps it should have been – this is what these publications help explain. In any case, "the reform of the reform" is also the way the Church *has* to go from here, given the fact that Vatican II *did* decide to reform the liturgy.

The Constitution on the Sacred Liturgy, *Sacrosanctum Concilium*, must accordingly now be considered a permanent part of the Church's long and rich heritage. If the liturgical reforms carried out in response to the mandate contained in this document have been less than satisfactory in some respects – which no one can really dispute, and instances of which we have sadly been obliged to show in some detail – then the obvious response to that fact is to go back and pick up where the reforms diverged from what the Council wished, and this time get it right!

Thus, neither the idea of the traditionalists that we have to abandon what Vatican II decided because things turned out so badly, nor the idea of the liberals that what Vatican II decided was a "creative," do-your-own-thing liturgy, can be credited or followed. What has to be followed is what the Church finally decides – even sometimes after missteps and false starts!

It is fitting now to conclude what has become our rather lengthy discussion of Vatican II's major enactments on liturgy and worship with the conciliar document *Sacrosanctum Concilium*'s own conclusion that:

> . . . from the liturgy . . . and especially from the Eucharist, grace is poured forth upon us as from a fountain, and the sanctification of men in Christ and the glorification of God to which all other activities of the Church are directed, as toward their end, are achieved with maximum effectiveness. But in order that the liturgy may be able to produce its full effects, it is necessary that the faithful come to it with proper dispositions, that their minds be attuned to their voices, and they cooperate with heavenly grace lest they receive it in vain (SC 10–11).

This is sage advice. We should never lose sight of the fact that, again in the eloquent words of Vatican Council II's Constitution on the Sacred Liturgy, *Sacrosanctum Concilium*:

> Christ is always present in his Church, especially in her liturgical celebrations. He is present in the sacrifice of the Mass, not only in the person of his minister, "the same now offering through the ministry of priests, who formerly offered Himself on the cross" [Council of Trent], but especially in the Eucharistic species. By his power he is present in the sacraments so that when anybody baptizes, it is really Christ himself who baptizes. He is present in his Word since it is he himself who speaks when the Holy Scriptures are read in the Church. Lastly, he is present when the Church prays and sings, for he has promised that "where two or three are gathered together in my name, there am I in the midst of them" (Mt 18:20) (SC 7).

The Mass misunderstandings that followed the Second Vatican Council did not result from what the Council itself decided and said; they resulted from the children of the Church not paying close enough attention and following what the Council decided and said.

Selected Bibliography

Abbott, Walter M., s.j., General Editor. *The Documents of Vatican II.* New York: Herder and Herder/Association Press, 1966.

Anzevui, Abbé Jean. *Le Drame d'Écône: Analyse et Dossier.* Sion (Switzerland), Valprint, S.A., 1976.

Bunson, Matthew. *2008 Catholic Almanac.* Huntington, IN: Our Sunday Visitor Publishing Division, 2008 (and similar volumes from previous years).

Congar, Yves M.-J., o.p., *La Crise dans l'Église et Mgr. Lefebvre.* Paris: Les Éditions du Cerf, 1976.

Crouan, Denis. *The Liturgy Betrayed.* San Francisco: Ignatius Press, 2000.

Crouan, Denis and Sebanc, Mark, *The Liturgy after Vatican II.* San Francisco: Ignatius Press, 2001.

Fesquet, Henri. *The Drama of Vatican II: The Ecumenical Council - June, 1962 – December, 1965.* New York: Random House, 1967.

Finn, Peter C., and Schellman, James M., Editors. *Shaping English Liturgy: Studies in Honor of Archbishop Denis Hurley.* Washington, D.C.: The Pastoral Press, 1990.

Flannery, Austin, o.p., General Editor. *Vatican Council: The Conciliar and Post Conciliar Documents.* Northport, NY: Costello Publishing Company, 1975. *Vatican Council II: More Post Conciliar Documents* (Volume 2). Northport, NY: Costello Publishing Company, 1982.

Gamber, Klaus. *The Reform of the Roman Liturgy: Its Problems and Background.* Harrison, NY: The Foundation for Catholic Reform, and San Juan Capistrano, CA: *Una Voce* Press, 1993.

Hebblethwaite, Peter. *Pope John XXIII: Shepherd of the Modern World.* New York: Doubleday and Company, 1985 – *Paul VI: The First Modern Pope.* New York/Mahwah, NJ: Paulist Press, 1993.

Hitchcock, Helen Hull, Editor. *The Politics of Prayer: Feminist Language and the Worship of God*. San Francisco: Ignatius Press, 1992.

Hitchcock, James. *The Recovery of the Sacred*. New York: The Seabury Press, 1974.

Jenkins, Philip. *The Next Christendom: The Coming of Global Christianity*. New York: Oxford University Press, 2002.

Jungmann, Joseph A., s.j. *The Mass of the Roman Rite: Its Origins and Development*. Westminster, MD, Christian Classics, 1974 (Reprint of the 1959 Benziger Brothers edition).

Kocik, Thomas M. *The Reform of the Reform? A Liturgical Debate: Reform or Return*. San Francisco: Ignatius Press, 2003.

Likoudis, James, and Whitehead, Kenneth D. *The Pope, the Council, and the Mass: Answers to Questions the 'Traditionalists' Have Asked* (Third Edition, Revised). Steubenville, OH: Emmaus Road Publishing, 2006.

Marini, Piero. *A Challenging Reform: Realizing the Vision of the Liturgical Renewal – 1963–1975*. Collegeville, MN: Liturgical Press, 2007.

Martimort, Aimé-Georges. *Deaconesses: An Historical Study*. Translated by Kenneth D. Whitehead. San Francisco: Ignatius Press, 1986.

Newman, John Henry Cardinal. *Certain Difficulties Felt by Anglicans in Catholic Teaching* (Twelve Lectures). London: Longmans, Green, and Co., 1901.

Nichols, Aidan, o.p. *Looking at the Liturgy: A Critical View of Its Contemporary Form*. San Francisco: Ignatius Press, 1996.

Prendergast, Michael R., and Ridge, M.D. *Voices from the Council*. Portland: Pastoral Press, 2004.

Ratzinger, Cardinal Joseph (with Vittorio Messori). *The Ratzinger Report: An Exclusive Interview on the State of the Church*. San Francisco: Ignatius Press, 1985.

– *Milestones: Memoirs 1927–1977*. San Francisco: Ignatius Press, 1997.

– *The Spirit of the Liturgy*. San Francisco: Ignatius Press, 2000.

– *Feast of Faith*. San Francisco: Ignatius Press, 1986.

– *God and the World: Believing and Living in Our Time* (A Conversation with Peter Seewald). San Francisco: Ignatius Press, 2002.

– *A New Song for the Lord*. New York: the Crossroad Publishing Company, 1996.

Ratzinger, Joseph (Pope Benedict XVI). *Jesus of Nazareth: From the Baptism in the Jordan to the Transfiguration*. New York: Doubleday, 2007.

Rynne, Xavier. *Vatican Council II*. New York: Farrar, Straus and Giroux, 1968.

Stacpoole, Allberic, O.S.B. Editor, *Vatican II Revisited: By Those Who Were There*. Minneapolis: Winston Press, 1986.

Weigel, George. *Witness to Hope: The Biography of Pope John Paul II*. New York: HarperCollins Publishers, 1999.

Wiltgen, Rev. Ralph M., S.V.D. *The Rhine Flows into the Tiber: The Unknown Council*. New York: Hawthorn Books, Inc., 1967.

Wojtyla, Karol (Pope John Paul II). *Sources of Renewal: The Implementation of Vatican II*. San Francisco: Harper & Row Publishers, 1979.

Wrenn, Msgr. Michael J., and Whitehead, Kenneth D. *Flawed Expectations: The Reception of the Catechism of the Catholic Church*. San Francisco: Ignatius Press, 1996.

ABOUT THE AUTHOR

Kenneth D. Whitehead is a former career Foreign Service Officer who completed his federal government career in the U. S. Department of Education as an Assistant Secretary of Education for Postsecondary Education (appointed by President Ronald Reagan). He now works as a writer, editor, and translator in Falls Church, Virginia. He is the author, most recently, of *One, Holy, Catholic, and Apostolic: The Early Church Was the Catholic Church* (Ignatius Press, 2000); and the co-author, with James Likoudis of *The Pope, the Council, and the Mass* (Emmaus Road Publishing, 2006). He has authored, co-authored, or edited a number of other books, mostly of Catholic interest, including, most recently, *After 40 Years: Vatican Council's Diverse Legacy* (St. Augustine's Press, 2007). He has translated more than 20 books from French, German, or Italian.

Index